ADVANCE PRAISE FOR

A BLESSING TO EACH OTHER

"Rebecca Moore's book is a courageous excursion into Jewish-Christian relations. Moore constructively examines the historical relationship between Jews and Christians and proposes a way forward that acknowledges the past and builds a new future. Rebecca Moore moves the reader from conflict and problem to cooperation and solution through her forthright and thoughtful analysis. At a time when antisemitism is on the rise, Moore offers a much needed, accessible, and powerful map for the future through her exploration of alternative narratives of deep equality."

—LORI G. BEAMAN
UNIVERSITY OF OTTAWA

"This is a groundbreaking book that will revolutionize the discussion on Christian-Jewish relations. Rebecca Moore departs from prevailing paradigms that emphasize discord, persecution, and ill will between the two communities. Instead, the book suggests a move to a more positive, constructive, and optimistic evaluation of the interaction between the two faiths. It points to elements that Christians and Jews shared, the exchanges between them and the manner they have influenced each other. The book also narrates how Jews and Christians lived near, and with, each other for long generations, and that in spite of differences and bad blood, they have shared a great deal on many levels. Moore's brilliant analysis is highly instructive, and should be read by every person interested in Christian-Jewish relations."

—YAAKOV ARIEL, PROFESSOR OF RELIGIOUS STUDIES
THE UNIVERSITY OF NORTH CAROLINA AT CHAPEL HILL

"Moore offers a fresh approach to contemporary Christian-Jewish dialogue and its history, accentuating positive gains as much as the legacy of hostility and misunderstanding. Without overlooking the very real differences and conflicts between Jews and Christians, she critiques 'lachrymose histories' of Jewish-Christian relations as historical constructs that conceal as much as they reveal. She recognizes that Jews' and Christians' 'complex identities' blur, or at least complicate, the overly rigid boundaries drawn between what is 'Jewish' and what is 'Christian.' Her passionate, nuanced, and convincing call here for 'deep equality' is yet one more positive advance in Christian-Jewish dialogue."

—Rabbi Jonathan Brumberg-Kraus
Professor of Religion, Wheaton College (Massachusetts)

"Customary certitudes about Jewish-Christian relations have been challenged by more recent hopeful discoveries which enabled Rebecca Moore to build a solid case for a newer, more equitable relationship. She set out to challenge the notion that relationships between Jews and Christians are overwhelmingly dreadful. Many scholars and religious leaders are cognizant of these insights which Dr. Moore now makes accessible to non-experts. She succeeds emphatically in this task."

—Paul Mojzes
Emeritus co-editor of the *Journal of Ecumenical Studies*

A BLESSING
TO EACH OTHER

A BLESSING
TO EACH OTHER

A NEW ACCOUNT
OF JEWISH AND
CHRISTIAN RELATIONS

REBECCA MOORE

A Herder & Herder Book
The Crossroad Publishing Company
New York

A Herder & Herder Book
The Crossroad Publishing Company
www.crossroadpublishing.com

© 2021 by Rebecca Moore

The text of this book is set in 12/15 Adobe Garamond Pro.

Composition by Sophie Appel
Cover design by Sophie Appel
Cover image by Paul Haring/Catholic News Service

Library of Congress Cataloging-in-Publication Data
available upon request from the Library of Congress.
ISBN 978-0-8245-9500-5 paperback
ISBN 978-0-8245-0492-2 epub
ISBN 978-0-8245-0498-4 mobi

Books published by The Crossroad Publishing Company may be purchased at special quantity discount rates for classes and institutional use. For information, please e-mail sales@crossroadpublishing.com.

CONTENTS

PART 4. PRESENT PROSPECTS

12. Finding Deep Equality in Jewish
    and Christian Relations   205

    Notes   211

    Works Cited   249

    Source Index   277

    Subject Index   279

ACKNOWLEDGMENTS

I wrote most of this book in 2020, the year of the COVID-19 lockdown. That is why I deeply appreciate all of the assistance I received from so many people who were dealing with life and death issues. Some answered questions by email, talked with me by phone or on Zoom, and some read the entire book in manuscript form.

The following scholars answered many questions, large and small: Philip J. Cunningham, Robert Harris, Daniel Langton, Alan T. Levenson, Risa Levitt, Michael McGarry, Paul Mojzes, David Rosen, R. Kendall Soulen, and Leonard Swidler. I especially thank peer reviewers Yaakov Ariel and Mary C. Boys for their close reading of the book and their helpful comments.

Librarians continued to work during the year of COVID, and their help allowed me to finish the book in a timely manner. Appreciation goes to Heidi Lewis and Jen Fleming at the San Juan Island Public Library, particularly for their help obtaining items through interlibrary loan; Stephanie Morgan and Amy Sedovic at Western Washington University Library; Anna Culbertson at San Diego State University Special Collections; and Eli Gandour-Rood at the University of Puget Sound.

I am greatly indebted to Lori G. Beaman and her amazing book *Deep Equality in an Era of Religious Diversity.* Dr. Beaman kindly read and commented on the manuscript and generously gave of her time and experience.

I enlisted a diverse group of friends—Jewish, Christian, Buddhist, Agnostic, Atheist—to read and comment on the book. Their insights and suggestions have made this a better book than what I gave them. My deepest gratitude goes to Pat Boni, Patrick Clary, Aaron Duggan, Richard Freeman, Noah Hadas, Dianne and Bruce Hall, Idell Kesselman, Duncan McGehee, Robert Ray, Pat

Sanborn, and Father Cosmas Shartz. E. Nick Genovese deserves special mention for carefully reading the manuscript twice and for his erudition in all things classical, linguistic, and grammatical.

It is a pleasure to work with the staff at Herder and Herder. I thank Chris Myers for his ongoing encouragement and support, Julie Boddorf for shepherding the project to completion, copy-editor Tom Bechtle for saving me from some embarrassing typos, and Sophie Appel for her wonderful cover design and book composition.

As ever I am thankful for having Fielding M. McGehee III as my life partner for more than forty years. And while he is an outstanding copyeditor and indexer, that is not the reason I married him.

I dedicate this book to our children, Tim Edgar and December Pomerenke, and to the memory of their sister Hillary Ann Moore. And to my parents, John V Moore and Barbara C. Moore, who raised me in a home that embodied deep equality. May their memory be a blessing.

TERMS AND ABBREVIATIONS
USED IN THIS BOOK

aggadic interpretation—nonlegal rabbinic literature that provides commentary on the biblical text, e.g. ethics, instructions, meaning.

agonistic respect—the sometimes painful recognition that other people have different faith commitments and beliefs about ultimate truth.

allosemitism—setting Jews apart from all other people as being in need of distinct language and treatment in order to understand them. Allosemitism contains the seeds of both antisemitism and philosemitism because allosemites perceive Jews as somehow "other" in either a bad way or a good way.

anti-Judaism, Christian—belief that Christianity is superior to Judaism. Anti-Judaism differs from antisemitism because it focuses on religion rather than race.

antisemitism—prejudice toward or hatred of Jews based on race rather than on religion. Spelled without a hyphen by scholars of Jewish and Christian relations. In this book, antisemitism encompasses any form of Jew hatred, whether grounded on religion, race, or other factors.

apocalypticism—the expectation that the world will end imminently and catastrophically as part of God's plan for final judgment and ultimate redemption.

BCE—Before Common Era, the nonsectarian designation for BC (Before Christ).

Byzantine Palestina—the geographical region of Palestine under Byzantine Christian control, 400–700 CE, prior to the Muslim conquest of the seventh century. A center of Christian and Jewish intellectual life.

canon—lit. rule or measuring stick; a collection of books or texts considered authoritative, as in the canon of scripture.

CE—Common Era, the nonsectarian designation for AD (Anno Domini, Latin for Year of [the] Lord).

Christ event—shorthand way Christians use to state that the life, death, and resurrection of Jesus provide salvation.

Christian Hebraism—the interest in and study of Hebrew language and literature by Christians, particularly the Christian Old Testament.

Christology—in Christian theology, the explanation of the nature and person of Jesus Christ, especially in his relationship to God.

contaminated diversity—the principle that religious identities are complex and diverse rather than pure and unadulterated.

Danby—English translation of the Mishnah by Herbert Danby.

Diaspora—lit. scattering about; the community of Jews living outside the Land of Israel.

dispensationalism—a Christian categorization in which history is divided into seven eras or dispensations. The Church and Israel are given distinct functions, and Israel will play a significant role in the final, Messianic era.

double-covenant theology—the post-Holocaust theology that sees Judaism and Christianity as two distinct religions with a shared biblical heritage.

Endtime—period of turmoil and disruption preparatory to the coming of the Messiah, or the Advent of Christ.

eschatology—study of last things or Endtime; or the study of an individual's ultimate destiny. For Jews and Christians, the coming, or return, of the Messiah is the central eschatological expectation.

exegesis—bringing out the meaning of a text; frequently used synonymously with commentary.

fl.—flourished, indicating the lack of specific dates to mark an individual's life.

Gemara—lit. to finish or complete; analysis and commentary on the Mishnah given by rabbis; together Mishnah and Gemara comprise the Talmud.

gentile—Jewish term for non-Jew.

gnosticism—variety of beliefs that posit an imperfect world and the necessity of knowledge as the means of redemption. Christian Gnostics see Jesus as a divine being who brings awareness of humanity's true, spiritual nature.

God-fearer—a non-Jew in Late Antiquity who respects Jewish customs and may observe some practices.

halakhah—general term for rabbinic law, which may include religious and ritual matters as well as civil and criminal law.

Haskalah—lit. wisdom, erudition; the Jewish Enlightenment; an intellectual movement that ran through the eighteenth and nineteenth centuries.

Hebrews—biblical term for the people Israel, generally used by foreigners rather than as self-identification. Hebrews can also simply refer to the Jewish people, although its use today is rare.

Hellenism—the Greek-speaking civilization that dominated Mediterranean culture from the fourth through first centuries BCE. Hellenization is the process of incorporating regional peoples into a common, universal society.

Hellenistic Judaism—a type of Judaism prevalent in the Mediterranean world from 250 BCE to 250 CE, in which Jews adopt and adapt elements from the wider Greco-Roman culture, including the Greek language.

hermeneutics—the study of meaning in a text; a hermeneutical key would be the overarching idea or ideas that guide the interpretive process.

historical criticism—a method of interpretation in which religious texts are read and understood apart from sectarian commitments.

Holocaust—lit. whole burnt offering; the genocide of European Jews that occurred during World War II. See also *Shoah*.

Holy Land—the area between the Mediterranean Sea and the Jordan River most sacred to Jews, Christians, and Muslims; roughly the area of Israel, Palestine, Jordan, Lebanon, and Syria.

Incarnation—the belief in Christianity that God became human (enfleshed) in Jesus Christ.

intertextuality—the interpretation of one text by another text.

Israel, Land of—term referring to the geographical area of biblical Israel; in Hebrew *eretz Israel*. As distinct from the biblical area of the Northern Kingdom, Land of Israel encompasses both Northern and Southern Kingdoms.

Israel, the nation—political state created in 1947 by a United Nations mandate that formally came into existence in 1948.

Israel, the people—term referring to the biblical people with whom God made a covenant at Mount Sinai. Israel can also simply refer to the Jewish people as a religious group.

Israeli—a citizen of the modern political nation Israel.

Israelite—term describing a descendant of the biblical figure Jacob, also called *Israel*. The Israelites were made up of *b'nai Israel*, the sons of Israel. Jews were called "Israelites" well into the nineteenth century.

Israelite religion—the beliefs and practices of biblical Israel, as distinct from Rabbinic Judaism and Christianity.

Jew—the religious and cultural designation of an individual belonging to an ethnic group that claims biblical origins. Originally the term *Judean*, from which we get the English word *Jew*, signified people who lived in Judea. Later on, it became the identification for practitioners of the religion of Judaism.

Judaize—a term of disapprobation used by Christians that refers to the adoption of Jewish beliefs or practices by Christians.

Judea—variant of Judah. A Roman province in the first century CE in the land once known as the Southern Kingdom in the period of the Israelites. More broadly, a term for the first-century geographical region that encompassed several Roman provinces that now comprise Israel and Palestine.

Judenmission—German word that describes missionary efforts to convert Jews to Christianity.

Kabbalah—a mystical branch of Judaism popular in the Medieval and Renaissance eras that relies extensively on symbolic interpretation of scripture.

KJV—King James Version of the Bible.

Late Antiquity—the era in European history that runs from the second to the eighth centuries CE.

lit.—literally; usually indicating the original definition of a word rather than its meaning in general usage.

liturgy—lit. work of the people; communal worship according to prescribed forms rather than private devotion.

Logos—lit. word, reason; in Greek philosophy, the creative principle of the One; in Jewish philosophy, a divine being or principle who assists God in creation; in Christian theology, the Word of God incarnate in Jesus Christ.

Masorah—lit. tradition; textual apparatus developed between the seventh and tenth centuries CE that standardized spelling and grammar in the Hebrew Bible.

Messiah—lit. anointed one; in Judaism, traditionally seen as a political figure who will restore the Jewish kingdom on earth. In Christianity, a salvific figure, namely Jesus Christ, who will return to bring about the kingdom of God on earth.

Messianic Judaism—the branch of Judaism in which Jesus is accepted as the Jewish Messiah. Messianic Jews continue to observe Jewish rites, rituals, and customs.

midrash—lit. explanation through study; rabbinic mode of biblical commentary that examines letters, words, sentences, and stories to deduce meaning in the text.

millenialism—belief in collective redemption on earth or in heaven brought about by God or God's agent working with or without human assistance; also called millenarianism.

millennium—the time of the collective redemption of all people; in Christianity, the thousand-year reign of Christ (Revelation 20).

Mishnah—lit. repetition; the oldest collection of rabbinic traditions, compiled in the early third century CE.

NJPS—New Jewish Publication Society translation of Tanakh.

NRSV—New Revised Standard Version of the Bible.

Noachide Laws—laws of Noah's offspring; the seven biblical laws given to Adam and Noah prior to the revelation at Mount Sinai incumbent upon non-Jews. The laws prohibit idolatry, blasphemy, bloodshed, sexual sins, theft, and eating from a living animal (since some cultures amputated limbs to consume but still kept the animal alive); a final instruction is to establish a legal system to enforce the other laws.

Oral Torah—traditions of scripture interpretation, especially legal judgments, believed to have been received by Moses at Mount Sinai at the same time that he received Written Torah; committed to writing in the early third century.

p.—papacy; that is, the duration of the rule of a pope.

Palestine, nation of—political state created in 1947 by a United Nations mandate and acknowledged by the UN as an independent nation in 1988.

Palestine, territory of—historically, a large geographical area extending from the Mediterranean Sea into what is modern Palestine, Israel, Jordan, and Syria. This name was used from the seventh-century Muslim conquest until 1947. See also *Byzantine Palestina*.

Pentateuch—the first five books of the Bible; also known as Torah.

philosemitism—the sentiment or action by non-Jews of appreciation, respect, or support of Jews and Jewish culture.

Pirkei Avot—Sayings (or Ethics) of the Fathers, a collection of aphorisms said by Jewish sages prior to the early third century.

post-Holocaust theology—a movement among Christian theologians that attempts to reformulate Christian teachings to eliminate elements of antisemitism; arose in response to the recognition of Christian guilt for the Holocaust.

Pseudepigrapha—Jewish and Christian books written anonymously ca. 250 BCE to 200 CE and attributed to biblical figures such as Moses, Noah, Enoch, and others.

r.—reign; dates follow the r. to indicate when a ruler reigned.

Rabbinic Judaism—Jewish thought and practice centered on interpretation of Torah and postbiblical traditions by sages and then rabbis that developed in the first centuries after the destruction of the temple in Jerusalem, 70 CE; distinct from Israelite religion.

Revised Common Lectionary—a list of Bible texts to be used in churches based on a three-year cycle of readings.

Roman Empire—extensive political and social structure that dominated the entire Mediterranean basin and parts of Europe, North Africa, and the Near East, 27 BCE–476 CE.

sages—Hebrew *chachamim*; learned teachers and interpreters of Torah in the pre-rabbinic period of Judaism.

salvation—preservation or deliverance from evil, sin, or death. In Christianity, the work of God through the Incarnation and the atoning death of Christ. In Judaism, God's ultimate redemption of Israel.

Second Temple Judaism—the period from the building of the second temple in Jerusalem ca. 515 BCE to its destruction by the Romans in 70 CE; a time of spiritual development in Judaic religions.

Sefaria—online collection of Jewish texts, https://www.sefaria.org/.

Seleucid Empire—hellenistic rule of the eastern Mediterranean basin from 312–63 BCE, founded by Seleucus I Nicator, a general in Alexander the Great's army.

Septuagint—Greek translation of Jewish Scripture, completed in third century BCE.

Shoah—lit. catastrophe; the genocide of European Jews during World War II. See also *Holocaust*.

single-covenant theology—the post-Holocaust theology that asserts that God's original covenant with Israel includes salvation of the gentiles with the coming of Christ.

supersessionism—belief that with the coming of Christ, Christianity replaced Judaism, with Christians supplanting Jews as the New Israel. Also called *triumphalism*.

Synoptic Gospels—the first three gospels in the New Testament. Matthew, Mark, and Luke have many of the same stories and can be seen together.

Talmud—lit. learning; the central text of Rabbinic Judaism, composed of the Gemara and the Mishnah. The *Talmud Yerushalmi* (Jerusalem Talmud, or Palestinian Talmud) was composed in Aramaic in Palestine by the late fourth or early fifth centuries CE. The *Talmud Bavli* (Babylonian Talmud) was written in Hebrew in Babylonia and completed between the late fifth and late eight centuries CE.

Tanakh—acronym for Torah (Instruction or Law), Nevi'im (Prophets), and Ketuvim (Writings) that comprise the Jewish Bible.

Targumim—Aramaic translations and interpretations of Hebrew scriptures; singular is Targum.

teaching of contempt—term used by Jewish historian Jules Isaac to characterize antisemitic traditions that Christians hold about Jews.

tikkun olam—lit. mending, fixing; the Jewish concept of working to repair or perfect the world.

Torah—lit. instruction, law; the first five books of the Bible. Torah also refers to all instruction revealed by God at Mount Sinai, both written and oral.

triumphalism—see *supersessionism*.

typology—the symbolic reading of texts in which people or events are understood as "types" or "figures" anticipating something to come later; e.g., the priest Melchizedek (Genesis 14:18, Psalms 110:4) as a type or prefiguration of Jesus.

Vulgate—the Latin translation of the Old and New Testaments completed by the Christian theologian Jerome in the fourth century CE. The Vulgate served as the Bible in the West until the Protestant Reformation and Roman Catholics continued to use it into the twentieth century.

Zionism—a diverse movement that has the goal of securing and defending a nation-state for the Jewish people.

Introduction

DEEP EQUALITY: A WAY BEYOND ANTISEMITISM AND PHILOSEMITISM

Historically speaking, there have always been alternatives to antipathy, hatred and violence even in the troubled history of Jewish-Christian relations. Yet the full picture of this history still remains to be painted.

—WOLFRAM KINZIG[1]

Bence Illyés was troubled when he encountered the collapsed tombstones and waist-high weeds in the Jewish cemetery of Tállya in northeastern Hungary. So in the fall of 2020, the Christian activist and scholar organized a team of volunteers to restore and rehabilitate the cemetery. Composed primarily of non-Jews, the team cleaned fallen markers, pruned trees, cleared out weeds, and discovered some rare Sephardic tombstones. As in many places throughout Europe, the Tállya cemetery bears mute witness to a once-thriving Jewish community. Illyés sees his task as nurturing the memory of Jews from the past and safeguarding Jewish culture in the present. "As a Christian," he writes, "it is also important for me to preserve the meaning of the traditional Jewish world."[2] Illyés hopes to restore other rural and historic Jewish cemeteries through-out Hungary. He is optimistic since more than 140 international donors supported his crowdfunding campaign for the Tállya cemetery.

In 2019, when fire damaged Trinity African Methodist Episcopal Zion Church in Birmingham, Alabama, the congregation of Temple Emanu-el welcomed the displaced Christians to their facility, saying "Our space is your space." This was not the first time the Reform Jewish congregation—the largest Jewish assembly in the state—had opened its building to a church in search of worship and meeting rooms. This was merely an example of tikkun olam, the Jewish commitment to repairing the world, according to the temple's cantor Jessica Roskin. "What that means is to act and to do as we would wish ourselves to be treated and to welcome the stranger."[3] Although Trinity AMEZ members had temporarily been meeting in another church, the move to the Jewish facility gave them more space and more freedom, especially since the temple was not used on Sundays. "They have opened their arms, not just their doors," said the church pastor, the Rev. Erskine Faush, Jr.[4]

These are just two of countless examples of Jews and Christians working together in common cause. Stories abound of cooperative efforts—from mutual efforts in 2004 protesting Mel Gibson's antisemitic depiction of Jesus's death in his movie *The Passion of the Christ,* to joint campaigns to fight food insecurity in the United Kingdom in 2020. On the seventy-fifth anniversary of the end of World War II, Jews and Christians held memorial services for Holocaust victims through interfaith virtual connections on a global scale during the COVID-19 pandemic. Major instructional ventures focus on Holocaust education, antisemitism awareness, and programs that teach respect for religious difference. Alongside the many high-profile projects, Jews and Christians in thousands of small groups around the world are engaged in interfaith dialogue, including scripture study, book clubs, and informal discussions.

These facts are obscured, however, by the international growth in antisemitism expressed in violence directed at Jews and Jewish institutions. Antisemitic graffiti, vandalism, harassment, verbal abuse, and physical assaults are on the rise. In the United States alone, FBI data from 2019 showed an escalation in the total number of hate crimes, with a large increase in those directed at Jews. T-shirts bearing antisemitic slogans—such as 6MWNE (Six Million Were Not Enough) and Camp Auschwitz, with the subhead Work Brings Freedom (*Arbeit Macht Frei* was the slogan that appeared at the gates of concentration and death camps)—show the visibility and mainstreaming of white supremacists in America today. As historian Deborah Lipstadt observes, antisemitism exists "here and now."[5]

Positive depictions of Jewish and Christian relations go unnoticed for another reason. What I am calling a "master narrative" has dictated considerations of the history of Jews and Christians since the nineteenth century. This narrative emphasizes problems, with conflict driving the conversation and antagonism taking center stage. It begins with the earliest debates between Jesus and the Pharisees in the New Testament. It continues with Christian hostility toward the people who refused to accept Jesus as the Messiah, that is, the Jews. This animosity flares into persecution in the late Middle Ages, with massacres of Jewish communities occurring in Europe as crusaders made their way to the Holy Land. Although the Age of Enlightenment brings some reprieve from the mistreatment that Jews suffer at the hands of Christians, discrimination remains widespread. Paradoxically, as Jews enter the mainstream, antisemitism does as well.[6] Christian tradition promotes a persistent and virulent "teaching of contempt" that demonizes Jews and serves as the backdrop to the rise of Nazism and the ensuing Holocaust in the twentieth century.[7] In our own era, anti-Israel sentiment stokes anti-Jewish hatred in the Muslim world, while economic hardship fuels hatred of Jews in the Christian world.

It is certainly imperative to understand this history in view of two millennia of Jewish suffering at the hands of non-Jews, culminating in the catastrophe—the Shoah—in which more than six million Jews are systematically murdered. Christian culpability for the centuries of persecution must be exposed in order to eliminate inhumanity in the future. A glance at the titles of popular books written by Christians and Jews throughout the twentieth and into the twenty-first centuries documents that record: *The Teaching of Contempt, Faith and Fratricide, The Christian Jewish Tragedy, The Crucifixion of the Jews, Constantine's Sword*, and *Betrayal*, to list just a few. These books are appropriate and necessary, given the hardships that Jews have experienced at the hands of Christians.

But they do not tell the whole story. Their melancholy account of Jewish and Christian relations is incomplete and even inaccurate. The Jewish historian Salo Baron uses the expression "lachrymose"—that is, tearful or sad—to criticize certain depictions of Jewish history. In contrast to accounts that present Jewish life in the Middle Ages as irredeemably tragic, Baron argues that Jews were better off in the medieval era than in the modern period.[8] His primary point is relevant: the history of interactions between Jews and Christians varies as to time and place. In contrast, the traditional story of Jewish and Christian relations tends to ignore fluctuations in the treatment and status of the Jews and stresses only conflict and competition.

What if we were to tell the story of Jewish and Christian relations in a new way, taking into account some of the variables that Baron notes? We might adopt a different stance and claim that antisemitism is the minority opinion.[9] We might see that friendship is the norm and antisemitism is the aberration.[10]

A generation of Christian and Jewish scholars writing at the end of the twentieth and into the twenty-first centuries is revisiting the melancholy history in exactly this way. First, they are recovering the records hiding in plain sight, the manuscripts and documents that were always there and just needed some attention. Examination of these items is generating new perspectives on timeworn conventions. Re-evaluation of old assumptions and the study of new evidence reveal that similarities far outweigh differences between members of the two religions. Jews and Christians frequently seem to be working on parallel tracks if not actually in tandem. New appraisals also illuminate the friendship and cooperation that exist between adherents of the two faiths. Second, scholars themselves are part of the new history. Engaging in candid dialogue as they study shared interests and concerns—from Jesus and the sages of early Judaism to post-Holocaust religious developments—Jewish and Christian academics, theologians, and clergy are enlarging our knowledge of the past in significant ways.

Nevertheless, the enormity of the Holocaust appears to engulf any attempt to challenge the master narrative. Is it too soon to outline a counter history when most Christians have not even come to understand how their dogma has justified oppression of Jews or to accept their culpability for the Holocaust? Despite these concerns—and they are big ones—I argue that the time is ripe for a fresh look at the history of Jewish and Christian relations. Paradoxically, this is because the Holocaust serves as the impetus for a new and unforeseen friendship to develop between Jews and Christians. A cohort of Christian denominations and individuals actively pursue not only reconciliation with Jews but genuine repentance for the sin of antisemitism. Convinced of the sincerity of their Christian counterparts, Jews cautiously enter into conversation. The small steps taken in the 1960s and 1970s lead to dramatic changes in considerations of Judaism and Christianity by the end of the twentieth century. Christian seminaries introduce Jewish Studies into their curriculum to locate Jesus and the early church in their religious context. Jewish seminaries include the New Testament as required reading for understanding first-century Judaic thought. Scholars of both faiths, and no faith, undertake critical investigation of the history of Christian antisemitism. While there is more to be done in that regard, those surveys pave the way for explorations into the ways in which Christians and Jews have cooperated and assisted each other across the centuries.

We are currently witnessing an upsurge in the study of philosemitism, a phenomenon few can name and fewer still can identify. Philosemitism "is that sentiment or action which supports or discriminates in favor of persons called Jewish on the grounds that, being Jewish, they possess certain desirable traits."[11] It denotes the existence of regard for rather than hostility toward Jews.

Fewer than a handful of books about philosemitism are published for general audiences after World War II, and most of those focus on individuals and significant events.[12] Similarly, only a few scholars take up the subject.[13] Since the turn of the twenty-first century, however, many are publishing analyses of a variety of primary sources, examining diaries, journals, letters, and other documents that illuminate the day-to-day contacts Jews and Christians have had with each other. Their findings frequently subvert long-held opinions that the two groups had few interactions at all, and mainly negative ones when they did. The numerous books and countless articles on philosemitism today tell a different story.[14]

Beyond the Dialectic to Deep Equality

A shift in the focus from the tension of antisemitism–philosemitism to the consideration of regard–engagement ought to affect our understanding of the history of Jewish and Christian relations. In her book *Deep Equality in an Era of Religious Diversity*, Lori Beaman laments the fact that society tends to turn religious distinctions into problems by emphasizing contention and competition. Trained in law, philosophy, and sociology, Beaman directed the University of Ottawa's Religion and Diversity Project from 2010 to 2017. This international study collected narratives of success, rather than failure, in the encounters that ordinary people have as they negotiate religious variance on a daily basis outside the realm of law and public policy. Beaman observes, "Narratives of conflict and controversy dominate both scholarship and media coverage of religious difference."[15] The Diversity Project demonstrates that in daily interactions, people frequently minimize differences, especially religious ones, rather than emphasize them simply in order to get along.

Relying on her findings, Beaman introduces the concept of deep equality as a preferable alternative to legal and political demands for tolerance and accommodation. As praiseworthy and necessary as they are, tolerance and accommodation suggest a hierarchy that retains the status quo for the religious majority while protecting, but not fully accepting, religious minorities. At the same time, though tolerance can foster resentment and hostility between those doing the tolerating and the ones being tolerated, it should not be abandoned as an impossibly idealistic maximum approach.[16] Nevertheless, shifting the focus to deep equality from public policy and social norms "relocates equality as a process rather than a definition, and as lived rather than prescribed,"[17] according to Beaman. She contrasts the idea of simply "living together," which tolerance and accommodation provide, with Jacques Derrida's idea of "living well together," which characterizes deep equality.[18] Everyone flourishes, rather than simply survives, in a culture of deep equality.

By using the principle of deep equality as a guide throughout this book, I will recount the times that Christians and Jews who, working together, have demonstrated instances of this process. I make no attempt to cover all two thousand years of history and in no way claim to be comprehensive. In fact, I focus largely on the developments in scholarship and dialogue in the twentieth and twenty-first centuries. I adopt a thematic approach that treats particular moments or movements that have contributed to Derrida's concept of "living well together" as I tell this new story in rough chronological order. Some readers may wonder why certain important individuals or events go unremarked upon, while little-known people and incidents are highlighted. No one is more aware of what is "missing" than I am, but other books address the large personalities and significant episodes. I confess to being selective and partial, rather than exhaustive and impartial, in my presentation of evidence. I admit to concentrating on positive rather than negative examples. My goal is to tell the story of Jewish and Christian relations in a fresh way, utilizing Beaman's framework. My profound debt to her theorizing is evident throughout this book.

Deep equality is characterized by a number of factors. These include:

- Recognition of similarity and acceptance of difference
- Acknowledgment of complex identity
- Cooperation and neighborliness
- Repentance and forgiveness
- Agonistic respect and courage
- Generosity

Each chapter in this book demonstrates at least one element from this list by providing examples drawn from past and present.

Part 1, Reading Scripture Anew, discusses the component of recognition of similarity and acceptance of difference. It focuses on three things that seem to set Christians apart from Jews: the Bible, Jesus, and Paul. Chapter 1 looks at how critical biblical studies have created opportunities for Jews and Christians to work together to gain new insights on ancient truths. Inquiries into the issue of anti-semitism in the New Testament have also created greater awareness of problematic texts and traditions. Similarly, research into the historical Jesus, as discussed in Chapter 2, has recovered the Jewishness of Jesus, to the benefit of Christians and Jews alike. Jesus is easier for Jews to accept than is Paul, but Chapter 3 shows how new readings of the apostle's letters have recovered his Jewishness as well. Sharing insights and information, scholars of both faiths are identifying the ways in which their earliest traditions reveal a common heritage that nonetheless generates existential differences between Jews and Christians.

Part 2, Complex Identity, takes an important concept developed by Beaman and applies it to three historical situations. Individuals are complex beings who navigate between multiple identities, goals, and purposes. Rarely are they completely Jewish, totally Irish, or entirely Republican. Impurity, rather than purity, characterizes human society and individuality, and it is only by accepting the reality of complicated personalities with mixed motives that deep equality can emerge. Beaman calls this fact of social interaction "contaminated diversity," which she sees as a disruption of imagined notions of purity of identity. "It is contamination, rather than purity, that predominates and circulates widely in social life," she writes.[19] Although I agree with this sentiment, the word *contamination* and its synonyms—pollution, adulteration, corruption, infection, uncleanness, impurity—are so negative that I have softened the expression to "complex identity." I think that complex identity captures the reality in which an individual can, and frequently does, endorse two or more opposing opinions or practices at the same time. This is especially true of religious adherents whose observances may conflict with orthodoxy—such as Catholics who use birth control, Jews who place a menorah next to a Christmas tree (or Hanukkah bush), or Mormons who enjoy a cup of coffee.

Chapter 4 thus considers the complicated paths that lead to the emergence of Rabbinic Judaism and Christianity. The complex identities of early Jews and Christians make it difficult at times for outsiders to tell the difference between the two, even though religious authorities are outlining clear distinctions. Chapter 5 investigates the paradox of Christian Hebraism, that is, the abiding interest that Christian scholars have in the Hebrew text of the Bible. Jewish scholars help their non-Jewish counterparts with language, linguistics, and grammar. Christians work with Jews to print Hebrew literature and religious texts. No one's motives in these endeavors are entirely altruistic. They are complex. Yet the cooperation between Jews and Christians produces a remarkable literature that resonates even today. The King James Bible is just one of many examples of this. Finally, Chapter 6 discusses the puzzle that is Christian Zionism and the evangelical impulse that prompts Christians in the nineteenth century to support resettlement of Jews in Palestine. These missionary endeavors encourage Jewish assimilation, conversion to Christianity, and Jewish nationalism as Christians sponsor the restoration of a homeland and advocate for Jews against mounting antisemitism.

Complex identity helps to explain why some Christians firmly believe that Christianity supersedes Judaism and, at the same time, value individual Jews and Jewish culture. The purity of their love of Jews is contaminated by their desire to convert them. Their esteem for Hebrew is polluted by their dislike, or even hatred, of Jews. A Christian might well have "positive feelings toward Judaism as a religion, friendly feelings toward actual, living Jews, or reverence for Hebrew as the sacred language of the Hebrew Bible or 'Old' Testament"[20] and still be committed to beliefs and opinions that Jews find appalling. We find occasions of complex identity among Jews as well. Certainly complicated reasons inspire some Jews to study the Bible in order to refute Christian claims, rather than to read it for spiritual edification. The first Hebrew Bible concordance, in fact, is written to counter Christian arguments. In the nineteenth century, the *Taufjuden* (baptized Jews) unquestionably have mixed motives and feelings concerning their Christian baptism—some out of conviction, others to obtain university appointments, political positions, and economic opportunities otherwise unavailable to them.

Part 3 devotes four chapters to Transformations after the Holocaust. Chapter 7 analyzes Christian response, and lack of response, to the growing violence against Jews before World War II and the near-annihilation of European Jews during the war. Chapter 8 describes the ways in which Christians attempt to repent and atone for their silence during the Holocaust, focusing primarily on Vatican Council II in the early 1960s. At this ecumenical council, the Roman Catholic Church issues a groundbreaking statement on its relationship with Jews. Although criticized by Jews and Christians alike as not going far enough, *Nostra Aetate* (In Our Age) creates a strong foundation for ongoing dialogue between Christians and Jews. Chapter 9 reviews the early efforts to engage in this dialogue, noting the concerns a number of Jews have about such participation, given the history of enforced disputations. Concluding this part is Chapter 10, which outlines the elements of post-Holocaust Christian theology—the approach to understanding Christian doctrine that avoids antisemitic presuppositions. But Jewish theology also undergoes a significant shift after the Holocaust, and this, too, is explored.

Several themes relating to deep equality arise throughout Part 3. Although it seems a miniscule thing in light of the enormity of the Holocaust, it is neighborliness that leads many rescuers to their work. A sense of community and common cause—in short, a feeling of friendship and concern for their neighbors—causes Danish citizens to rescue the nation's 7,000 to 8,000 Jews during World War II. Although King Christian never parades through the streets of Copenhagen wearing a yellow badge, as mythology has it, he nonetheless declares that, in Denmark, Jews are Danes first and Jews second.[21] More significantly, it is ordinary people who stage the October 1943 rescue by hiding Jews in their homes or taking them by boat to Sweden, where they are concealed in private residences. "The crucial point is that the refugees could count on their countrymen and engage friends, colleagues, and neighbors, as a matter of course, in their efforts to find a way out."[22]

Additional transformations that take place after the Holocaust relate to the work of deep equality. First is the work of repentance and forgiveness that occurs between Christians and Jews after the Holocaust. Only a few churches issue statements of atonement in the decades following World War II, but eventually virtually every denomination and branch of Christianity expresses sorrow and remorse over its failure to protect Jews. And as recently as 2020, the Dutch Protestant Church has admitted for the first time its failure to condemn antisemitism before and during World War II. Second, Beaman's concept of agonistic respect is an apt characterization of the interactions that occur in response to the Holocaust. "Respect is 'agonistic' because it requires an abandonment of 'rightness' and the conviction that one is imbued with the truth through some sort of transcendent authority."[23] Such respect opens up the possibility for dialogue. It is agonistic, or argumentative, in the sense that as we respectfully listen to others with whom we disagree, they respectfully listen to us in their own disagreement. This kind of engagement requires the courage to listen, learn, and to be able to live with an appreciation for indeterminacy, that is, the possibility that we may not yet have all the answers. Finally, the spirit of generosity exhibited by participants in Jewish and Christian dialogue exemplifies deep equality. Kind, thoughtful, and unselfish but honest discussions create a number of breakthroughs in relationships between Jews and Christians.

Part 4 closes with Present Prospects. Chapter 11 contends that Zionism and evangelism are two similar religious impulses driving in opposite directions. Zionism is the inward drive of Jews to the land and nationhood, and evangelism is the outward propulsion of Christians into the world. Cooperation between Jews and Christians has resulted in support for the establishment of the state of Israel and the ongoing backing of Christian Zionists. Meanwhile, Christian encouragement for the nation of Palestine and Palestinians creates tensions between Jews and Christians. Chapter 12 concludes the book by outlining the place that a history of Jewish and Christian relations finds in the study of Judaism and Christianity. The last fifty years demonstrate that things really can change. Through personal and professional dialogue, collaboration on scholarly projects, and partnerships in modifying worship and teaching materials, Jews and Christians are fashioning a new narrative based on mutual regard and appreciation.

Concluding Introductory Notes

Popular works highlighting the tragic past have overshadowed the prodigious work of scholars—which numbers in the thousands of books, monographs, articles, and lectures—that offer an alternative to the chronicle of Jewish victimization and Christian oppression. This neglect of countervailing accounts not only distorts the past but contributes to misunderstanding in the present. If ordinary Jews and Christians do not become aware of ideas that contest their prejudices and stereotypes, then academicians are talking only to each other. That is why I have written this book specifically for a nonspecialist audience. I hope to interpret and report on the important scholarship that has occurred over the past fifty years in a way that lay readers can understand and appreciate.

I have written on the assumption that some Jewish readers may be unfamiliar with Christian terminology, such as justification by faith, works righteousness, and Incarnation. I also presuppose that there are Christian readers unfamiliar with Jewish concepts, like halakhah, Tanakh, and Oral Torah. This is why a table of terms used in the book appears at the very outset and why I try to explain theological expressions when they first appear.

Although it is anachronistic to equate anti-Judaism (hatred of Judaism as a religion) with antisemitism (hatred of Jews as a race), I have chosen to use a single term—antisemitism—to encompass all forms of Jew hatred, simply to avoid confusion. In their efforts to differentiate Christianity from Judaism, early Christian theologians write anti-Jewish tracts attempting to demonstrate the superiority of their faith over that of the Jews. Christians assert that Judaism is a religion of worthless superstitions and outmoded customs. By the nineteenth century, Protestant biblical theologians seem to believe that Judaism is long dead, calling the religion of Jesus's era "Late Judaism." The message is clear: Judaism is an inferior religion that has been superseded by Christianity. This widespread, cultural anti-Judaism operates primarily at a theological and philosophical, rather than a personal, level. On the one hand, it frequently exists within the ecclesiastical hierarchy rather than in the populace, though sometimes, on the other hand, the church must protect Jews from the hatred of the local parishioners. In theory, a person could disdain Judaism and still like Jews, along the lines of the "hate the sin, love the sinner" theology of some present-day Christians. Anti-Judaism appropriately describes this religious antipathy. In reality, however, the distinction between religion and its adherents is blurred, and in the end, violence against Jews—rather than the abstract concept of Judaism—is the result. This is why I prefer using antisemitism to cover all forms of hatred of Jews.

I am generally avoiding the words *philosemitic* or *philosemitism* because they meet with, at best, ambivalence among Jews and, at worst, antipathy. I agree that the term philosemitism is problematic, given the philosemite's stereotypical and at times obsessive fascination with Jews as Jews rather than as individuals. One scholar believes that the search for "unadulterated philosemitism" may be akin to the quest for the Holy Grail.[24] There is no entry for the subject of philosemitism, or philo-Semitism with a hyphen, in the *Encyclopedia Judaica*, the *New Catholic Encyclopedia*, or on the U.S. Holocaust Memorial Museum website. This suggests that mainstream sources reject the term. Even spellcheck on the computer does not recognize a philosemite, offering Phil Semite as an alternative.

Scholars have yet another term at their disposal: *allosemitism*, which "refers to the practice of setting the Jews apart as people radically different from all the others."[25] Allosemites perceive Jews as somehow "other" in either a bad way or a good way. They maintain a deep ambivalence toward Jews. For example, people may either admire the perseverance of the Jews in overcoming centuries of dispersion and discrimination, or despise that same perseverance as a symptom of stubborn antisocial clannishness. This ambivalence may ultimately lead to antisemitism. It is worth knowing this expression but, like the words philosemitism and anti-Judaism, I have chosen not to make use of it.

Finally, I'd like to make it clear that my purpose in writing this book is not to assert that a sunny storyline should replace the timeworn melancholy recital. I simply wish to illuminate a perspective on Jewish and Christian relations well-known in scholarly circles but generally unfamiliar to popular audiences, especially readers attentive to interreligious dialogue and rapport. It is a truism that we find what we are looking for. If we search for instances of oppression and violence, we will most surely find them. If we search for examples of mutual aid and assistance, we will find those as well.

Part I

READING SCRIPTURE ANEW

Chapter 1

THE BIBLE: BARRIER
AND BRIDGE

The deepest bond between Judaism and Christianity is a common text, the Hebrew Bible.

—MICHAEL WYSCHOGROD[1]

When Jews and Christians disagree over the meaning of scripture, the Bible may serve as a barrier to respect and friendship. Are the commandments given on Mount Sinai eternally enduring? Does the Suffering Servant prophesied by Isaiah represent the people Israel or Jesus? Do the Israelites crossing the Red Sea prefigure Christians in the waters of baptism? But when Christians and Jews consider what they have in common, the Bible becomes a bridge that overcomes the divide. Members of the two faiths see that they share the patriarchs and matriarchs, the tales of kings and kingdoms, the prophets and their wisdom, the Psalms and the writings. Though they may understand their mutual heritage differently, they retain a profound and unbreakable connection.

But what exactly is the text that Jews and Christians both claim? The Jewish Tanakh and the Protestant Old Testament contain the same books originally written in Hebrew (with a few parts composed in Aramaic), although the order of the books differs. The Catholic and Orthodox Old Testaments also include a half dozen books written in Greek. Tanakh is the acronym for Torah, Nevi'im, and Ketuvim, that is, Instruction, Prophets, Writings. Instruction

17

or teaching is a more accurate rendering of Torah than law, and when Jews say "*the* Torah," they usually mean the first five books of the Bible. It may sound simplistic, but it is true that Jews and Christians fundamentally part company over the interpretation of this collection of texts. Everything that each holds most dear and most sacred depends upon how the Old Testament and Tanakh are read. These scriptures relate the saga of the Israelites and their understanding of God's role in history. It is not the story of Rabbinic Judaism or Christianity, but an account of antecedents.

The revelation of God described in Tanakh and the Old Testament continues, however, recounted in additional texts and explicated in layers of interpretation. For Christians, collections of oral teachings given by Jesus, along with letters sent by various apostles written in the first century, begin to be compiled in the second century. These eventually form the basis of the New Testament, which, in effect, is an interpretation of the Old Testament in light of a belief in God's new revelation in Jesus Christ. Subsequent interpretations of the Old and the New Testaments written in succeeding centuries by church leaders and scholars become authoritative, particularly for Catholic and Orthodox Christians. Jews follow a similar process, in which collections of oral teachings about torah given by sages in the first century BCE and the first and second centuries CE are compiled by the third century. (The lowercase *torah,* without the definite article *the,* usually refers to the entire body of Jewish law and instruction, rather than to scripture alone.) These make up the Mishnah, a compendium of legal traditions. Later interpretations of Torah and of the Mishnah, developed in Palestine and in Babylonia, are collected into what is called the Gemara (literally, to finish or to complete). Mishnah and Gemara together make up the Talmud, a body of writings known as Oral Torah and believed to have been given by God on Mount Sinai. (There are two Talmuds: one compiled in the Land of Israel by the end of the fourth century CE and a second compiled in Babylonia by the end of the eighth.) The Oral Torah complements the Written Torah of the Tanakh, just as the interpretation of church leaders complements the Old and New Testaments. In short, God speaks in Tanakh and Old Testament and continues to speak in Talmud and New Testament. Although Jews treasure Moses and the revelation at Sinai, and Christians treasure the apostles and the revelation in Jesus, their respective religions grow organically out of the interpretations of subsequent Jewish rabbis and Christian theologians.

There are a number of exegetical issues—that is, questions of biblical interpretation—that either bring Jews and Christians together or drive them apart. Sectarian labels for scripture have caused division and distress—Tanakh or Old Testament? Hebrew Bible or Jewish Scripture? Although Jews and Christians share a number of exegetical styles and methods, the content of interpretation is widely divergent. Jewish New Testament scholars Amy-Jill Levine and Marc Zvi Brettler skillfully capture this issue with the title of their book *The Bible With and Without Jesus,* which examines how Christians and Jews read the same stories differently—Christians through the eyes of the New Testament and Jews through the rabbinic tradition.[2] Nevertheless, we find remarkable parallels, if not actual accord, when we look at the process of interpretation. The introduction of historical criticism—a new way of reading religious texts (discussed below)—skirts this issue by providing all parties a common set of ground rules and exegetical language. The question of who gets to interpret, however, remains. From the earliest times, Jews and Christians attempt to control interpretation chiefly by limiting interpretive authority. Again, a similar approach leads to widely differing results. A final issue in examining the ways in which the Bible can be either a barrier or a bridge is the apparent antisemitism of the New Testament. Christians have only just begun to face this problem directly, with the support and encouragement of Jewish scholars. At times this move has questioned the very authority of scripture.

The difficult and sometimes challenging work of biblical scholars and those with a personal and spiritual interest in understanding the Bible reveals areas of convergence and divergence between Jews and Christians. Both the academic field of biblical studies and the individual spiritual quest in Bible or Talmud study serve as the locus for encountering difference in positive and constructive ways. Recognizing similarities and accepting differences contribute to the process of deep equality.

Terms of Estrangement

To understand the interpretive battle over scripture, it is necessary to review some of the factors that have contributed to the history of animosity, oppression, fear, and suspicion that exists between Jews and Christians. Jews refer to Written Torah as Tanakh, which consists of thirty-nine books. Jewish tradition holds, however, that there are only twenty-four, counting the minor prophets as a single book, and 1 and 2 Kings, Ezra and Nehemiah, and 1 and 2 Chronicles as single books. The Protestant Old Testament contains the same thirty-nine books, while the Catholic and Orthodox Old Testaments include six additional books that are written by Greek-speaking Jews before the second century of the Common Era. In the world of biblical studies, the term "Hebrew Bible" is preferred to acknowledge, or include, Jews in their own scripture. Though in conversation, Catholic and Orthodox Christians may say "Hebrew Bible" to acknowledge the Bible's Jewish origins, for them this term is not interchangeable with "Old Testament."

Hebrew Bible is problematic in another way, since a Greek translation of Jewish scripture influences Jews and Christians for centuries. Called the Septuagint and abbreviated LXX, or 70, after a legend concerning its divinely inspired origin, this version is widely used by Jews in the Diaspora from the early second century BCE and by Christians in the first century CE. Aware of the LXX's shortcomings, Jews in the second century CE begin correcting mistranslations, expunging Christian additions, conforming the Greek text to existing Hebrew texts, and developing entirely new Greek translations. Writing in Greek, the authors of the books of the New

Testament read the LXX as prophesying the life, death, and resurrection of Jesus. Other translations or versions of Hebrew scripture appear both in Palestine and in the Diaspora. Most notable are the Targumim, which convert Hebrew texts into Aramaic and interpret them at the same time. For any number of reasons, therefore, Tanakh might be preferable terminology to Hebrew Bible.

But how do Christians respond to the concern expressed by Jews about calling their scripture an "old" testament? The language of testament originates in Jesus's words at the Last Supper: "This cup is the new testament in my blood, which is poured out for you" (Luke 22:20, KJV). For linguistic reasons, modern translators render "testament" as "covenant" most of the time, but retain testament where it is more appropriate—for example, Hebrews 9:16: "For where there is a testament, there must also of necessity be the death of the testator" (KJV). Jesus is clearly referring to the new covenant promised in the book of Jeremiah:

> See, a time is coming—declares the Lord—when I will make a new covenant with the House of Israel and the House of Judah. It will not be like the covenant I made with their fathers, when I took them by the hand to lead them out of the land of Egypt.... I will put My Teaching into their inmost being and inscribe it upon their hearts. (Jeremiah 31:31, 33 NJPS)

Followers of Jesus pick up the new covenant language very early, since Paul reports the tradition in his first letter to the church at Corinth. He presents Jesus's words at the Lord's Supper as "This cup is the new covenant in my blood" (1 Corinthians 11:25 NRSV). The "old" covenant is the one given by God on Mount Sinai, and the "new" covenant is the one given by Jesus at Mount Calvary.

Those engaged in dialogue with Jews attempt to provide euphemisms for the Old Testament. Some call it the First Testament, which has biblical warrant (Hebrews 9:1, 15).[3] Others call it the Prime Testament.[4] Original Testament might catch on, if internet usage is any indication. It seems unlikely, however, that Christians will ever abandon the centuries-old name, despite the best efforts of those sensitized to how offensive Old Testament and New Testament may sound to Jews.

While we take the form of the Tanakh and the Christian Bible for granted, it requires centuries for a canon, or official listing, of scripture to be settled for both Jews and Christians. By the first century CE, the Jewish historian Josephus says there are twenty-two books in scripture. By the fourth century, Christians adopt twenty-two books for their Old Testament and accept the twenty-seven books that appear in the New Testament today. By the eighth century, the Babylonian Talmud includes a discussion of Torah scrolls and other sacred texts, their authors, and the order in which they should appear. And by the end of the sixteenth century, Protestant and Catholic Christians develop their own catalogs of canonical books, excluding some and including others.

Although Jews and Christians use the same texts, they disagree over the canon of the Tanakh and the Old Testament in three areas: the arrangement of the books, the inclusion of Greek Jewish texts, and their translations. The form of the canon undoubtedly shapes interpretation. The Tanakh concludes with the return of the Judahites to Judah, with the mandate from the Lord God of Heaven, per King Cyrus of Persia, to build the temple in Jerusalem. The Old Testament ends with several prophetic works predicting the coming of the Lord of Hosts and a time of judgment, preceded by the arrival of the prophet Elijah. Both endings point to the future, but in radically different ways. This is exactly the crux of the ancient dispute. The Bible exists within the interpretive traditions of both faiths. It has no life outside of human reading and consideration. This raises several provocative questions: Is there only one way to read the Bible? Can its meaning change? And, most importantly, can Jews and Christians accept each other's markedly different interpretations of the same texts?

"You Have Heard It Said..."

Debates over the meaning of sacred writings do not begin with the early Jewish sages, or with the Pharisees and Jesus, or with Paul and the Jerusalem Church. The Bible interprets itself in a process called "intertextuality," whereby a later passage of scripture comments upon an earlier one. This is most evident in the New Testament's dependence upon the Old. Jesus himself frequently comments on the Law and the Prophets, as when he compares the judgment of Sodom and Gomorrah in the book of Genesis (19:1–29) to that of the towns that do not show hospitality to the disciples (Matthew 10:5–15, Luke 10:1–12). But the Tanakh also interprets the Sodom and Gomorrah story, with references to it appearing in Deuteronomy, Isaiah, Jeremiah, Ezekiel, Amos, and Zephaniah.

The text itself, therefore, is one interpretive source. A variety of religious groups claiming adherence to the Law and the Prophets is another. Judaic communities that expect an apocalyptic end to the oppression they experience under foreign domination—from the Seleucid Empire in the second century BCE to the Roman Empire in the second century CE—write a range of books foretelling a violent future that will eventually have a happy ending. The community at Qumran is one such apocalyptic group, writing biblical commentaries that explain prophetic works as describing their own leader and present situation. Other apocalyptic authors write in the voices of biblical figures such as Abraham, Moses, Job, and Enoch to lend authority to their visionary statements. This literature is called the Pseudepigrapha, a body of Jewish and Christian literature written anonymously ca. 250 BCE to 200 CE and attributed to biblical figures.

Jewish believers in Jesus Christ—yet another community expecting the imminent reign of God—understand their scriptures as predicting a Messiah who would suffer. Their interpretive claims make up the New Testament. In some of the oldest New Testament writings, the apostle Paul provides his own hermeneutical key, or guide, to reading scripture—namely, Christ—and criticizes Jews for not seeing this. "Indeed, to this very day whenever Moses is read, a veil lies over their minds; but when one turns to the Lord, the veil is removed" (2 Corinthians 3:15–16 NRSV). Similarly, in the Gospel of Luke, the risen Christ explains to two disciples how to understand scripture: "Beginning with Moses and all the prophets, [Jesus] interpreted to them the things about himself in all the scriptures" (Luke 24:25–27 NRSV).

Interpretive freedom is rather great before clear boundary lines between Christianity and Judaism are drawn. One of the ironies of history is that the allegorical, or symbolic, interpretation of scripture, used so much by Christians, is a gift from the Jews. Philo of Alexandria (fl. ca. first century BCE–first century CE) is a Greek-speaking Jew who wants to explicate the Torah in a way that makes sense to hellenized Jews familiar with Greek philosophy. (Hellenized Jews speak Greek and adopt a number of Greco-Roman cultural practices. Chapter 3 discusses Hellenism and hellenization further.) Philo explains the spiritual meaning of the commandments by means of symbolism, which is a method of interpretation in widespread use in Greek-speaking society. Later Christian commentators find Philo's allegorical procedure extremely helpful in reading the Old Testament christologically, that is, as being about Jesus Christ, and we have Christian monks to thank for preserving the Greek texts of Philo's work. But Philo himself never abandons literal observance of the Jewish commandments or the significance of their literal meaning since he merely seeks to reconcile Jewish law with Greek philosophy.

Well aware of Philo's work, Christian exegetes in the early church follow his system of allegorizing. Others disdain allegory, however, and propose typology as an alternative, by which they read the Old Testament as anticipating the New. They find prefigurations of Jesus and Christian life in events such as Abraham planning to sacrifice Isaac or Joshua holding back the sun, and in elements such as water, mountains, and deserts. Thus, the mysterious priest-king Melchizedek (Genesis 14:18, Psalms 110:4) is a "type" that foreshadows Jesus (Hebrews 7). Typological interpretation exists in the Old Testament itself, when it sees Joshua as the new Moses, or when Second Isaiah uses the Exodus theme to describe the return of Israel from Babylon to Zion.

Jews also read scripture symbolically and allegorically, but their interpretive project tends to fall into two main categories: halakhic, or legal; and aggadic, or homiletic. Halakhic commentary focuses on understanding the commandments given in the Torah and applying them to the ritual life of all Jews, not just the priesthood. This is one of the innovations introduced by the Pharisees of Jesus's day, and especially by Yohanan ben Zakkai and other sages at the end of the first century. Aggadic commentary concentrates on determining the moral messages in scripture that present the ways to live an ethical life. First- and second-century sages, such as Rabbi Hillel and Rabbi Ishmael, develop hermeneutical rules to guide the process of understanding scripture.

Despite their different theological concerns, Christian and Jewish commentators tend to follow a fourfold method of interpretation well into the modern period. On the Christian side, readings are split into historical and spiritual, with the latter encompassing allegory (symbolism); tropology (morality); and anagogy (mysticism). Spiritual interpretation enlarges the literal meaning of scripture by introducing symbolic, moral, and mystical readings. A medieval example is thus: "Historically, Jerusalem is an earthly city, allegorically she signifies the Church, tropologically the faithful soul, and anagogically the Celestial City."[5] A parallel interpretive system exists in Judaism called Pardes or PaRDeS (par-désh), an acronym that signifies four senses of scripture: the plain or literal meaning (Peshat); the allegorical or symbolic meaning (Remez); the moral meaning (Derash); and the esoteric or mystical sense (Sod). Jews might therefore read the first verse of the first chapter of Song of Songs, an erotic poem symbolically interpreted, as meaning that the speaker longs intensely for a kiss (Peshat), the kiss expresses the longing for contact with God (Remez), the site of the kiss is Mount Sinai (Derash), and the spiritual quest begins with intense yearning, denoted by a kiss (Sod).[6]

Jews have a lively tradition of symbolic biblical interpretation. The Song of Songs becomes part of the biblical canon because it is understood as describing God's love for the people Israel and their love for God. During the Renaissance, Jewish interest in scriptural symbolism reaches its height in the Kabbalah, a mystical branch of Judaism. Therefore, those who assert that Jewish interpretation is always literal or historical are mistaken. Conversely, those who think that Christian interpretation is always symbolic are also in error. Jews and Christians share a capacious interpretive toolkit from which to draw meaning.

The Turn to History

For more than a millennium, biblical interpretation remains largely unchanged, until several Christians and, most importantly, a Jew transform the rules of the game. The French Calvinist Isaac la Peyrère (ca. 1596–1676) maintains that the Old Testament is simply the history of the Jewish people, rather than any sort of divine revelation. He questions Mosaic authorship of the Pentateuch, noting repetitions and contradictions in the text. Richard Simon (1638–1712), a French Oratorian priest, also sees the biblical text as imperfect, but is contending—against the Calvinists—that infallible Catholic tradition is superior to scripture alone.

It is an apostate Jew, Baruch de Spinoza (1632–1677), who introduces what might be called a truly modern reading of the Bible. Influenced by the work of la Peyrère and Thomas Hobbes, Spinoza calls for deducing the sense of biblical texts through techniques that include knowing biblical grammar, vocabulary, phraseology; studying the life, character, and pursuits of biblical authors; and analyzing textual history, including the record of reception, variant editions, and canonicity. Spinoza argues in his *Theologico-Political Treatise* that reason alone is required to interpret scripture properly. We might examine a text in the same way we would study nature—that is, through empirical science.[7] Ordinary people need not rely on religious authorities, since the original "unlearned people" understand the language of prophets and apostles full well, and scripture teaches simple doctrines.

While Spinoza, Simon, and other Enlightenment thinkers construct the foundations for a new way to read the Bible, the turn to historical thinking in the nineteenth century creates still more radical openings. Imperialistic conquests bring treasures from antiquity to the attention of scholars: the Cairo Genizah, a storeroom in an Egyptian synagogue that holds a collection of thousands of Jewish texts, initially found around 1752 and rediscovered by two Scottish sisters in 1896; the Codex Sinaiticus, a fourth-century Greek version of the entire New Testament, located in the Monastery of Saint Catherine in the Sinai Peninsula and first mentioned in the West in 1761; the Rosetta Stone, found in Egypt in 1799; the Epic of Gilgamesh, discovered in 1853 in the ancient Mesopotamian city of Nineveh; and much more. These ancient texts generate curiosity about the people who write them, about the substance of the thoughts they contain, and about the connections they have with other religious texts and traditions. In other words, they provide the underpinning for the academic and comparative study of religions. Can we not ask the same historical questions of an ancient text like the Bible? they wonder.

Historical criticism, which attempts to read religious texts apart from sectarian commitments, becomes the dominant system for biblical study, but comes under intense criticism by the end of the twentieth century. Ostensibly a neutral methodology, historical criticism still bears the biases of the scholar. Detractors charge that it atomizes scripture into unrecognizable bits, focuses on minutiae and irrelevant details, forgets the larger context, ignores centuries of interpretation, and denies the unity of divine revelation. Jewish critics find that the method displaces Jewish tradition in favor of a universalistic and rationalistic reading of scripture. Some fear that such interpretations undermine halakhic life.[8] Christian critics complain that historical criticism does not give the faithful "the solid doctrinal and religious nourishment needed."[9]

Yet for all its drawbacks, the historical-critical method brings Christians and Jews together by providing a shared language and a set of mutual presuppositions for the study of scripture. "Only in the rise of modern critical biblical scholarship," writes Jewish New Testament scholar Samuel Sandmel, "with its goal to recover the pristine meaning of the Old Testament free from both Jewish and Christian interpretation, have scholars, whether Christian or Jewish, read and understood Scripture in any common way."[10] The Pontifical Biblical Commission seemed to agree in its 1993 declaration: "The historical-critical method is the indispensable method for the scientific study of the meaning of ancient texts."[11] Historical criticism allows Jews and Christians to read their sacred texts in ways that encourage dialogue and build bridges.

Who Decides?

Despite the challenges posed by the historical-critical method, belief in the divine origin of scripture protects the integrity of the written word for Jew and Christian alike. With God as author or inspiration, the biblical text is necessarily infallible regarding religious truths. For Christians, the Old and New Testaments form a complete unity, mutually interpreting and enhancing the other— yet ultimately pointing to the revelation of God in Christ. For Jews, the Oral and Written Torah are also a unity, mutually interpreting and enhancing as well—yet ultimately being the revelation of God. What is essential for Jews and Christians is not authorship or date or provenance, but the text's divine wholeness.[12] But who decides which interpretation of the divinely given text is the right one?

For Jews, *Torah min ha-Shamayim* (Torah from Heaven) embraces the entirety of Jewish tradition—both written and oral—which is believed to have been given by God to Moses on Mount Sinai. Oral Torah preserves the authority of the revelation embodied in the sages who render opinions on halakhah—that is, questions of law, practice, and ritual. By the first quarter of the second century, an authoritative lineage is included in the Mishnah. The Pirkei Avot (Sayings, or Ethics, of the Fathers) begins by presenting a chain of tradition that runs from God to Moses to Joshua, to the elders, to the prophets, to the "men of the Great Synagogue." It then continues to list individuals in the chain well into the second century CE (Mishnah Avot 1.1–15). This puts the sages in a direct line of succession from Moses and thus makes them reliable interpreters of Written Torah. The first verse of Pirkei Avot concludes with the admonition to "make a fence around the Law." This is exactly what the rabbis do. They build an interpretive wall against those outside the chain of tradition, like gnostics, heretics, and followers of Jesus.

By the end of the first century, Christians develop their own chain of tradition. The New Testament first suggests this in the Epistle to the Ephesians: "You are citizens with the saints and also members of the household of God, built upon the foundation of the apostles and prophets, with Christ Jesus himself as the cornerstone" (2:19b–20 NRSV). A letter attributed to Clement, Bishop of Rome (ca. 90–100 CE), develops the Christian pedigree further: from God to Christ to the apostles and thence to bishops and deacons (1 Clement 42:1–4). With unorthodox teachings circulating widely, Christians need an interpretive fence as well. One New Testament writer admonishes Christians to "guard the good treasure entrusted to you, with the help of the Holy Spirit living in us" (2 Timothy 1:14, NRSV).

In Catholic Christianity, this treasure is known as the deposit of faith, in which scripture and tradition flow "out from the same divine well-spring, come together in some fashion to form one thing, and move towards the same goal."[13] Together scripture and tradition make up a single sacred reservoir of the Word of God, which the church maintains and protects through its teaching office, the magisterium. "It is clear, therefore, that in the supremely wise arrangement of God, sacred Tradition, sacred Scripture and the Magisterium of the Church are so connected and associated that one of them cannot stand without the others."[14]

Orthodox Christians also value scripture and tradition equally, though not quite so formally. "The final criterion for our interpretation of Scripture is the *mind of the Church,*" according to Bishop Kallistos Ware, by which he means "keeping constantly in view how the meaning of Scripture is explained and applied in Holy Tradition" (italics in original).[15] This tradition includes the writings of all theologians throughout the history of the church, the creeds adopted at ecumenical councils, and the liturgy of worship. The outlook of Catholic and Orthodox Christians does not seem so far removed from the Jewish fence around Torah that protects its written and oral manifestations. Tradition in this context functions as a type of Oral Torah for Christians. In contrast, Protestants emphasize the centrality of scripture, moderating the impact of tradition. They tend to favor a personal and individual encounter with the Bible apart from church teachings. Nevertheless, traditional interpretation usually guides Protestant "Bible Study." Moreover, scripture imbues church liturgy in all branches of Christianity— from daily readings of Psalms, to litanies, prayers, and rituals of baptism and communion in worship services.

Christians part company not only with Jews over interpretive authority, but with each other. This dispute is one of the driving factors of the Protestant Reformation of the sixteenth century. The development of Reform Judaism in the nineteenth century prompts a similar kind of fracture within Judaism. How is scripture best interpreted, and to whom should the interpretive function be invested? Though Christians and Jews may diverge in their understanding of shared texts, they nevertheless converge in their wrestling with questions of authority within their respective religious traditions.

Is the New Testament Antisemitic?

Questions of interpretation act as one barrier between Jews and Christians. Another obstacle is the New Testament itself and whether it is antisemitic. If we are asking, "Do the authors of the New Testament hate Jews for religious or racial reasons?," the answer must be no. The vast majority of the writers themselves are Jewish, and the texts represent internal conflicts rather than discord between Jews and non-Jews. However, if we are asking, "Does the New Testament divorce Jews from their biblical inheritance? Has it been used historically in antisemitic ways? Does it make statements offensive to the ears of modern Jews?," then the answer is an unequivocal yes.

The Gospel of John is particularly problematic. With its use of the word *Jew* or *Jews* 63 times—as opposed to a half dozen or fewer times in each of the three Synoptic Gospels—John has generated great concern. This gospel adopts a particularly combative tone toward Jews, and scholars have categorized the many ways Christians have attempted to ameliorate this problem.[16] They range from emphasizing the positive elements of the gospel to stating that John cannot be antisemitic because it presents an intra-Jewish argument. They also claim that "the Jews" refers only to religious authorities and leaders. They maintain that the translation of the Greek *hoi Ioudaioi* should be "Judeans," a geographical or ethnic designation, rather than "Jews," with its religious connotations. Moreover, some argue that references to "the Jews" really designate unbelief in general, or the unbelieving world. Historical explanations consist of examining the situation of John's community or regarding the polemic in John as mild by comparison to other ancient literature. But the plain meaning of Jesus's words to his Jewish interlocutors in John 8:44—"You belong to your father, the devil"—seems to defy any attempts to explain them away. (The New International Version of the New Testament even includes the subhead "The Children of the Devil" to identify this section.) It does not appear that scholarship alone can solve the problem.

What are Christians to do with sacred texts that elicit misunderstanding, outrage, and distress on the part of Jews? How should they handle scripture that contributes to antisemitic feelings on the part of their coreligionists? Jewish scholars propose a number of solutions. One is to remind Christians that the passion narrative, which describes Jesus's last week on earth, has its origins in liturgy rather than history.[17] Pointing out the gospels' whitewashing of Pilate, who by all historical accounts is unlikely to have shown any anguish or remorse over executing Jewish rebels, is also helpful. Jewish scholar Michael Cook (1942–2021) recommends creating pedagogical techniques for reaching lay Christians to help them understand the anti-Jewish tendencies evident in Christian exegesis, that is, Bible commentary.[18] He presents a program of studying gospel parallels that graphically reveals how each gospel handles the conflicts Jesus has with Jewish religious authorities. Becoming informed about Judaism and studying Jesus in his Jewish context also helps Christians avoid the pitfall of antisemitism.

Christians offer additional solutions to the problem of New Testament antisemitism. Alternative translations may help. For example, rendering "the virgin shall conceive" in Matthew 1:23 (NRSV) as "a young woman will have a child in her womb" deftly blends the original Hebrew of Isaiah 7:15 with the Greek of Matthew.[19] More accurate translations may solve some problems, though others remain. Simply removing inflammatory passages from worship language is another measure. Changes in Holy Week liturgies have occurred as a result of interfaith dialogue. (Holy Week is the seven days between Palm Sunday and Easter during which there are a number of worship services for Christians.) Some of the most antisemitic texts—such as the Jews declaring "His blood be on us and on our children" (Matthew 27:25 NRSV) after calling for the crucifixion of Jesus—have simply been expunged from the liturgy. Much more can be done, however, to mitigate the centuries-long tradition of repeating creeds and confessions that many believers assume come directly from God rather than from church councils.[20]

The fundamental questions are, however, what is essential to the New Testament, and what can be set aside? One Catholic theologian asserts that anti-Judaic statements in scripture have no authoritative status in Christianity.[21] There is no theological need for them.

Just as Christians (and Jews) have rejected the biblical practices of stoning adulterous couples or owning slaves, other first-century assumptions no longer hold in the twenty-first. Other Christians draw an "inexorable link" between antisemitic sentiments in the New Testament and the Holocaust, noting the contrast between the inclusive teachings of Jesus and the exclusive, even vicious, writings in the New Testament.[22] Christians must decide what is nonnegotiable and what is essential.

Deep Equality in Biblical Studies

Critical New Testament studies dramatically reveal antisemitic elements to Christian readers and increase their sensitivity to Jewish perspectives concerning these controversial texts. As a result, the Revised Common Lectionary used by most Catholic and mainline Protestant churches to guide weekly scripture readings excludes the most onerous ones, including the passage from John 8:44, noted above. Romans 9:6–33, in which Paul bitterly criticizes the Jews who have not turned to Christ, is also missing. These changes occur as a result of dialogue through which Christians become sensitized to the way some statements might sound to Jewish ears.

Historical studies reveal points of convergence, as well as points of divergence. A common canon, shared interpretive methods, and theologies that protect and preserve traditions of revelation demonstrate some similarities between Judaism and Christianity. It is far easier to embrace the methods than to accept the interpretations, which, by definition, are what distinguish Christians from Jews. The Bible therefore can serve as either a barrier against, or a bridge to, deep equality. If there were no common text, however, the magnitude of disagreements would be far greater.[23]

Questions of biblical authority and the authenticity of revelation in the Tanakh and Old Testament are not what divide Jews and Christians, since "Jews and Christians seek authority from the same book."[24] Rather, the interpretive differences between

Christians and Jews center on which commandments are eternally binding, which prophecies, if any, can be read as foretelling the coming of Jesus, and, at the core, which interpretation is correct. Does the Old Testament allow only a single reading? Certainly Jewish tradition yields multiple interpretations, as a glance at rabbinic literature reveals. Christian commentaries also furnish multiple readings, as can be seen in the New Testament, among other sources. "A single text necessarily gives rise to multiple interpretations," note Amy-Jill Levine and Marc Zvi Brettler.[25]

The rabbis in the Babylonian Talmud recognize this fact in their interpretation of Jeremiah 23:29. The original verse reads, "Behold, My word is like fire—declares the Lord—and like a hammer that shatters rock" (NJPS). Taking this a bit further, the school of Rabbi Ishmael teaches that the verse means:

> "Is not My word like as fire? says the Lord; and like a hammer that breaks the rock in pieces." Just as this hammer breaks a stone into several fragments, so too, one verse is stated by God and from it emerge several explanations. (Babylonian Talmud Sanhedrin 34a:12 Sefaria)

The rabbis seem to suggest that varying interpretations of the Bible emerge through divine will from the same Word of God. To extrapolate a bit, might Jews and Christians see that their different readings of Holy Writ are a gift, rather than a curse, from God?

Chapter 2

JESUS THE JEW

Jesus of Nazareth, called the Christ, embodies the paradox of uniting Jews with Christians and of separating Jews from Christians. There is simply no way around or beyond this stern fact.

—A. Roy Eckardt[1]

Although Old Testament studies are frequently the source of conflict and contention, contemporary New Testament studies have proven to bring Jews and Christians together by showing their common origins. In some respects, this is a more painful process for Jews than for Christians, since historical investigations question the existence of a normative, or single, Judaism in the first century, and include the Jesus movement and the early church under the umbrella of Judaic religion. But the process is also difficult for Christians since they must reconsider almost every doctrine they have ever received about Judaism, the Law, Paul's message, and Jesus's self-understanding. Nevertheless, opening the New Testament to Jewish scholars enlarges their understanding of postbiblical literature as well as early Judaism. Contemporary Christians, in turn, are looking to Jews for help in understanding the language and thought-world of the New Testament and later Christian literature. Perhaps it should not be so surprising, then, that Jesus, the Jewish man of Nazareth, might point toward deep equality.

For almost two millennia, most Jews have seen Jesus as a false Messiah—a misguided prophet at best and a blasphemer at worst.

Jewish polemic, anxiety, and terror turned upon this strange figure, the crucified God, and understandably so. Christians have blamed Jews for killing Jesus, pointing to their dispersion as proof of God's punishment for the heinous act. At times they would rise up against Jews in mob violence or state-sponsored pogroms. Thus, many Jews consider Jesus, the Prince of Peace, as the instigator of persecution. At the same time, Paul the apostle was virtually unknown in Jewish circles. He did not replace Jesus as the target of Jewish animosity and angst until the nineteenth century, and even then continued—and continues—to receive criticism for his apparent failure to understand Jewish observance and for his contribution to the break between Judaism and Christianity. Scholarly and popular examinations challenge all of these views, but long-held convictions remain deeply ingrained among adherents of both faiths.

While these opinions have ongoing power in the pews of churches, synagogues, and temples, they have been contested ever since the nineteenth century. The European Enlightenment greatly transforms the theological landscape in which Christian scholars are studying, just as the Jewish Enlightenment, called Haskalah, offers intellectual freedom to Jews. With emancipation and full civil equality, Jews feel at liberty to revisit their own religious traditions. German Jews in particular advocate for critical readings of the Tanakh. They depart from traditional homiletic interpretations and even commence reading Hebrew scripture in German translation. Newfound freedom leads to the reappraisal of Judaism and Jewish history. Jews begin to write histories of Judaism in their own voices, no longer silenced by Christian interpretations of their past. Historians lift up the accomplishments of Jews along with accounts of their suffering. Jewish writers in continental Europe, England, and the United States begin to include Jesus as a key figure in the history of Judaism. These developments allow scholars to turn their attention to Jesus as a figure of importance in Jewish history.

Historical Jesus studies contribute to deep equality by revealing a surprising number of ideas and beliefs that early Jews and early Christians share. They also locate the first-century charismatic preacher in his Jewish context. Jewish New Testament scholars are also enlarging both Christian and Jewish understanding of the holy man from Nazareth. They are even questioning traditional Jewish teachings about who and what the Messiah might be, allowing room for Christian messianic beliefs—within Christianity. Some Jews, as well as Christians, feel their faith to be threatened in the new environment that regards Jesus within his Jewish culture and belief. This "rejudaizing" of Jesus is not entirely welcomed. Still, it is clear that Jesus has begun to serve as one way into deep equality, rather than as a wedge dividing Jews and Christians.[2]

The Quest of the Historical Jesus

Using the methodology of historical criticism, Christians begin to re-evaluate Jesus and his religion. Albert Schweitzer (1875–1965) summarizes numerous portraits of Jesus in his appraisal of eighteenth- and nineteenth-century depictions of the "historical Jesus," that is, the human figure Jesus of Nazareth instead of the Risen Christ of dogmatic Christianity.[3] He reports on a wide variety of Christian perspectives—from the analytical view that claims that the miracles of Jesus can be explained rationally as natural phenomena rather than as divine marvels, to the "mythological" explanation. From this latter angle, the gospels do not present facts but provide ideas that reflect the cultural context in which they are written. This interpretation of Jesus exchanges literal history for metaphorical truth. Schweitzer concludes his assessment of historical Jesus reconstructions with his own, in which he declares that Jesus is a Jewish prophet who preaches the end of the present evil age and the coming reign of God.

A Jewish "reclamation of Jesus" begins at the same time, indebted to Protestant historical studies. Abraham Geiger (1810–1874), the leader of Reform Judaism in Germany and an accomplished New Testament scholar, writes extensively about Jesus and Christianity. In his history of the Jewish people, Geiger sees "early Christianity as a paganization and ultimate betrayal of Jesus's Jewish message" since he understands Jesus to be a Pharisaic Jew and a reformer.[4] Indeed, he sees Jesus as a Reform Jew. "While Geiger's life of Jesus was not an entirely new creation in the history of Jewish thought, his intellectual involvement in Christian scholarship gave it nuances not previously present in Jewish thought."[5] His studies at the time are so important that New Testament scholars review his work in the major theological journals, often critically.

Another Reform Jew and a friend of Geiger, Kaufmann Kohler (1843–1926) writes that Jesus is inspired by the Essenes, an ascetical Judaic group, perhaps even living among them for a while. But the rabbi and educator sees influence of the *hasidim* (pious ones) on Jesus as well. He concludes that Jesus is a "typical Jew" of his era and states that in order to understand the sayings attributed to him in the New Testament, one must also study the Talmud and the midrash.[6]

The historian whose work continues to influence Jews today is Heinrich Graetz (1817–1891), a history professor at Breslau Seminary for many years. Drawing upon Christian scholarship and sources, Graetz integrates both Jesus and the history of the early church into a complex account of the history of Jews.[7] He sees Jesus as an Essene, a strictly observant and even austere Jew. "In Graetz's depiction, Jesus is an earnest, gentle, moral figure who ... inspired Jews with piety and fervor, belief in God, and the values of humility."[8]

Writing in the early twentieth century, Jewish Zionists adopt and reshape Jesus as a model for the "New Jew," an integral and even necessary part of the nationalistic project.[9] Jewish historian and Hebraist Joseph Klausner (1874–1958), whose book *Jesus of Nazareth* (1922) is the first account of Jesus written in modern Hebrew, sees Jesus as a Galilean "prophet-dreamer." He is a Jew to his "fingertips," who sends disciples only to the House of Israel, that is, to other Jews. For Klausner, "Jesus was not simply a Jew, but a Jew who belonged to his own land, aware of his mission to claim the land for his people."[10]

Claiming Jesus for Judaism is both a conciliatory and a polemical project: conciliatory in that the central figure for Christians becomes important for Jews; polemical in that Jews argue that Jesus was a great man, but no greater than any other Jewish rabbi. One Jewish writer adopts both approaches. He asks fellow Jews, "Why should we not accept Jesus?" He does not mean that Jews should accept Christian dogma about the Christ; rather, they should welcome the sayings and parables of Jesus along with those of other rabbis.[11] Thus, in Jewish eyes, Jesus is no more, but no less, than any other Jewish luminary. Clearly this is not a belief Christians can accept.

The Demise of the Historical Jesus

Despite Christian fascination with the man from Nazareth in the nineteenth century, Karl Barth's insistence on the priority of revelation over history abruptly halts discussion of the humanity of Jesus for several decades following World War I. The Swiss theologian (1886–1968) asserts that we can know nothing about Jesus apart from God-given faith; thus, the historical Jesus is not only irrelevant, but actually impossible.[12] After World War II, the German theologian Rudolf Bultmann (1884–1976) continues the demythologizing project he begins in the 1920s and 1930s, which dismisses the historical Jesus. All that can be known about Jesus, he claims, is the kerygma, the proclamation the early church makes about its savior and lord. Little can be known about the human person since the gospels are ideological, rather than historical, documents.[13] Many, if not most Jews today might agree with Barth and Bultmann.

Christians rediscover the historical Jesus after World War II, however. A new quest, sometimes called the second quest, emerges in reaction to Bultmann. German Protestant theologians return Jesus to his Jewish origins. This does not necessarily lead them to an appreciation of Judaism, however; on the contrary, some judge the authenticity of sayings of Jesus by their *dissimilarity* from his contemporaries. Thus, they find that it is divergence from Jesus's Jewish heritage that characterizes the essence of his career.[14] The second quest of the historical Jesus thereby rescues the man of Nazareth from the radical skepticism inherent in the dogmatics of Karl Barth and the demythologizing of Rudolf Bultmann. But it does not recover the Judaism of Jesus. Scholars continue to accept the historicity of gospel accounts of Jesus's conflicts with Pharisees and Sadducees. Very soon, however, New Testament scholars will see these conflicts as describing encounters between early church members and Jewish religious authorities after the destruction of the temple in Jerusalem in 70 CE, rather than as tensions between Jesus and his contemporaries.

A third quest of the historical Jesus begins in the 1980s, when a conviction becomes widespread among Christian scholars that the Judaism from which Jesus comes contributes to his self-understanding. Paradoxically, the third quest is more skeptical of canonical texts that appear in the New Testament and, at the same time, more accepting of nonbiblical texts, such as gnostic gospels. The Jesus Seminar, organized in 1985, gathers together scholars on a regular basis to discuss, and then vote on, the historicity of sayings and parables of Jesus; the group eventually votes on events and activities in which Jesus may have been involved. Because the system of weighting the rankings makes it difficult to opt for absolute authenticity, seminar participants rarely assign a "red letter" to Jesus sayings. Members of the group vote on the authenticity of each Jesus saying by selecting a red, pink, gray, or black bead to drop into an urn. In order to use a red marble, the participant would have to agree with the statement, "I would include this item unequivocally in the database for determining who Jesus was." The parable of the Good Samaritan (Luke 20:30–35) and the parable of the Shrewd Manager (Luke 16:1–8a) are among the very few parables that receive an unqualified red from the seminar.

Although skeptical of biblical texts, those in the third quest value nonbiblical texts. They particularly prize gnostic gospels, such as the Gospel of Thomas, which provides sayings found in the canonical New Testament gospels, but also includes other aphorisms. For example, the Gospel of Thomas contains the saying, "What goes into your mouth will not defile you; rather, it's what comes out of your mouth that will defile you" (Thomas 14), which parallels sayings in Mark (7:15) and Matthew (15:11). But it also has "Lord, there are many around the drinking trough, but there is nothing in the well" (Thomas 74), which has no parallels. But relying on noncanonical texts such as the Gospel of Thomas does not bring these particular scholars any closer to an understanding of the Jewish Jesus.

Jesus and Judaism

E.P. Sanders is the Christian who returns Jesus to his Jewish roots, locating the man from Nazareth within Jewish restoration theology. The Protestant New Testament scholar presents Jesus as a prophet of the coming kingdom on earth, much as Albert Schweitzer had. Sanders's study of Jewish and rabbinic sources leads him to conclude that nothing Jesus says is outside or at odds with the Judaism of his day. "The material in the Gospels reveals no transgression [of Jewish Law] by Jesus," with one exception—let the dead bury the dead (Matthew 8:22).[15] Moreover, the gospels present no disputes outside the normal range of give-and-take found in Jewish religious debates. The fact that Jesus's disciples continue to observe Torah requirements in Jerusalem after his death and resurrection also subverts any notion that Jesus comes to set aside God's Law. Yet, among Christian New Testament scholars, as Sanders laments, "There seems to have developed a greater willingness to see Jesus as consciously setting himself against the law and the other essentials of Judaism."[16] As we shall see, things have changed significantly since Sanders made his gloomy assessment in 1985.

With the introduction of sociological, anthropological, liberationist, feminist, and other approaches to historical Jesus studies, the Jewish Jesus remains elusive. Jesus is seen as a spirit-filled mystic, a teacher of wisdom, a political revolutionary, and an apocalyptic prophet, as well as a heavenly savior, a divine man, and even a mythological figure. Christian feminist New Testament scholars regard Jesus as the defender of women in an oppressive patriarchal society, that is, a Jewish society; this is a posture that Jewish feminist scholars criticize, noting the anti-Jewish tropes embedded in the presentation of "Jesus as a feminist."[17]

It takes a new generation of Jewish scholars, schooled in New Testament studies after World War II as well as in the language and traditions of Judaism, to bring a fresh understanding of the man of Nazareth to Jews and Christians. Less skeptical than the Jesus Seminar about the New Testament as a historical source, Jews also read it from a different starting point. Steeped in both academic and practical knowledge of Judaism, they are able to identify much in Jesus and his teachings that Christian writers have missed.

One startling development is their identification of Jesus as a Pharisee. Nineteenth-century Jewish scholars already make this assertion. Abraham Geiger views him as part of the liberal house of Hillel, which probably would have allowed a healing on the Sabbath.[18] Many have pointed to the similarities between Hillel's maxim—"That which is hateful to you do not do to another"—and the Golden Rule of Jesus—"Do unto others as you would have them do unto you." Claude G. Montefiore (1858–1938), a leader of Liberal Judaism in England, thinks Jesus may have followed the strict teachings of Rabbi Shammai.[19] Jewish scholars today differ on what kind of Pharisee Jesus might have been, though they seem to agree that he was Pharisaic in outlook and practice. Like Montefiore, some claim that his prohibition of divorce puts Jesus close to the Shammai camp.[20] Others point out that representatives of Rabbi Shammai oppose Jesus throughout his ministry and are responsible for handing him over to the Romans for execution. One scholar claims that the Talmud records the actual debates between Jesus and representatives of Rabbi Hillel and Rabbi Shammai, with Jesus adopting the views of Hillel.[21]

A towering figure in Jewish New Testament studies, with a clear and convincing commitment to Jewish and Christian dialogue, is Samuel Sandmel (1911–1979). The only Jew before 2011 to treat the entire New Testament to an extended analysis, Sandmel writes widely and prolifically for both scholarly and popular audiences throughout the 1950s and 1960s. He designs his groundbreaking book *A Jewish Understanding of the New Testament* "to introduce the literature of the New Testament to Jews."[22] The irenic scholar-rabbi examines the books of the New Testament in chronological, rather than canonical, order, beginning with the apostle Paul before turning to the four gospels and asking who Jesus was—Prophet? Messianic claimant? Political rebel? Mythic figure? Liberal rabbi? Sandmel expresses skepticism about ever arriving at the historical Jesus, however, since he writes that it is not possible to derive history from literature that provides supernaturalistic evidence.[23] We hear echoes of Barth and Bultmann and their conviction that the New Testament in particular, and the Bible in general, are ideological rather than historical documents.

Sandmel develops this position further in *We Jews and Jesus* as he traces the history of New Testament scholarship and historical Jesus studies within both Christianity and Judaism. He states that he is writing "for those thoughtful Jewish people who seek to arrive at a calm and balanced understanding of where Jews can reasonably stand with respect to Jesus."[24] Jesus is an important figure in western culture—no less, but no more, than Plato—and should be appreciated on those grounds. But what we can know of the actual person is very little, Sandmel concludes, "Thus he was in part a teacher, a Jewish loyalist, a leader of men, with a personality unquestionably striking enough to be a leader, and his career must have been exceedingly singular for his followers to say that he had been resurrected."[25] He himself admits, however, that he cannot see anything special or superlative in Jesus in the same way that Christians do.

Geza Vermes (1924–2013) is another significant Jewish New Testament scholar. Both his study of the Dead Sea Scrolls and his investigations into the interpretive practices of those in the

Qumran community and subsequent rabbis lay the groundwork for a series of remarkable books about Jesus. Like Sandmel, Vermes approaches the study of Jesus as a New Testament scholar, which the subtitle of his first book emphasizes—"A historian's reading of the Gospels." In *Jesus the Jew*, Vermes examines the various titles given to Jesus in the New Testament. He places Jesus within the milieu of charismatic Judaism and identifies him as a Galilean Hasid, or holy man.[26] Jesus's activities as healer, exorcist, wonder worker, and teacher, coupled with his emphasis on ethics rather than rituals, all confirm this conclusion, as does his use of Abba/ Father to refer to God. By reading Jesus in light of first-century Galilean charismatic religion, we see him as "Jesus the just man, the *zaddik*, Jesus the helper and healer, Jesus the teacher and leader, venerated by his intimates and less committed admirers alike as prophet, lord, and *son of God*" (italics in original).[27]

While it is unusual in the twentieth century to be a Jewish scholar of the New Testament or early Christianity, there are many in the twenty-first. One who has particularly contributed to Christian understanding of Jesus today is Amy-Jill Levine, a professor of Jewish Studies and New Testament at Vanderbilt Divinity School. Levine has numerous scholarly books and articles to her credit, but her major contribution to historical Jesus studies is her work helping Christians understand their own tradition by looking at the religious culture in which Jesus found himself. *The Misunderstood Jew* and *Short Stories by Jesus* target Christian readers who may never have known any Jews personally and certainly don't know Judaism. Levine demonstrates a kind of tough love toward Christians. She is critical of their misunderstanding of Judaism, but compassionate about their attempt to come to grips with the tragedies of the past. "One need not have to believe in Jesus as Lord and Savior in order to realize that he had some extraordinary things to say," she writes. "If I can find such genius in his parables, how much more so should those who worship him be able to listen with more finely attuned ears to hear."[28]

The Messiah

Of all the christological titles that have been mentioned in this chapter—and there have been many—the most contentious is the identification of Jesus as the Messiah. It is practically axiomatic that the question of the Messiah is a major issue that divides Christians and Jews. Is the promised Messiah primarily a political figure? Certainly the Romans consider Jesus a potential rival, executing him as a first-century terrorist and writing somewhat sarcastically "King of the Jews" above and below the cross. Is the Messiah chiefly a heavenly savior, a divine being? Certainly some first-century Jews see Jesus in this light. Qumran literature, apocalyptic texts, and the Bible itself bear witness to a variety of messianic conceptions in the first century. Even among Jewish scholars today, there is disagreement over what type of Messiah is expected.

For example, the Jewish New Testament scholar Paula Fredriksen firmly rejects the notion of any kind of nonpolitical Messiah. The biblical prophets anticipate a historical event for the people Israel, namely, a return to the land and the restoration of the kingdom. Admitting that multiple messianic types appear in first-century Judaic thought, Fredriksen nonetheless concludes that "this diversity of messianic figures and their function should not obscure the prime importance of the Davidic messiah ... the best and most widely attested figure."[29] (Fredriksen is best known for her 1988 book *From Jesus to Christ*, which served as the foundation for the popular PBS television series of the same name. The programs introduce millions of viewers to historical Jesus studies and become a staple in college and university courses on gospel formation.)

The Jewish historian and talmudist Daniel Boyarin takes quite a different stance. He argues that many Jews at the time expect a divine Messiah to come to earth in the form of a human.[30] Jewish traditions about a Davidic, human Messiah, and a divine Redeemer merge into a divine-human Messiah known as the Son of Man. This ancient belief goes back to Daniel 7. Many Jews come to accept that Jesus is a divine and human Messiah because they already have this concept within their tradition.[31] Boyarin argues that later rabbis deliberately expunge the Jewish belief in a divine Son of Man—held by the esteemed Rabbi Akiva himself (50–135 CE).[32] By seeing the Son of God as a human, kingly figure and the Son of Man as a divine Redeemer, Boyarin turns both Christian and Jewish traditions on their heads. Rather than Son of God being a divine title, it is earthly, while Son of Man, usually understood to refer to Jesus's humanity, becomes an exalted identification.

Although early Christian writers put acceptance or rejection of Jesus as the Messiah at or near the center of their self-definition, Jews of that era do not see messianism as the overriding distinction. The first-century Jewish historian Josephus mentions numerous charismatic figures, and there are instances where faithful, observant Jews remain well within Judaism despite their belief in a messianic leader. Some fourth-century literature even puts Jesus in the trajectory of Moses, a prophet and teacher predicted in Torah to challenge the practices of the Sadducees, the priestly party.[33] Thus, Jews and Christians may be closer than they realize on the messianic issue.

Rejudaizing Jesus

In its 2008 issue devoted to "10 ideas that are changing the world," *Time* Magazine ranks rejudaizing Jesus as number 10.[34] The one-page article notes that most seminaries are teaching the Jewish context for Jesus, Paul, and the New Testament writings and concludes by asking if Christians will accept Jesus the Jew. Another question—unasked—might be, Will Jews accept the Jewish Jesus? So far, the answer to these two questions is mixed.

The congenial interplay between Jewish and Christian scholars described in this chapter does not generally appear on the internet. There, a well-developed polemical approach on both, or all, sides continues to churn out old myths in new packaging. Rabbi Tovia Singer, for example, loves to debate Christians to prove their errors regarding Jesus as the Messiah and to write articles demonstrating the thousands of inconsistencies that exist in New Testament manuscripts (outreachjudaism.org). Meanwhile, an internet search on the "Jewish Jesus" turns up a number of Messianic Jewish sites. (Messianic Jews accept Jesus as the Messiah but continue to observe Torah commandments.) Christian apologetic websites in turn reject historical-critical analyses that may jeopardize the divinity of Jesus or the uniqueness of Christianity.

Some Christian scholars resist the apparent desanctification of the Son of God in historical Jesus studies. One skeptic's book in 2014 on the historical Jesus, *How Jesus Became God*, quickly prompts a volume in response the same year. *How God Became Jesus* presents the opinions of New Testament scholars who attempt to demonstrate that the exaltation of Jesus appears in the earliest Christian sources. The claim that devotion to Christ is a pagan import is vigorously rejected. From the beginning, some state, the primitive Christian community worshipped both the God of Israel and Jesus the Messiah. But, as noted, there are Jewish scholars who go even further and claim that early Judaism also features reverence for multiple divine beings.[35]

Contemporary Jewish interest in Jesus may actually reflect internal debates about Jewish identity within Judaism. It seems evident that Reform Jews in the nineteenth and early twentieth centuries reclaim Jesus as a Reform Jew in their argument against Orthodox Judaism. They also recover the Jesus of Christian culture as if to say, "Look, your hero is a Jew."[36] Some modern scholars, however, seem to adopt a deliberately provocative stance when they advocate alternatives to the usual Jewish ways of understanding the early church.[37] The debate ultimately falls upon constructions of Jewish and Christian origins, and whether there is a normative, or single, Judaism in the first century: liberal Jews would deny such existed, while traditionalists would assume its presence. Lacking a clear-cut Judaism blurs the dividing line(s) between early Judaism and Christianity. For many Jews, this is preposterous, and even monstrous; for many Christians, this is equally outrageous.

Nevertheless, the entry of Jewish scholars into New Testament studies opens a number of new and surprising vistas. They provide Christians with insight into the social, religious, and political setting in which Jesus lived and taught. *The Jewish Annotated New Testament* is one example of this.[38] Using the New Revised Standard Version as its text, the JANT supplies an introduction by a Jewish scholar to each book of the New Testament and presents commentary notes throughout. Extended thematic essays on topics ranging from archaeology to baptism to marriage and divorce give the historical context for understanding Jesus, Paul, and the world of early Judaism and early Christianity. Christians and Jews alike use the JANT to deepen their understanding of their own traditions.

By restoring Jesus to Judaism, Jewish and Christian scholars disclose a number of unexpected similarities between the two historic faiths. Seeing Jesus as a first-century Jew requires reading New Testament texts in a new light, with a different set of theological presuppositions. While the discovery of similarities helps soften the boundaries between Christians and Jews, there is also the danger that the quest for similarity may erase differences that matter to people.[39] Yet it is possible to engage in historical studies that search for common ground without creating sameness. "Put another way: there is no reason for Jews and Christians to sacrifice their particular beliefs on the altar of interfaith sensitivity."[40] Understanding, sympathy, and appreciation for the other's viewpoint does not require agreement. Historical Jesus studies demonstrate the truth of this.

Chapter 3

THE PROBLEM OF PAUL

I would like to reclaim Paul as an important Jewish thinker.
—DANIEL BOYARIN[1]

Jesus may be easy for Jews to accept, not as the expected Messiah or the divine Son of God, but as a first-century Jew who understands, and even observes, Torah. Paul is a different story. Most Jewish scholars emphatically assert that Jesus was Jewish, though they disagree on what kind of Jew he was; but they consider Paul "goyish," that is, more gentile than Jewish.[2] Despite recent reinterpretations of Paul, the general attitude of Jews toward him "is overwhelmingly hostile, even pathologically so."[3] By characterizing Judaism as legalistic, imperfect, impermanent, and inferior, Paul's interpreters make it difficult for any Jew to take the apostle seriously. Jews can easily love Jesus, and just as easily hate Paul. Even Christians find Paul hard to like. In addition, those engaged in dialogue with Jews have a problem with Paul—or rather with his interpreters—in their apparent misunderstanding of both the apostle and Judaism.

Sometimes considered the founder of Christianity, Saul of Tarsus (d. 64/67 CE) is a Greek-speaking Jew who lives in the Diaspora and does not arrive in Judea until he is an adult. The New Testament Acts of the Apostles describe Saul undergoing a dramatic, life-changing experience—from oppressor of Christ-believing Jews to promoter of Christ belief to gentiles, that is, non-Jews. Afterward he is known as Paul. By his own account, he is a Pharisee of the tribe of Benjamin who is strictly observant of the Law: "As to zeal a persecutor of the church, as to righteousness under the law blameless" (Philippians 3:6 NRSV). But the new Paul renounces his previous career and embarks on a number of missionary journeys throughout the eastern Mediterranean, planting churches among pagans, God-fearers (non-Jews who nonetheless observe Jewish Law), and Jews.

The New Testament is largely a compendium of letters written to these churches and other groups of Christ-believers. (I am using the term *Christ-believers*, rather than *Christians*, to avoid being anachronistic and to indicate the fluid religious boundaries that exist in the first century.) Scholars attribute seven epistles to Paul with certainty, three more with uncertainty, and a final three—the Pastoral Letters comprising 1 and 2 Timothy and Titus—to a pseudonymous author. Undoubtedly other letters Paul writes have disappeared since he mentions them in the letters we do have. Nor do Paul's letters present a coherent, unified theology, because each is written to address a specific issue: a runaway slave in the letter to Philemon, dissension in Philippi, libertinism in Corinth, scrupulousness in Galatia, and other problems each church is facing. Of course, most Christians throughout history read Paul as a unity, harmonizing contradictions and emphasizing apparent distinctions between Pauline thought and their conception of early Judaism. The theologian Augustine of Hippo (354–430) reads Paul through the lens of his own personal experiences, emphasizing human bondage to sin rather than human capacity for freedom. This sets the stage for Christian understanding of Paul for nearly sixteen centuries.

Paul languishes in obscurity for Jews until nineteenth-century Jewish historians turn their attention to the renegade from Tarsus. Although Heinrich Graetz is willing to admit that Paul is a Pharisee, he also argues that Paul is unfamiliar with Jewish scripture and tradition. Graetz depicts a hellenistic Jew who welcomes the opportunity to forsake Torah observance because it is onerous. Kaufmann Kohler, who appreciates Jesus, takes a decidedly more negative position when he maintains that Paul knows virtually nothing about Judaism. Kohler argues that Paul relies upon gnostic and pagan elements to create Christianity, a religion completely alien to the spirit of Judaism.

Not all nineteenth- and early twentieth-century Jewish appraisals are negative, particularly those of Reform rabbis. In the United States, Isaac Mayer Wise (1819–1900) admires Paul's universalism, his rejection of Jewish nationalism, and his willingness to compromise the Law for progress—all tenets of the Reform Judaism that Wise is intent on developing.[4] Another North American Reform rabbi, Joseph Krauskopf (1858–1923), also praises Paul's universalist outlook and his attempt to share Jewish ethics with the gentile world.[5] Claude G. Montefiore uses the word "genius" five times in the first fifteen pages of his essay on the religion of St. Paul.[6] He explains that Paul's Judaism is far from the Rabbinic Judaism of the twentieth century, or even of the sixth century, when the Babylonian Talmud is finalized.[7] The leader of Liberal Judaism in England concludes that the apostle is a hellenistic Jew with apocalyptic sentiments who practices a somber, pessimistic form of Judaism in which God is distant and less loving than the God recognized by subsequent rabbis. Yet, in a companion essay that addresses the relation of Paul to Reform Judaism, Montefiore praises Paul's universalism, his willingness to make compromises so as to be inclusive, and his devotion to the spirit of the Law.

A great variety of perspectives on Paul has emerged over the last two centuries. Jews find much to commend in the man from Tarsus, while Christians identify much to criticize. Evaluations of the apostle and his theology reveal shifting dynamics in scholarship. Evoking a major change, a number of archeological studies show that the sharp distinctions scholars draw between Hellenism and Judaism are unwarranted. Hellenism is the Greek-speaking civilization that dominates Mediterranean life from the fourth through first centuries BCE and remains influential into the Roman period. Hellenistic Jews, both in Judea and in the Diaspora, adopt some of the customs of the non-Jewish culture in which they exist. They balance the hellenistic drive for a universal culture and the covenantal emphasis on Jewish particularity. Paul's theology poses questions about this quandary that remain especially relevant today: What are the boundaries of universalism and particularism? Can a religion recognize the unity of all peoples and, at the same time, retain ethnic and cultural distinctions?

Jewish Perspectives on Paul

Jewish scholars working after World War II continue to divorce Paul from first-century Judaism. In *The Genius of Paul*, Samuel Sandmel presents Paul as a hellenistic Jew with little or nothing in common with Palestinian Judaism.[8] His apocalypticism requires a savior for individual salvation rather than collective restoration. But, at the same time, he anticipates universal rather than ethnic redemption. These views are Greek, rather than Jewish, according to Sandmel. Taking a more combative approach, Hyam Maccoby (1924–2004) argues that Paul hellenized the Jesus movement by introducing foreign beliefs and practices.[9] The British classicist and polemicist interprets Paul's experience of Christ on the road to Damascus as a psychological breakdown. Were it not for the apostle's dismissal of Torah and its commandments, Jewish believers in Jesus would remain observant. According to Maccoby, Paul asserts that the Torah is abrogated, and that the apostle elevates Jesus to divine status and reinterprets the death of Jesus in gnostic terms. The gospels then reproduce Pauline doctrine and are written through the lenses of beliefs in dualism, predestination, atonement, and original sin. Maccoby's portrait of Paul remains influential among both Jewish and nonreligious readers.[10]

Other Jews place Paul firmly within Judaism. In *Paul the Convert*, Alan F. Segal (1945–2011) describes Paul as moving from one religious and cultural community, that of Pharisaism, to another, gentile Christianity. He argues that all of Paul's agony, conflict, and rhetoric stems from this life-shattering event, in which his concern becomes unity between Jewish and gentile Christians.

Righteousness is not at stake but, rather, living together: "The issue was not how the gentiles could be saved but how to eat with them and marry them."[11] What ultimately puts Paul outside of Judaism is his desire to create a single community in which everyone has an encounter with Christ in the Spirit. Christian identity thus comes from a transformative experience similar to that of Paul's, rather than from ritual identity markers such as circumcision or kashrut (observing kosher requirements). Nevertheless, Segal sees Paul as an exceptionally important figure within Jewish history, being one of two Pharisees to leave personal writings (the other is the historian Josephus). "As the only first-century Jew to have left confessional reports of mystical experience (2 Corinthians 12:1–10), Paul should be treated as a major source in the study of first-century Judaism."[12]

Daniel Boyarin agrees that Paul is integral to understanding Judaism in Late Antiquity, the era running from the second to the eighth centuries CE. He also agrees that identity is central to Paul's thinking. But in *A Radical Jew*, Boyarin sees Paul as a cultural critic within Judaism rather than a convert to Christianity. Paul's hellenistic upbringing in the Diaspora creates his desire to eradicate the ethnocentrism that erects barriers based on nation, race, and gender, while his Jewish background provides his commitment to the one God of Israel. "What motivated Paul ultimately was a profound concern for the one-ness of humanity."[13] Paul's psychological tension is relieved by his realization that unity exists as a spiritual, rather than a material, or carnal, reality. The way to surmount difference, therefore, is to live in the spirit (by faith) rather than in the flesh (by works of the Law, that is, rituals that separate ethnic groups). Paul's quest for oneness and for overcoming difference has important implications for the process of deep equality. The contrast between the universal and the particular, or spirit and flesh in Paul's words, becomes a significant distinction between Christians and Jews, one that can either facilitate or impede working toward deep equality.

Christian Perspectives on Paul

While Jews assess Paul in a variety of ways, Christian interpreters tend to stick with the received traditions—that he has a remarkable conversion experience on the road to Damascus (Acts 9:1–19; 22:6–21; 26:9–18) as a result of which he abandons Judaism because he has found a better way in Christ (Philippians 3:7–11), and that Jews need to relinquish Torah observance as well, because they are bound to its legalistic precepts, the means by which they can earn their way into God's good graces (Galatians 3). The Christian doctrine of justification by faith—the belief that God redeems individuals solely by divine grace rather than human merit—is constructed upon this understanding of Paul. We have Martin Luther (1485–1546) to thank for making this idea central to Paul. The sixteenth-century reformer uses the apostle's letters to mount an attack on Catholic practices, especially the sale of indulgences. (Indulgences are tokens that one can buy to shorten the time one's relatives, or oneself, might spend in Purgatory.) Luther personally identifies with what he believes is Paul's agony over sin and feelings of unworthiness enumerated in the apostle's letter to the Romans (Romans 7).[14] But, more importantly for understanding Paul and Judaism, Luther believes that Paul rejects Torah observance for Jews, not just for Jewish or non-Jewish believers in Christ.

Two nineteenth-century scholars, William Wrede (1859–1906) and Albert Schweitzer, stand apart from other Christians in their interpretations of Paul. Both of them decenter the doctrine of justification by faith. Wrede criticizes Luther's depiction of the apostle as being self-portraiture.[15] Paul emphasizes faith over works (that is, loyalty to Christ over Torah observance) because he is concerned about gentile inclusion in the church. But that is a side issue, according to the Lutheran theologian. Paul's real concern is human enslavement to elemental forces such as angels, powers, and spirits, which separate humanity from God. Only a superhuman, celestial being like Christ can release the entire cosmos from the evil forces controlling it. By taking on flesh and dying, Christ can defeat death for the entire human race, in Wrede's view.

Albert Schweitzer offers an alternative vision of Paul, seeing him as a mystic who believes that "putting on Christ" is a literal transformation of body and soul that nullifies all precepts and beliefs, whether Jewish or pagan. "His great achievement was to grasp, as the thing essential to being a Christian, the experience of union with Christ."[16] This union makes the future kingdom of God into a present reality in Paul's mind. According to Schweitzer, righteousness by faith, rather than works of the Law, is peripheral to Paul's understanding of redemption. The apostle mentions it only when there is some controversy concerning ritual observance. What is central is "being in Christ" and transcending the transient, sinful world.

Twentieth-century Christian historians, theologians, and biblical exegetes are also revisiting Paul. Finding fault with Luther's reading of the apostle, they have a "problem of Paul," that is, a problem of interpreting Paul's letters correctly apart from Martin Luther. Krister Stendahl (1921–2008) is one of the first postwar Christian scholars to contest the received tradition. In a series of lectures delivered in the early 1960s, the Swedish theologian makes a pointed critique of Luther's illegitimate use of Paul, rejecting the view that the apostle had a mind tormented by sin.[17] According to Stendahl, as for Segal and Boyarin three decades later, the critical problem for Paul is not sin but rather gentile inclusion in the covenant of Israel. Jews can continue to be observant, as is their inheritance, but gentiles need only have faith in Christ to enter the covenant since Paul does not want to encourage any activity that might bar gentiles from the God of Israel. The early church understands Paul in exactly this way—that he is discussing the relationship between Jews and gentiles.[18]

One of the most influential twentieth-century evaluations of Paul by a Christian comes from historian E.P. Sanders and his magisterial book *Paul and Palestinian Judaism*. Sanders, who had studied Rabbinic Judaism in Jerusalem, generates a "Copernican revolution in Pauline studies"[19] by examining a wide range of Jewish texts before turning to the writings of Paul himself. Sanders painstakingly refutes the Christian notion that Judaism of the first century (or of later centuries, for that matter) is a legalistic religion dependent upon observance of the Law to win God's grace. In Luther's words, and in subsequent Christianity, this is "works righteousness," the belief that we can earn a place in heaven by what we do. On the contrary, according to Sanders, Jews perform the commandments because of their loyalty to (or faith in) the covenant that the Israelites make with God at Mount Sinai. He introduces the expression "covenantal nomism" to characterize the connection between covenant and Law for Jews. Sanders's investigations persuade him that Paul's attitude toward the Law changes as a result of his mystical experience of Christ. As the historian sees it, the solution precedes the problem. Paul has no difficulty accepting, revering, and observing the Law until he perceives Christ as the mediator of salvation for Jew and gentile alike. At that point, whatever separates Jew and Greek, male and female, free and slave is to be abandoned, since all are one in Christ Jesus (Galatians 3:28; 1 Corinthians 12:13; Colossians 3:11). According to Paul, if Torah observance causes divisions in the early Christian community, then it needs to be set aside.

New Perspectives on Paul

Sanders inaugurates what is called the New Perspective on Paul (NPP) by considering Paul and Judaism on their own terms rather than through the eyes of sixteenth-century debates between Protestants and Catholics. It is not really a new perspective on Paul, but rather a new perspective on the Judaism of Paul's day.[20] This approach assumes that first-century Jews do not believe that performing good works on earth earns them heavenly rewards. God's grace to Israel is evident in the covenant made at Mount Sinai, and faithful observance of the covenant is simply part of the bargain. Even those who are critical of Sanders admit that there is now a scholarly consensus against the view that first-century Jews attempted to balance transgressions against good deeds.[21]

With other theologians developing it further, the New Perspective on Paul is now an old perspective, with a Paul Within Judaism school of thought superseding it. One of the prominent voices is Pamela Eisenbaum, who argues in her book *Paul Was Not a Christian* that Paul never converts from Judaism, but rather receives a prophetic call to extend the covenant to non-Jews—exactly what Krister Stendahl claims half a century earlier.[22] The Jewish scholar, who teaches at a Protestant seminary, says that Paul is not concerned about salvation for Jews since they are already part of the covenant; it is Paul's belief in Jesus's imminent return that drives his concern about gentile inclusion in that covenant. Seeing himself as "the new Abraham," Paul hopes to bring the nations of the world to monotheism as history draws to a close.[23] Just as the people Israel enjoy God's grace through the faith of Abraham, gentiles may hope to receive God's favor through the faithfulness of Jesus.[24] In Eisenbaum's interpretation of Paul, it is Jesus's faithfulness, not the believer's, that justifies non-Jews before God.

Mark D. Nanos, another Jewish New Testament scholar, also insists that Paul remains a Torah-observant Jew even after his vision of Christ. The apostle "keeps Torah fully as a matter of fidelity, that is, as an expression of faithfulness, since he is a Jew."[25] Paul's letters are full of behavioral advice, reminiscent of rabbinic elaborations of Torah. After reviewing the evidence in Galatians, for example, and against most traditional readings, Nanos concludes that Paul's opponents are Jews, and that the dispute in Galatia concerns gentile claims for full inclusion in Jewish communities without benefit of proselyte conversion. The "influencers," as Nanos calls the Jewish communities advocating for circumcision, merely call for complete conversion of gentiles in order to gain Jewish rights and privileges.

Christian scholars are also part of the Paul Within Judaism school. Much like their Jewish associates, they note Paul's overwhelming anguish over the plight of those living outside God's plan of redemption. According to one academic, Paul sees the solution to this dilemma in Christ's atoning death, by which gentiles are incorporated into the people of God, that is, Israel.[26] Another argues that Paul wants gentiles to be integrated into Israel as gentiles, without first becoming Jews.[27] "Torah remains the path of righteousness for Israel; Christ has become the promised way of righteousness for Gentiles."[28]

While the argument that Paul is contesting gentile conversion to Judaism—rather than Torah observance by Jews—is persuasive, many, if not most, Christians resist the new Paul. Donald A. Hagner, a longtime professor of New Testament studies, provides perhaps the clearest and most articulate defense of traditional interpretations of Paul's apparently negative view of Judaism. Hagner argues that Jewish "works of the Law" for Paul are more than identity markers that separate Jew from gentile, a major claim that NPP proponents make. His emphatic conclusion that "Paul ... knows of no salvation—not even for Israel—apart from the cross of Jesus" summarizes the opinions of other Christians who defend what they see as Paul's abolishing of Jewish Law in favor of a "higher" or more universal moral law.[29] Many Christian scholars continue to hold a distorted view of first-century Judaism,[30] and most Pauline studies conducted in local Bible study groups reflect an outdated view of so-called "legalistic Judaism." They ignore the groundbreaking work of Sanders and others. Beliefs about salvation, rather than historical data, seem to drive this interpretation of Paul.

If Christians still use Paul to attack Judaism as excessively concerned with rules and regulations, Jews persist in using Paul to attack Christianity as pagan, idolatrous, and irrational. Hyam Maccoby is the prime example of this evaluation, but others accept and adopt his polemical approach. Paul also appears as part of an ongoing internal Jewish controversy in which the recognition of Paul as a fellow Jew fuels a debate between traditionalists and progressives over what constitutes Jewish identity. A number of Jewish scholars use Paul as a platform to argue against conventional views of Jewish authenticity.[31] They relax fixed notions of what it means to be Jewish by including the writings of Paul within the canon of Jewish literature. Yet this moderating of Jewish identity is exactly what troubles many Jews today. The concern goes back to the long-held conviction that Paul is a Hellenist whose thinking contrasts starkly with the Judaism of his day. Historical evidence no longer supports this standpoint.

Blurring the Boundaries

A basic operating assumption among writers in the nineteenth and most of the twentieth centuries is that there is a sharp distinction between the religion practiced by Jews in Judea and that practiced by Judeans in the wider Greco-Roman world. The Judaism of Jesus is considered to be pure, uncontaminated by foreign elements, while the Judaism of Paul of Tarsus, and more broadly, outside the Land of Israel, is polluted by the culture of Hellenism. Apocalyptic Judaism, which arises within Palestine and characterizes the expectations of Jesus and Paul, falls somewhere in the middle. Until the twentieth century, most scholars reject the possibility of a Hellenistic Judaism, even though the greatest postbiblical text of Judaism—the Babylonian Talmud—is composed outside of Palestine. But as early as 1914, Claude Montefiore admits that "as regards the Jewish world of 50 A.D., these divisions, Rabbinic, Apocalyptic, Hellenistic, are not water-tight or cut and dry."[32]

Three key archaeological discoveries in the twentieth century demonstrate how correct Montefiore is and generate a paradigm shift in understanding the earliest centuries of Christianity and Judaism. The first is the discovery in 1932 of the Dura-Europos synagogue, located high above the Euphrates River in modern Syria. Of note in the world's oldest synagogue outside of Israel is the presence of images of biblical figures, such as Moses and Aaron, Mordechai and Esther, the prophet Samuel anointing King David, and others. The iconography at Dura-Europos, dating from 246 CE, reveals that Jews have not always opposed the use of images, at least of human beings. Indeed, the synagogue at Tiberias in modern-day Israel features a third- or fourth-century mosaic with human figures on it, including the sun god Helios and the signs of the zodiac.

A second find is the Nag Hammadi Library. Thirteen ancient books, called codices, are found in upper Egypt along the Nile River in 1945. They contain 52 texts, including secret gospels that never make it into the New Testament canon.[33] The items themselves are Coptic translations made around 350–400 CE of older Greek writings, possibly dating to around 140 CE. Some of the texts discuss Jesus and the disciples, including Mary Magdalene, and presumably come from Christian authors. Others reinterpret or retell biblical stories in striking new ways and may have their origins in either Jewish or Christian communities.

A final archaeological breakthrough comes in 1947, with the discovery of ceramic jars containing scrolls in the desert near the western shores of the Dead Sea in a place called Qumran. Thousands of fragments, along with partial or complete parchment scrolls, are found. Access to the documents is severely limited by protective—and ambitious—scholars for many decades until two primary stakeholders—one Christian and one Jewish—publish the fragments independently and without official permission in the early 1990s.[34] The collection comprises a variety of texts: scrolls of books from the Hebrew Bible, nonbiblical scrolls such as hymns, psalms, prayers, and items called "sectarian," that is, unique to the Judaic group—probably the Essenes, an ascetical sect—that collects the other scrolls. Some of the documents are apocalyptic, describing an impending war between the sons of light, under the archangel Michael and the sons of darkness; some present rules of the community; and some provide commentaries in which biblical texts are interpreted as being about the community itself. According to Geza Vermes, these and other discoveries "have altered beyond recognition our documentation regarding the Judaism of that period." He notes that "instead of restricting the boundaries of the Jewish background to the New Testament, the Dead Sea Scrolls have enlarged them."[35]

These three archaeological discoveries, among others, blur the boundaries not only between Judaism and Christianity, but also between paganism and the two emerging faiths. Images of humans not only in the Diaspora but in the Galilee show that the phenomenon of Hellenistic Judaism is widespread. The presence of pseudepigraphal literature at Qumran—such as books attributed to biblical figures like Moses, Noah, Enoch, and others—reveal Judaic attention to a variety of apocalyptic and imaginative texts. This is a side of early Judaism not bound by either Torah and Prophets or the traditions of the elders.

Thus, by the second century CE—nearly four centuries after the Maccabean Revolt against hellenization—"a hellenizing process had so long been proceeding within Judaism itself that Judaism no longer presented a sharply contrasting culture."[36] Analyses of the apostle Paul therefore need to be evaluated within a radically new framework. Paul is hellenistic, a category that encompasses Judaism throughout the Roman Empire. Paul is apocalyptic, but that thought-world falls well within the norms of Second Temple Judaism. And though Paul himself does not have affinity with the texts from Nag Hammadi, many of his followers subsequently embrace the theology represented in those codices. The problem of Paul must therefore be framed differently.

Universalism and Particularism

If the fundamental distinction between Pauline Judaism and Rabbinic Judaism is neither abrogation of Torah, nor hellenistic philosophy, nor mystical encounters with heavenly beings, nor belief in a divine savior, nor any one of a number of common conceptions Jews and Christians hold, then why is Paul so troublesome? I think that Daniel Boyarin identifies the key issue, which is found in Paul's letter to the Galatians, particularly the following passage:

> For in Christ Jesus you are all children of God through
> faith. As many of you as were baptized into Christ have
> clothed yourselves with Christ. There is no longer Jew or
> Greek, there is no longer slave or free, there is no longer
> male and female; for all of you are one in Christ Jesus.
> And if you belong to Christ, then you are Abraham's
> offspring, heirs according to the promise. (Galatians
> 3:26–29 NRSV)

Boyarin deconstructs the ways in which Paul attempts to overcome
the ethnic (Jew/Greek), social class (slave/free), and gender (male/
female) barriers that separate people, not only from each other but
from God. "Paul was motivated by a Hellenistic desire for the One,
which among other things produced an ideal of a universal human
essence, beyond difference and hierarchy."[37] The danger, Boyarin
continues, is that Paul associates equality with sameness, eradicat-
ing difference in the quest for human liberation.

In reaction to Paul's universalizing claims, the rabbis emphasize
the particularity, and even exclusivity, of their practices, cherishing
historical memory, sexuality, and ethnic difference.[38] The striking
parallel between Paul's statement in Galatians and its apparent
refutation in the Jewish Morning Prayer is a case in point. The
Morning Prayer states, "Blessed art Thou, O Lord our God, King of
the Universe, who has not made me a Gentile ... who has not made
me a slave ... who has not made me a woman."[39] (Jews today have
modified the prayer to fit modern sensibilities, revising misogynistic
or marginalizing language.) Even if Paul and the rabbis draw from
the same original source, the Morning Blessings that take shape
in the Babylonian Talmud follow Paul's exact format and seem
designed to refute the apostle.[40] One possible conclusion is that the
rabbis meet Paul's challenge of a universal religion with a sectarian
response that emphasizes chosenness and distinctiveness.[41]

Other texts, however, show the rabbis including non-Jews
among those with a share in the world to come. They draw upon
traditions of inclusion. Jews, especially in the Diaspora, welcome

gentile interest and participation. The prophecies of Third Isaiah foretell all the nations in the world worshiping the God of Israel:

> As for the foreigners who attach themselves to the Lord, to minister to him, to love the name of the Lord, to be his servants—all who keep the sabbath and do not profane it, and who hold fast to My covenant—I will bring them to My sacred mount and let them rejoice in My house of prayer. Their burnt offerings and sacrifices shall be welcome on My altar; for My House shall be called a house of prayer for all peoples. (Isaiah 56:6–7, NJPS)

There is a push-and-pull between the universalizing mission of Israel to be a light unto the nations (Isaiah 49:6) and the particularizing goal of maintaining faithfulness to God's covenant in a non-Jewish world. The relative emphases—Paul on the God of the Nations and the rabbis on the God of Israel—place in sharp relief the advantages and disadvantages of each perspective. The one dissolves all distinctions; the other heightens them.

Paul's dismissal of difference as unimportant, and even as destructive of the unity he seeks, is what Jews find so dangerous. Such tolerance deprives people of the right to be different.[42] Although tolerance provides restraint and some resource sharing, the balance of power "lies predominantly with religious and cultural majorities."[43] Religious freedom, as well as tolerance and accommodation, all seem to be universal goods, but they reflect and promote Christian dominance of religious life and discourse. "Universalism is in fact a particularism that frames religion in very specific ways."[44] In other words, the traditional Christian criticism of Jewish particularism ignores the particularism of the Christian worldview. None of us stands outside time, history, or culture. Our own universalizing cosmopolitanism is itself a type of tribalism, which we condemn in others but not in ourselves.

Does Paul transcend this dichotomy to head in the direction of deep equality? Or do Pauline scholars? The Paul Within Judaism approach may steer a course past the shoals of universalism and particularism by keeping Paul a Torah-observant Jew who nonetheless sees God acting in and through Jesus Christ to extend the covenant to all the nations. Moreover, this perspective sees Paul as including gentiles as gentiles—without conversion to Judaism—which means that they retain their ethnic identity. Christians have integrated local customs, languages, and liturgies into the universal church. Can they also accept and embrace those who say "no" to Christianity? Can Jews embrace those who say "yes" to Jesus the Messiah?

Part II

COMPLEX IDENTITY

Chapter 4

JEWISH CHRISTIANS, CHRISTIAN JEWS, AND THE QUEST FOR PURITY

Christianity and Judaism, viewed from outside, probably appeared very much alike: they were distinguished in their doctrines, but neither in their social status nor in their attitude to the heathen world.

—JAMES PARKES[1]

We take it for granted that we know who and what Jews and Christians are. The differences between Christianity and Judaism seem crystal clear. Practitioners, especially the devout, have no doubt as to the tenets of the faith—what they believe and how they should act according to those beliefs. It therefore may come as a surprise to learn that the sharp distinctions that we presuppose today develop over a period of centuries. Far from there being definitive separation at the time of Jesus or Paul, or even in the second and third centuries, it is not until the late fourth century that religious leaders stake out the firm boundaries of their respective doctrines. And even then, religious identity is far from certain, with gentile Christians continuing to Judaize—that is, to adopt Jewish practices—and observant Jews continuing to believe in Jesus the Messiah. Scholars use the expression Jewish Christianity—and, more recently, Christian Judaism—to encapsulate a hybrid collection of texts that are neither entirely Christian nor entirely Jewish.

67

But as questions of identity and religious practice arise, these expressions have come to be interrogated.

A large part of the rethinking of early Judaism and Christianity
comes as a result of studies in Late Antiquity. Far from there being
a straight-line trajectory from biblical Israel to Rabbinic Judaism
to Christianity, many pathways materialize, one of which becomes
Rabbinic Judaism and another of which becomes Christianity.
Other tracks lead to the apocalyptic community at Qumran on
the shores of the Dead Sea, to the movement started by John the
Baptizer, to the Samaritans who worship God at Mount Gerizim
rather than at Mount Zion, and to the Gnostics, who rewrite the
Bible in order to refute it.

We tend to think that religious commitment is firm and fixed, but
new research suggests that the formation and maintenance of identity,
including religious identity, is a dynamic process. This is not to
flatten or dismiss real differences. Instead, it describes the theological
fluidity that characterizes the era of Jewish and Christian origins, as
well as our own. While religious leaders attempt to guide, influence,
and control the activities of lay practitioners, those at the bottom of
the hierarchy engage in practices they find meaningful, regardless of
origin. It isn't religious difference that causes difficulties, so much as
the belief in religious purity that is problematic. "It is contamination,
rather than purity, that predominates and circulates widely in social
life," according to Lori Beaman.[2] I am, however, substituting the
expression "complex identity" for Beaman's theory of "contaminated
diversity" as a preferable descriptor for the range of emotions and
motivations people exhibit in their religious commitments. We gain
a different understanding of Jewish and Christian relations when we
keep complex identity and social relations in mind rather than when
we concentrate on theological texts alone.

What factors, then, do contribute to a "parting of the ways" when
Judaism and Christianity become truly separate and distinctive?[3]
Certainly the world of paganism, the cultural milieu in which the
two faiths emerge, has an impact. It has been asserted that Christian antisemitism grows out of pagan prejudice, but other evidence

tells a different story. Within the pagan environment, Christians try to differentiate themselves from Jews, and Jews from Christians. This dialectical relationship creates what has been called a rivalry of genius, with all parties demonstrating interactions not only with texts but with each other. Their literary output serves as the foundation for later biblical interpretation. Because Jews and Christians converge and diverge for centuries, the date(s) of the final separation between the two keep getting pushed later and later. As a result, scholars are continually enlarging the borderlines of what are "Jewish" texts and what are "Christian." Complex identity helps to explain this amazing diversity.

Pagan Antisemitism?

Textual evidence, coupled with inscriptions gathered from throughout the Mediterranean, shows that Jews participated in all aspects of civic life in hellenistic society for many centuries, including those following the legalization of Christianity in the Roman Empire in the fourth century. Jewish resistance to hellenization occurs from time to time—most notably the Maccabean Revolt of 167–160 BCE, but also in reaction to Emperor Hadrian's settling Romans in Jerusalem and placing a temple to Jupiter on the site of the Jewish temple in the second century CE. Jewish rebellions transpire in response to the direct provocation of the desecration of the temple, the Lord's dwelling house. But these unique events mark the exceptions rather than the rule to Jewish and pagan relations, which are generally amicable. In fact, Jewish culture in the Diaspora is Greek-speaking and extremely hellenized. Although Hellenism and Judaism do hold distinctive features, it is inaccurate to think of them as coherent, consistent, and strongly opposing systems.[4]

While some pagan intellectuals are critical of Jews, first-century literature shows that a remarkable number of gentiles are both interested in Judaism and sympathetic to it.[5] There is evidence of

Jewish financing of pagan temples and pagan funding of Jewish synagogues, such as that given in the New Testament, where a Roman centurion is praised for building a synagogue (Luke 7:4–5). Jews attend pagan shrines to conduct legal transactions and adopt Ptolemaic loan procedures in Egypt. Greek funerary practice influences Jewish methods, as witnessed in the addition of epitaphs in Diaspora communities of Asia Minor. There is extensive documentary confirmation that pagans in the ancient world find Judaism attractive—its antiquity, its virtues, and its leader, Moses. Jewish proselytism wins sympathizers as late as the fifth century CE. Contradicting long-held stereotypes and beliefs, it appears that Jews are not despised after all.[6]

Even after Emperor Constantine allows the practice of Christianity, the legal status of Jews remains more or less unchanged. Although Jews lose some privileges with the Theodosian Code of 438 CE, many others are restored or even enhanced. The code establishes that "the sect of the Jews" is not prohibited by law, and observes that "we are gravely disturbed that their assemblies have been banned in some places."[7] The order goes on to mandate "repression" of "the excesses" of those who attempt to destroy and plunder synagogues in the name of Christianity, adding later that no Jewish synagogues are to be seized or set on fire. If they have been appropriated for Christian usage, Jews must be compensated. Nevertheless, the code prohibits future construction of new synagogues or repair of existing ones.

The Theodosian Code outlawing paganism and limiting Judaism in the Latin West meets with mixed success, but the institutions of traditional hellenic culture remain alive and well in the Greek-speaking East. There Jewish and Christian communities and individuals maintain generally friendly contacts, despite the opposition of their respective religious leaders. An analysis of architecture and artwork in Byzantine Palestina reveals great similarities in style and design of Jewish synagogues and Christian churches—so many as to defy coincidence and to suggest that Jewish and Christian relations between 400 and 700 CE are generally

peaceful and amicable, not only in the Holy Land but throughout the Byzantine Empire.[8] This departs dramatically from written
documents from this time and place, in which Christian sermons
and theological tracts seem to express malicious hatred for Jews
and historical records chronicle revolts by Jews and Samaritans
against Byzantine rule. The archaeological record from Palestina
shows Christians and Jews living side by side and gives the impression of overall expansion of prosperity and population—"Indeed a
veritable golden age."[9]

There is also convincing evidence of the relatively high status
that Jews hold in Antioch for many centuries, a city they probably
helped found during the Seleucid Period (312–63 BCE). Although
Emperor Hadrian (r. 117–138 CE) bans circumcision, the edict is
modified to allow Jews to circumcise their own sons. Conditions
continue to improve, and by the beginning of the third century,
Jews in the Diaspora and Palestine are fully integrated into civic
life. "For the next several hundred years the Jews are a significant
factor in the life of the Greek-speaking cities of the East."[10] They
serve on councils in cities where they live, finance public works
projects such as road construction and bridge building, hold positions as magistrates, and labor as watchmen, clerks in markets, and
police officers. They send their sons to pagan schools to learn Greek
philosophy and rhetoric. In Sardis, Jews act as members of the pro-
vincial administration, where they construct a large synagogue.
Inscriptions on synagogues built in the third and fourth centuries
in cities scattered throughout Asia Minor, Syria, Greece, and Palestine show that Jews maintain their way of life comfortably, with
the resources to support religious, educational, and social structures and institutions.[11]

Why, then, has the view remained that pagans basically hold
antisemitic views and that the hellenistic world is antagonistic to
Jews? Such a position might well appeal to either Christians or
Jews. On the one hand, it supports the Christian view that Judaism
could not have succeeded in the Roman world, and that pagans,
rather than Christians, foster antisemitism.[12] On the other hand,

Jews argue that pagan antisemitism strengthens the cohesiveness of Judaism, which enables it to survive.[13] While both Christians and Jews benefit from the myth of pagan antisemitism, the reality is that periodic violent outbursts against Jews are rare and localized. Material culture, as opposed to literary texts, uncovers a largely hellenized culture in which different ethnic groups, including Jews, are able to prosper. Even when the Roman Empire comes under Christian control, Jews retain more privileges than do pagans.

Early Attempts at Self-Definition

Despite the relatively benign picture painted above, Christian philosophical polemic against Jewish beliefs becomes more heated and virulent in the second and third centuries, in part because a process of differentiation is underway. Christians feel it is particularly important to develop correct, that is, christological, methods of interpreting scripture and to create a coherently "Christian" way of life in homilies and tractates. The christological system of exegesis finds prophecies of Christ throughout the Old Testament. Meanwhile, Jewish sages are developing their own response to the end of the sacrificial system that occurs with the destruction of the temple in Jerusalem. A period of restoration—which scholars call Yavneh (Greek Jamnia) after an ancient city in Judea—essentially ends the sectarianism that characterizes Second Temple Judaism. Surprisingly, given the invective against the Pharisees that appears in the New Testament, neither the rabbis of this time nor their Christian counterparts identify the Pharisees as leaders in the emerging Rabbinic Judaism; this identification is not "secure and determinative until the early middle ages."[14] By the early third century, Jewish sages compile the Mishnah, a compendium of traditions concerning law, practice, and ritual. At about the same time, Christians assemble a list of the books of the New Testament, which appear in today's Christian Bibles. The process of self-definition is beginning for both groups.

Many scholars place the definitive split at the end of the fourth century. First, the Talmud Yerushalmi (Jerusalem Talmud) is redacted around then. It declares the opinion of particular sages to be correct while rejecting the opinions of other sages. Right or wrong, however, the judgments of all the sages appear in the Jerusalem Talmud. Second, ecumenical councils of Christian bishops adopt the Nicene Creed in 325, with further clarifications in 381, which outlines orthodox Trinitarian doctrine—the belief that God is three Persons in one divine Godhead. Unlike the sages, the bishops attempt to suppress and literally eradicate unacceptable doctrine, excommunicating those who espouse it. In these two ways, Jewish practice is clarified and Christian doctrine is solidified, apparently marking a definitive break between the two faiths. Several centuries later, the Babylonian Talmud seems to complete the split.

These attempts by religious leaders to define the orthodoxies called Christianity and Judaism do not necessarily impress or even affect Jews and Christians who are living and working together throughout the Roman Empire. The majority of Jews had lived in dispersion long before the destruction of the temple in 70 CE or their formal expulsion from Jerusalem after 136 CE. They toil in a variety of trades and crafts, as do their Christian neighbors. Given the number of imperial and local laws promulgated about Jews, "we get the impression of a Jewish community which is numerically large, geographically widespread, a force to be reckoned with in society."[15]

While Jews do not appear to engage in active missionizing of their pagan or Christian neighbors, they do welcome non-Jews and God-fearers into synagogue services and festivals. Non-Jews appreciate both the integrity with which Jews approach their work and the ethical system of Judaism, with its one deity who administers justice impartially. The attractiveness of Judaism is so great in the fourth and fifth centuries that various church councils issue repeated prohibitions against Judaizing—the practice of Christians engaging in Jewish practices. The anti-Jewish sermons and tracts frequently cited as evidence of Christian antisemitism are probably directed at gentile Judaizers rather than at Jews or Jewish followers of Christ. For example, John Chrysostom, Bishop of Antioch (d. 407), preaches a series of sermons once called *Against the Jews*. But recent examinations of their actual targets—Christian Judaizers— prompt scholars to correctly title them *Discourses against Judaizing Christians*.[16] The Christians whom Chrysostom attacks attend Sabbath and High Holy Days, go to synagogue, dance at certain Jewish festivals, erect tents for Sukkoth, attend ritual baths, and may even practice circumcision. Christians who Judaize call upon the authority of Jesus—the promised Messiah—to defend their practices, bypassing the Christian apostolic tradition and appealing to the older and, in their view, more authentic Jewish tradition.[17]

By the fourth century, Christian Judaizers in the Eastern Empire are clearly out of step with their orthodox counterparts in the West. One of the key issues that the Council of Nicea addresses in 325 is the date of Easter. Churches in the East observe the holy day on 14 Nisan, the same day as the Jewish Passover, although some eventually move it to the first Sunday after 14 Nisan. Celebrating Easter while Jews are commemorating Passover is intolerable to the western church, however, as is the fact that churches throughout the empire recognize Easter on different Sundays. A letter to the churches from Emperor Constantine, and subsequent local councils, repeatedly urges a single method of calculating the date of Easter. However, as late as the seventh century, Christians in the British Isles continue to follow the ancient traditions. Even today, Orthodox Christians use a somewhat different formula than do Catholic and Protestant Christians for calculating the date of Easter each year.

A Rivalry of Genius

Unlike Judaizers, who are gentile Christians engaged in Jewish practices, Jewish Christians are Christ-following Jews who continue to be observant and who have varying opinions on the nature of

Christ. The apostle Paul, for example, is a Jewish Christian who sees Jesus as a divine being, while James, the brother of Jesus, is a Jewish Christian who probably does not. The concept of Jewish Christianity, which originates with Enlightenment Deist John Toland (1670–1722), is further developed in the nineteenth century into a Hegelian synthesis: Jewish Christianity + gentile Christianity = Catholic Christianity. (Scholars use the term *Christian Jew* with less frequency than Jewish Christian, especially when discussing early Christianity.) The very category of Jewish Christianity is now questioned, however, since it assumes a clearly marked Judaism and Christianity from which it departs.

Many attempts have been made to locate the moment that Judaism and Christianity do become mutually exclusive. The quest for "the parting of the ways" in the late twentieth century is now replaced with skepticism over the possibility of identifying a specific time and place of separation, and it leads some to assert "the ways that never parted." The existence of Jewish-Christian texts, which do not manifest a clear-cut difference between the two faiths, complicates the process of determining when Christians are no longer Jews.

Jewish and Christian scholars today caution against applying modern categories of religion, Christianity, and Judaism to historical phenomena. We have to be careful about reading the present back into the past, they say. Regardless of what rabbinic schools of learning or church councils consider the bounds of acceptable belief and practice, Greco-Roman culture comprises a society in which religious identity is as much cultural and ethnic as it is theological. Moreover, there are Christians who believe Jesus was never human, or that the Old Testament is not part of the canon of scripture, just as there are Jews who believe that Jesus is the promised Messiah who will return, or that two divine powers exist in heaven. Thus we perceive a continuum of Jewish and Christian belief in Late Antiquity. On one end are the Marcionites, who have nothing to do with Judaism; on the other end are Jews for whom Jesus means nothing. "In the middle, however, were many gradations that provided social and cultural mobility from one end of this spectrum to the other."[18] The fact is, early Jews and Christians are in constant conversation—either directly in person as neighbors and co-workers or obliquely through texts—all against the backdrop of Greco-Roman culture. Pagan philosophy and practices such as magic and thaumaturgy (the working of miracles and wonders) exert ongoing influence on adherents of both religions well into the Middle Ages.

Marc Hirshman, professor of Rabbinics and Midrash, describes the ways in which theologians and sages in Late Antiquity respond to each other's assertions, calling these exchanges "rivalry of genius." Origen of Alexandria (d. 254), for example, composes a series of homilies on the book of Exodus that seem to wage "full-scale war" on his Jewish rivals. Yet Origen's Jewish opponents utilize the same kinds of "exegeses, word play, and contextual insight," and in at least one instance turn to Origen for some of the insights that appear in their commentary.[19] Links between Origen's homilies on the Song of Songs and rabbinic interpretations are also noticeable, with the Christian exegete explicitly citing concerns "the Hebrews" have over study of the erotic love poem.[20] Hirshman provides many additional examples of shared knowledge between the sages and the church fathers.

Although there is debate today over the extent of these contacts, it seems clear that Jewish and Christian religious authorities absorb, revise, or reject the wisdom and insights of each other, living as they do in overlapping cultures. The apostle Paul is undoubtedly influenced by traditions that later find expression in rabbinic literature. But the sages of Paul's day also know of his viewpoints and rework them "through an anti-Pauline prism" in their own judgments, particularly about justification by faith, the status of the uncircumcised, and divine favoritism.[21] The sages can ignore early Christian writings until long-held traditions become problems in need of clarification. The fact that recitation of the Ten Commandments is part of the Morning Prayer in the early third century (Mishnah Tamid 5.1) but is prohibited by the end of the fourth because of the "heretics" (Jerusalem Talmud Berakhot 1, fol.

3c) indicates rabbinic concern over Christian rejection of the entire Torah. Simultaneously, church leaders spurn any practice that hints at Judaization. Thus, the theologies of Judaism and Christianity develop in the midst of tensions over self-definition.

Many Partings

Even though "the ways" are diverging doctrinally over a period of centuries, popular piety looks pretty much the same for Christians and Jews. Religious identity is complex. Philo of Alexandria, for instance, is not a strict monotheist. He introduces the Greek concept of Logos—one of the subordinate powers that surrounds God—into Jewish philosophy. According to Philo, the Logos assists God in the creation of the world. (We can find Logos theology in John 1:1–4 and parallels in the Wisdom theology of Proverbs 8 and Wisdom of Solomon 7:21–8:6.). When the rabbis talk about the role creative angels play, they do not appear to be strict monotheists either.[22] Within the Christian fold, concern about the appearance of polytheism drives the clarification of Trinitarian doctrine, with many remaining concerned that the unity of God has been compromised.

Time and place dictate the level of friendship or animosity among Christians and Jews. "There were, in fact, many 'partings,' and they happened in different places at different times in different ways; furthermore, the Jewish and Christian communities continued to be intertwined in certain ways at certain times."[23] Well into the Middle Ages, the boundaries of religious identity are more fluid than we can imagine today. Jews visit Christian shrines for healing,[24] while Christians wear amulets with Hebrew inscriptions.[25] The name of the most famous knighthood, the Knights Templar, comes from Christian veneration of the temple in Jerusalem.[26] Christians and pagans alike consider Jewish scripture to have a numinous quality; oaths made in synagogues, with the Torah scrolls present, are believed to be more binding.[27] Jews apparently use, or at least collect, a magical text of Christian origins—the Legend of Saint Eustachius—and both communities employ magical formulas to find hidden treasure.[28] The prophet Muhammad (571–632) merges Jews and Christians together as "people of the Book," although he and his successors also have very firm ideas about the differences that already exist between the two groups.

Jews and Christians in Europe and the Near East live together in relative peace well into the Middle Ages. At a mundane level, scattered evidence from European sources "points toward routines of intimacy and intense interaction. Beyond commercial and juridical relations, conversation and confrontation, there were adjoining neighborhoods, servants going both ways, instances of intermarriage, and arrangements for burial places."[29] Jewish synagogues and ritual baths are located near Christian cathedrals and city halls. Jews live in the midst of Christian culture, while Christians live next door to Jews. Indeed, these close and friendly encounters prompt Pope Innocent III (p. 1198–1216) to demand that Jews wear distinctive clothing—such as a yellow badge on their outerwear—to differentiate them from their Christian neighbors. Few secular authorities attempt to enforce the edict, however.[30]

Scholars have tried to pinpoint the moment, or factors, when amicable relations take a decided, and almost irrevocable, turn for the worse. Many theories have been proposed: that the church hardens the boundaries of Christian culture, that the social distance between Jews and Christians increases due to shifting economics, that new religious orders like the Franciscans and the Dominicans who seek out heretics encourage antisemitism, that the First Crusade (1096) marks the change.[31] And yet, "the very search for such turning points has come into question."[32]

Indeed, a growing body of literature suggests that Jews find Europe in the Middle Ages "to be more or less congenial, since a flourishing Jewish civilization arose even under the relative constraints of Christian Europe."[33] Jews are not the only or even primary targets of medieval violence, which is also directed at heretics, lepers, Muslims, and apocalyptic Christians. And when it does occur, violence against Jews is contingent on local conditions "and not the result of unchanging hatred or an irrational structure of medieval society."[34] Time and place, rather than religious imperatives, influence the nature of Jewish and Christian relations. Just as the various partings between Judaism and Christianity are complicated, mixing high-minded intentions with mundane antagonism, so too is the nature of the medieval world. Complex identity is one way to understand how Jews and Christians successfully engage each other across a wide spectrum of experiences and relationships.

Chapter 5

THE PARADOX OF CHRISTIAN HEBRAISM

*When reading Hebrew I seem to see God himself speaking.
When I think that this is the language in which God and
the angels have told their minds to man from on high. And
so I tremble in dread and terror, not however, without some
unspeakable joy.*

—JOHANNES REUCHLIN[1]

*By the mid-seventeenth century, after much discussion, most
Englishmen agreed that God spoke Hebrew.*

—DAVID S. KATZ[2]

When Augustine of Hippo urges fellow Christians not to kill Jews,
he does so not out of love but rather out of theological imperatives.
He cites Psalm 59:11 as biblical warrant for protecting Jews in order
to maintain their degraded status—"Slay them not, lest my people
forget: scatter them by thy power; and bring them down, O Lord
our shield" (KJV). The church father sees the condition of living
Jews as proof of biblical prophecy. Their dispersion seems to indicate the truth of scripture ("scatter them"), and thus "Jews came to
be seen as witnesses in the very desperation of their status."[3] Yet,
they are also the heirs of scripture. Their divine security rests in
the ongoing commitment to their scriptures and customs.[4] Jews in

the Diaspora thereby testify both to the veracity and ultimacy of Christianity.

It isn't just any book that Jews carry, however, nor is it in just any language. It is the Bible and it is in Hebrew. Christian esteem for the Old Testament creates opportunities for communication and exchange between Jews and Christians and, ultimately, a measure of religious tolerance. Christians throughout the ages honor the heroes of the Old Testament. The Reformation and Renaissance— with their emphasis on scripture and original sources—renew fascination with both Hebrew and the Bible. While this interest does not alter Christian triumphalism, it does contribute in its own way to the readmission of Jews to various European nations in the seventeenth century, Jewish emancipation in the eighteenth, and proto-Zionism in the nineteenth.

The Christian turn to Hebrew oscillates between the twin poles of missionizing and Judaizing. On the one hand, Christian interest in learning the language of Jews and their holy scripture has an evangelistic and even polemical purpose at times. Many, if not most, of the translations of Jewish works—from grammars and lexicons to rabbinic texts—include a derogatory introduction about Judaism and an explanation of the necessity of, essentially, learning how to fight fire with fire. Jews study Christian texts and engage in interreligious talks for the same polemical purposes. Moreover, the identification of Christians with ancient Israel, particularly among the Puritans of New England, reinforces the supersessionist view that Christianity has replaced Judaism. On the other hand, the encounter with living Jews and their literature forges a new relationship between adherents of the two faiths. An uneasy but nonetheless authentic respect is the result.

Christian Hebraism, the interest in Hebrew language and literature, especially the Old Testament, therefore has a significant impact on Jewish and Christian relations. Although some Christians in Late Antiquity and the Middle Ages are interested in the Hebrew language, dedicated and devout study replaces curiosity in the Renaissance and the Reformation. There are a number of reasons for this shift, including religious fervor that anticipates the imminent arrival of the Messiah and republican movements seeking governmental models from the Bible and Talmud. Paradoxically, respect and regard for Judaism create the legitimate fear of being accused of Judaizing, which, in turn, leads some Christians to use antisemitic rhetoric to justify their study of Jewish texts. Jews, as well, must explain to other Jews their linguistic collaboration with Christians. Thus, both Christians and Jews walk a fine line among their coreligionists, who fail to understand how much they treasure their cooperative endeavors. This tension explains some of the inconsistency we see in the beliefs and behaviors of both Christians and Jews.[5] The remarkable collaboration of Jews and Christians demonstrates another instance of complex identity.

Christian Hebraism

Christian Hebraism has a long history. By the second century, some Christian scholars believe that the *Hebraica veritas*, the Hebrew truth, is a preferable, more accurate version of Jewish scripture than the Greek translation in use. In the third century, the Christian exegete Origen creates the Hexapla (Greek for sixfold), a chart that provides various Hebrew and Greek versions of the Bible in six columns. Origen's purposes in identifying differences flow in part from his controversies with the Jews, in which he wishes to argue from a source that his adversaries will accept. But even Jews recognize the usefulness of the Hexapla. This is demonstrated by the discovery of a fragment of it in a Jewish genizah (a storeroom for worn-out sacred works) in Cairo in the late nineteenth century.

Another Christian Hebraist, Jerome of Stridon (d. 420), translates the books of the Hebrew Bible into Latin. In the late fourth century, Pope Damasus I (p. 366–384) commissions a Latin version of the Christian Bible. A number of translators contribute to this Bible, called the Vulgate (Latin for common version), but Jerome is largely responsible for rendering the Hebrew into Latin.

Although Jerome also utilizes the Septuagint, he generally prefers the *Hebraica veritas*. The Vulgate functions as the Bible used by Christians in the West and, after the Protestant Reformation, by Catholic Christians until the twentieth century. Some continue to use the Vulgate today.

Christian attention to the *Hebraica veritas* emerges sporadically after Jerome until the twelfth-century renaissance, when Augustinian canons at the Abbey of St. Victor in Paris turn to Jewish neighbors to better understand the Bible. This interest is an outgrowth of their desire to understand the history of salvation from creation to the Incarnation—that is, everything up to the arrival of Christ. (The Incarnation is the Christian belief that God became human in Jesus Christ.) This salvation history is to be found in the Old Testament, which encourages them to emphasize the historical, or literal, sense of scripture, rather than its spiritual meaning. Well aware of problems with Jerome's Vulgate Bible, Hugh of St. Victor (d. 1141) and his students seek the advice of local experts in Hebrew—that is, the Jews. Hugh, for example, looks for help in resolving not only textual questions about words and grammar but exegetical ones about interpretation and meaning, peppering his own commentaries with references to Jews. Interpretations from Jewish contemporaries and near-contemporaries are found in his opinions.[6] Hugh's student Andrew of St. Victor (d. 1175) may have known a smattering of Hebrew, it being clear that he has firsthand knowledge about the customs and habits of local Jews. His commentaries present both Jewish and Christian interpretations. Usually Andrew sides with the Christian reading, but he often accepts the Jewish.[7] Andrew's student, Herbert of Bosham (1120?–1194?), apparently does know the Hebrew language. He discusses textual difficulties with his Jewish informants but also seems to use rabbinic texts on his own. He probably knows Aramaic as well since he quotes the Targumim.

Interest in the Bible, as opposed to study of rabbinic literature, is simultaneously growing among the Jews of northern France, where Jews and Christians remain on generally friendly terms. "[Jews] were neither shut into ghettoes nor restricted to shop-keeping and money-lending, but scattered among the towns and villages in small communities."[8] Like their Christian neighbors, they engage in agricultural pursuits, such as cultivating vineyards and tending horses. A parallel school of historical and literal commentary mounts among Jewish scholars alongside the Victorines. The most famous and influential of these is the school of Rabbi Solomon ben Isaac (1040–1105). Subsequently known as Rashi, he has a reputation for emphasizing the plain meaning of scripture rather than delving into rationalistic, mystical, or abstract concepts. He never abandons rabbinic midrash, which is sprinkled throughout his commentaries on the Bible, but incorporates it along with examples from everyday life. This explains the enduring popularity of Rashi's work, elements of which are found in the commentaries of Hugh of St. Victor. Rashi's successors may even have direct contact with the Victorines. For example, Rashi's grandson, Rabbi Samuel ben Meir (known by the acronym Rashbam, ca. 1085–ca. 1174), explicitly rebuts Hugh's interpretation of Genesis 49:10 in his own commentary on Genesis.[9] Others following in Rashi's footsteps "showed an increasing knowledge of Christian exegesis and an increasing desire to refute it."[10] Thus, Jews and Christians adopt a new way of reading scripture even as they retain commitments to their own traditions.

The Language of God

Christian fascination with Hebrew—believed to be the original language of humankind and the foundation of all theology in the Law and the Prophets—does not always affect Jews positively. The thirteenth century sees both increasing literacy in Hebrew, especially among new religious orders, and condemnations of rabbinic writings. Well-versed in the Talmud, Jewish converts to Christianity disclose the most salacious passages they know of—the ones that disrespect the Virgin Mary or mock the parentage of Jesus.

More broadly, their reliance upon rabbinic tradition rather than on
the Bible itself places Jews within the camp of heretics. Augustine
counseled protection of the Jews by virtue of their obligation to
scripture, but their faith in Oral Torah puts them outside the range
of shelter. Nevertheless, only the king of France complies with a
papal decree of 1239 that orders the confiscation of holy books of
the Jews.[11]

Given the rising tide of antisemitism in some areas of Western
Europe that continues into the fourteenth century, it is all the more
remarkable that the most-read Christian Bible commentary until
the early modern period is dependent upon rabbinic sources. The
Postilla litteralis super totam Bibliam (Literal Commentary on the
Whole Bible) by Nicholas of Lyra (1270–1379) not only emphasizes
the historical and literal sense of scripture, but relies extensively on
Jewish biblical interpretation and methods to prove the truth of
Christian doctrine. The Franciscan friar's use of Jewish sources is
so great, and at times the criticism of him so wide, that subsequent
iterations of his commentary include postscripts that emphasize his
orthodoxy. Although some scholars see Nicholas as writing in the
adversos Judeos tradition—the polemical "opposed to Jews" style—
the Franciscan is primarily arguing against other Christians. He
opposes the scholastic turn to philosophy to determine the truth
of dogma and instead advocates using scripture, and even rabbinic
interpretation of scripture.[12] Nicholas thereby presents Jewish biblical interpretation to a wide audience of Christians for the very first
time. His attention to the literal sense ultimately influences Martin
Luther's reading of scripture.

Meanwhile, a Jew creates the first concordance to the Hebrew
Bible and introduces Christian chapter-verse divisions into the
Tanakh. Isaac Nathan ben Kalonymus (fl. fifteenth century) is a
leading merchant and Jewish intellectual living in Arles, France. He
is also an ardent polemicist, whose early encounters with Franciscan
monks wound him with their rational arguments, which they see
as irrefutable.[13] His contacts with Christians lead to his discovery of
something they call a concordance, an index of words that guides

readers to particular citations in a text. Latin concordances to the Bible had been written in the fourteenth century, but no Hebrew concordance yet exists. Ben Kalonymus sees the concordance as the perfect weapon for successful disputation. "With that book there was no argument that was too sublime for me to eradicate and demolish," he writes.[14] Rather than translate the existing Latin concordance into Hebrew, Nathan hires a staff of scholars, supplies all of them with copies of the Hebrew Bible and Jewish commentaries, and works himself for more than ten years on the Hebrew concordance.

Ben Kalonymus's key contribution, for both polemical and homiletical purposes, is his adoption of the Christian numbering system and its division into particular books, thereby establishing the format used in the Jewish Tanakh today. (The Tanakh orders the books differently, however, from the Christian Old Testament.) When he finds discrepancies between the Vulgate Bible and the Jewish text, he sometimes adopts the Christian approach rather than automatically accepting the Jewish interpretation.[15] In this regard, he shares the open mind of Nicholas, who occasionally prefers the Jewish explanation to the Christian.

Christians can find theological truth not only in Jewish scripture and interpretation, but also in Jewish mystical texts known as the Kabbalah. Renaissance interest in philosophy and science prompts Christian Hebraists to investigate the Kabbalah. Both Jewish and Christian Kabbalists view Moses as the precursor to Plato and Pythagoras, to whom the esoteric secrets of the universe are revealed at Mount Sinai as part of the Oral Torah. Others see the Kabbalah as originating with Adam, to whom God discloses the mysteries of creation. Jews and Christians alike turn to mysticism seeking relief from, or flight from, the constraints of rationalism and biblicism. Kabbalistic texts, such as the Zohar, are essentially commentaries on scripture that transport readers into transcendent, rather than historical, realms. Jewish translators and interpreters open the mystical and magical doors to the Kabbalah to Christian humanists, who then find what they are looking for—proofs of the Trinity, the Incarnation, the divinity of the Messiah, and other dogmas.

Although the goal of Christian Kabbalism is to uncover ancient wisdom and to prove the truths of Christianity, scholarly attention to Hebrew nevertheless generates concern over Jewish books, if not over Jewish people. Johannes Reuchlin (1455–1522) writes several works of Christian Kabbalah as well as textbooks on the Hebrew language (largely indebted to David Kimhi, a medieval Jewish philologist). Reuchlin, a professor of Greek and Hebrew at the University of Ingolstadt, disavows any sympathy for Jews. At the same time, he strenuously argues against confiscating or burning any Hebrew books—unless they have blasphemous content—in a famous "Battle of the Books" that occurs in the early sixteenth century.

Reuchlin refuses to join efforts organized by Dominican friars to burn Jewish literature and in 1511 publishes an ardent defense of himself and of Hebrew learning. In his view, the burning of Jewish books "would mean the destruction of Jewish culture and with it the irreparable loss of knowledge not alone to Judaism but also imperative for the study of Christian texts."[16] Reuchlin's book provokes heresy charges against him and roils the humanist culture of Europe for a decade, with Reuchlinists going in and out of favor with the ecclesiastical hierarchy. In 1520, however, Pope Leo X (p. 1513–1521) declares the book heretical, and it is placed on the Index of Forbidden Books, along with all of Reuchlin's works. (Not until 1966 does the Catholic Church abandon the Index, and no such list exists today.) Thus, in the case of Reuchlin, Christian Hebraism leads to an ardent defense of Jewish culture.

Cardinal Egidio da Viterbo (1472–1532) shares Reuchlin's love of the Kabbalah. The cardinal, who heads the Order of Augustinian Friars, petitions the pope to add three Hebrew letters to the Roman alphabet.[17] Da Viterbo believes that God has set Hebrew apart from Greek and Latin to reveal sacred mysteries. He also sees meaning in numerals and in the arithmetic of literary devices found in scripture, such as acrostics in which the first letter of each line can be read vertically to form another word. He feels that "the only competent theologians are the Jews who grasp this principle."[18]

Facilitating the cardinal's study of Hebrew is the Jewish Hebraist Elijah Levita (ca. 1469–1558), who lives under the patronage of da Viterbo for more than a decade. While he produces grammars and lexicons of both Hebrew and Aramaic, Levita draws the line at sharing the mysteries of the Kabbalah with a gentile. As a result of his close connections with Christians, however, he receives criticism from the Jewish community for instructing them in the Talmud. Levita's response is that they would learn it from his books anyway. Somewhat paradoxically, Levita's scholarly freedom resides in his Christian milieu, though he never converts to Christianity. Operating outside of Jewish structures and norms, he is not constrained by traditional Jewish discourse in order to survive as a scholar. As a result, "Levita's ideas were instrumental in the development of early modern Biblical scholarship."[19]

Levita's contributions extend beyond the Kabbalah when he leaves Cardinal da Viterbo to work in the burgeoning printing industry. He first works as a proofreader with the influential Christian printer Daniel Bomberg (1483–1549) in Venice. Bomberg issues a range of Jewish texts, including the first printed edition of the Talmud. With Levita's assistance, the printer produces a third edition of the rabbinic Bible. Levita then moves to Isny, Germany, at the invitation of the Christian printer and Hebraist Paul Fagius (1504–1549), a former student of Levita. Fagius publishes one of Levita's lexicons with Hebrew and Latin pages facing each other— without changing a word, according to Levita. The two write mutually complimentary introductions to each version. Lest he be accused of Judaizing, Fagius includes critical comments about Judaism, but his comparison of Levita to "old wine"—an allusion to Jesus's comparison of old wine and new wine—seems to be a defense of Jewish teachers like Levita.[20] Undoubtedly his partnership with Levita piques the curiosity of Fagius and prompts him to write "an entire treatise analyzing and interpreting and translating standard Jewish table blessings, including benedictions over wine, a long and short version of grace, and other blessings recited over food."[21]

The association of Jews and Christians in the world of print is extraordinary. "When one considers that as late as 1500 Hebrew sources were virtually unknown in Christian circles, their immense popularity by 1550 is nothing short of a minor cultural revolution."[22] Like their Jewish counterparts, Christians see in the Bible the witness to their truth claims and thus recognize its usefulness in arguing against opponents. In addition, Catholics and Protestants engage in a number of intra-Christian debates over the reliance upon Jewish sources. The charge of Judaizing remains a distinct threat to Christians who publish Jewish books wherein the translators fail to include anti-Jewish remarks.[23]

Research into history, geography, cartography, customs, language, and other nontheological topics unavoidably brings Christians closer to understanding Jews and Judaism. And, for better or worse, Jews find their cultural heritage disseminated to a wide audience of non-Jewish readers. In turn, contacts with Christians profoundly influence the production of Jewish religious literature. Jewish printers today maintain much of the formatting of editions created for Christian readers during the Renaissance, thus demonstrating the ongoing impact of Christian Hebraica.[24]

The Second (or First) Coming

Another impetus for rising Hebraism among Christians is the Protestant emphasis on scripture, and hence, the need for a correct understanding of it. This causes a number of Protestants to read messianic prophecies literally and to believe in the imminent return of Jesus as Lord. Some literalists go so far as to follow Jewish practices and are accused of Judaizing the faith. Meanwhile, Jews see the fragmentation of Christendom during and after the Reformation, and its splintering into rival groups, as signs of the coming Messiah as well.

While medieval millenarianism—the belief that Jesus is coming soon to establish a thousand-year reign—occasionally provokes violent outbursts against Jews, this new Christian millenarianism sees Jews as a necessary part of God's ultimate plan. Whether as converts to Christ, as participants in the restoration of a Jewish kingdom, or as accurate interpreters of biblical prophecy for the present day, Jews are needed. Traditional Christian teaching holds that Jews do not understand the prophecies found in the Old Testament that foretell the coming of Jesus. But the breakup of ecclesiastical authority in the sixteenth and seventeenth centuries, supplemented by the political, economic, and social ferment of burgeoning republicanism, calls for fresh readings of scripture. Jewish participation in new mercantile endeavors challenges the timeworn claim that God has abandoned the Jews to dispersion. On the contrary, the Jews seem to thrive under the special providence of God, having survived as a people for so long. European colonization of North America, particularly the British colonies, also generates new interest in the Hebrew language. The settlers who sail to America see themselves as establishing a New Israel in the wilderness. The study of Hebrew is a key component of this project, especially with the founding of colleges that promote Puritan values.

A number of intriguing collaborations between Jews and Christians occur in England and the Netherlands in the seventeenth century. Both nations are embroiled in revolutionary changes— England in a civil war against the monarchy and the Netherlands breaking free from more than a century of Spanish rule. Large numbers of religious resisters and radicals—from Puritans and Separatists, to Quakers and Diggers—live in England or emigrate to Holland and the New World to escape oppression. A number envision a revamped political order that will provide a measure of justice to all people. Add to this mix those who expect the Messiah to arrive at any minute, and we get a unique situation for interreligious cooperation.

Called the Jerusalem of the North, Amsterdam is the capital of the Sephardic Diaspora in the seventeenth century.[25] Sephardic Jews, who have lived across North Africa and on the Iberian Peninsula for more than a thousand years, flee the Spanish Inquisition in the fifteenth century. They settle in Holland in large numbers and exert a positive influence on trade and culture. One such descendent of Sephardic immigrants, Menasseh ben Israel (1604–1657), becomes the rabbi for a Portuguese synagogue in Amsterdam. He establishes the first Hebrew publishing house in the city and engages in lively discussions with Christians about the coming Messiah. Ben Israel develops an Abramite theology, based on the biblical patriarch Abraham, in which he identifies the teachings common to both Judaism and Christianity. Written as a defense of the resurrection against those who are denying it, the book appears in a Latin version directed specifically at Christians and outlines the principles they share with Jews—"worship of the same God, following his commandments, and belief in life after death."[26]

Correspondence with the English millenarian John Dury fosters the publication of *Hope of Israel* (1650), ben Israel's most important work. *Hope of Israel* considers, but dismisses, the idea that some of the Native Americans in the new colonies belong to the lost tribes of Israel. The "Jewish Indian Theory" has excited Protestants who see conversion of indigenous peoples—in their minds, Jews—as a sign of the impending advent. But ben Israel also encourages the millenarians with his prediction that the restoration of Israel is near, as long as Jews are dispersed to the ends of the earth. For biblical prophecy to be fulfilled, this means that England needs to admit, or readmit, the Jews who had been expelled nearly four centuries earlier. Ben Israel sails to England in 1555 to make the case for readmission to Oliver Cromwell (1599–1658), Lord Protector of the English Commonwealth, and to the British Parliament. Although unsuccessful at the time, his hope later becomes realized when Cromwell quietly issues protections to the Sephardic Jews of London a few years later.

Menasseh ben Israel takes Jewish restorationist theology, blends it with Christian messianic expectation, and comes up with an inclusive eschatology. (Eschatology is the doctrine of last things or Endtime, frequently encompassing final judgment and ultimate destiny. For most Jews, eschatology encompasses the arrival of the

Messiah; for Christians, the return of the Christ.) Christian leaders frequent ben Israel's home in Amsterdam. Queen Christina of Sweden (1626–1689), for example, introduces him to the work of Isaac la Peyrère, quite possibly another Sephardic Jew, who is born in France and raised a Calvinist Christian. His theory of a pre-Adamic race results in his condemnation as a heretic, though he ultimately converts to Catholicism. La Peyrère argues in *Du rappel des Juifs* (The Calling Back of the Jews) that there are two Messiahs: one who came for gentiles in the spiritual person of Jesus and a second who is to come in the flesh to Jews in the present day. More specifically, la Peyrère advises Jews to settle in France to await their Messiah. There they should establish Jewish "churches" in which no objectionable (that is, Christian) beliefs or practices are required and then go with the Messiah to rebuild Jerusalem. From there they will rule the world with the Messiah and his viceroy, the Prince of Condé (1530–1569), a prominent French Huguenot.[27] The influence of *Du rappel des Juifs* can be seen in ben Israel's last published work, *Vindiciae Judaeorum* (Vindication of the Jews), in which he claims that Jews and Christians disagree only on the Messiah. They should really look to the future rather than the past, he argues. Citing la Peyrère, he writes that all will be redeemed, for while Christians expect a second appearance of the Messiah, and Jews hope for a first appearance, "by that faith they shall be saved, for the difference consists onely [only] in the circumstance of time."[28]

In the seventeenth century, many Protestants and most Jews expect the Messiah to assume a political leadership role on earth, a departure for Christians who believe in a spiritualized, heavenly being who exerts power from heaven. With political systems in turmoil, Protestants turn to the Bible for guidance on government. Israelite society under the leadership of Moses is closely examined. John Selden (1584–1654), "the most learned Englishman of his age,"[29] is just one of many Christians who scour the Bible and postbiblical Jewish tradition for contemporary guidance on political theory and international law. A talmudic scholar, Selden writes a half dozen rabbinic works covering topics as diverse as the theory and practice of marriage and divorce laws to laws relating to the (biblical) Jewish priesthood. In his study of the Sanhedrin (the supreme council of Jews during the Second Temple period), he argues that the Jewish body might serve as a model for the English parliament.

Selden's magisterial work *De jure naturali et gentium juxta disciplinam Ebraeorum* (On Natural Law and the Law of Nations according to Hebrew Teachings) compares Jewish Noachide commandments with the Christian concept of natural law. (The seven Noachide commandments are the biblical laws given to Adam and Noah prior to the revelation at Mount Sinai that are incumbent upon non-Jews. They are discussed further in Chapter 10.) Selden claims that both have divine, rather than rationalistic, warrant, and that following either leads to eternal life. He sees salvation as open to the entire human race, if people follow the Noachide commandments or obey the God-given natural law. Most noteworthy is Selden's generous vision, in which he expresses hope for universal salvation, rejects prejudices concerning Jewish nationalism, and emphasizes the humaneness of rabbinic thought.[30]

But New England Puritans depart from Selden's inclusivity, arrogating the biblical heritage strictly to themselves and enforcing a severe biblical code of conduct on secular society. "In their own mind, they were the Jews, the ultimate and total heirs of the promises that God had made in the Hebrew Bible."[31] As the New Israel, they make their way from Egypt (that is, Europe) to the wilderness (the colonies) to create a New Zion, a city on a hill. They disdain all other religions, but whereas they barely tolerate Jews in their midst, they execute Christian heretics. The Bible is their constitution, prayer book, and hymnal, which they read in the new English translation—another work of Christian Hebraism—commissioned by King James I and first published in 1611.

Despite a narrow outlook, Puritan devotion to the Old Testament also creates a legacy of valuing Hebrew in the colonies. Hebrew is integral to the curriculum at ten colleges founded before the American Revolution.[32] This follows the precedent set at some European universities—Cambridge, for instance, has required Hebrew language for the master's degree since 1549 and Oxford since 1575.[33] Along with Greek and Latin, Hebrew is one of the classical languages, the essential mark of all educated persons, and thus Hebrew is a required subject at Harvard, Yale, Dartmouth, Columbia, and other colonial universities. To graduate from Harvard at this time, a student has to translate both the Old and New Testaments from the original languages into Latin. Additionally, until 1817, at least one commencement speech is given in Hebrew each year.[34] A story circulates at the time of the American Revolution that some of the nation's founders recommend substituting Hebrew for English as the national language.[35]

Millenarian expectations in the colonies are channeled into the quest for independence from England and the vision of America as the New Israel. Meanwhile, messianic claimants flourish in Europe and Britain. News about the Jewish Messiah Shabbatai Zevi (1626–1676) blazes across Europe in letters, pamphlets, posters, and broadsides beginning in 1665. Zevi is well educated in rabbinic literature, passionate about the Kabbalah, and apparently mentally unstable. His charisma, enhanced by the testimony of his prophet, Nathan of Gaza (1643–1680), attracts followers in Palestine, modern Syria, and Turkey, and ignites millenarian fervor among not only Jews but Christians. When the Ottomans capture and incarcerate Zevi, he abruptly converts to Islam. Shabbateanism basically collapses, although some groups continue to believe in Zevi as Messiah until about 1700. The whole incident disappoints Jews and convinces Christians that Jews will never be able to recognize the true Messiah.[36] Christians are equally skeptical, however, about their own messianic claimants.

Cooperation within Complex Identity

Commercial, educational, and personal alliances in the world of Renaissance printing undoubtedly engender greater openness among Jews and Christians. Cooperation in working on a common project, one of the hallmarks of deep equality, brings Christians and Jews together despite themselves. The fact that they join forces to translate, print, and distribute a shared text of utmost importance is even more significant. The interreligious partnership exemplified by Renaissance Hebraism offers a counternarrative to the master account of conflict and antagonism.

But does Christian Hebraism actually lead to better relations with Jews?[37] The record is as mixed as are the motives of those involved. The concept of complex identity captures the ambivalent nature of the entire undertaking: paradoxical and ambiguous, but also open and dynamic. These terms characterize the feelings of Jews who collaborate with Christians on a wide array of projects, as well as of Christians who team up with Jews. Co-religionists of both faiths question this association. For Jews, their peers warn that the information they share may be used against them—and they are right in some instances. For Christians, their peers accuse them of being insufficiently Christian, that is, antisemitic. What would it be like to live among contemporaries who accept the proposition, "If it is Christian to hate the Jews, we are all Christian enough in this regard"?[38] We do not know the extent to which Christian Hebraists embed antisemitic polemic into their works because they sincerely believe it, or because such rhetoric is required for publication. There are consequences for supposed Judaizers.

Johannes Buxtorf the Elder (1564–1629), one of the most significant publishers of the early modern era, is a case in point. His great work, the *Bibliotheca Rabbinica*, brings the Hebrew Bible, the Aramaic Targumim, and commentaries by celebrated rabbis together into a single volume. Although designed for Christian readers, it is well received by Jewish scholars.[39] Yet a harsh condemnation of Judaism is found in another one of his books, the *Synagoga Judaica*. In the introduction, the printer informs the reader that he writes about Jewish customs merely to show how hollow and meaningless they are. This disclaimer "is difficult to reconcile with the meticulous and respectful explanation he gives of the theological significance of almost every aspect of Jewish practice."[40] His dismissal of the Talmud in the same introduction does not reflect the meticulous efforts he makes to accurately translate and interpret the text.[41] Moreover, Buxtorf's study of Jewish texts brings him into friendly contact with the Jews of Basel. He attends the *bris* (Jewish ceremony of circumcision) for the son of one of the Jewish printers with whom he works. As a consequence, the leading citizens of the Swiss city fine and severely reprimand him. The printer gains the right of residency for Jewish scholars who work for him, since the city is closed to Jewish inhabitants. He maintains a correspondence and apparent rapport with Jewish scholars in Germany, Holland, and Constantinople. "His seemingly close friendships with his Jewish collaborators ran against the grain of prejudices and expectations of his fellow citizens."[42]

Indeed, many Christian Hebraists justify their close reading of Jewish scripture, commentary, and halakhah by stating that their purposes are purely argumentative. They feel the need to excuse their fascination with rabbinic literature by denigrating its value.[43] Christian Hebraism nevertheless creates positive attitudes toward Jews and Jewish culture, providing an unprecedented framework for dialogue and exchange.[44] Many Christian Hebraists actually defend the rights of Jews, especially those whom they know personally, as does Buxtorf. Others, like Reuchlin, aim to safeguard Jewish culture because of their esteem for it.

The choices available to Christians and Jews at this time inevitably produce ambivalence about each other. Despite their mutual doubt and uncertainty, however, they manage to cooperate in ways that alter religious literature for centuries to come.

Chapter 6

THE PUZZLE OF CHRISTIAN ZIONISM

We respectfully petition His Excellency Benjamin Harrison, President of the United States ... to secure the holding, at an early date, of an international conference to consider the condition of the Israelites and their claims to Palestine as their ancient home.

—THE BLACKSTONE MEMORIAL, 1891[1]

Over the course of eight centuries, more than sixteen hundred Christian scholars in some thirty countries and regions devote themselves to the study of Hebrew language and rabbinic literature.[2] Rather than a steady stream of research, it is at times a roaring river and at others a small trickle. The same elements that contribute to the flowering of Christian Hebraism in the Reformation and Renaissance also cause its withering in the Enlightenment. Political, economic, social, cultural, philosophical, and religious ferment shift the focus from the authority of scripture—and therefore the importance of Hebrew—to the authority of reason. Radical skepticism over the validity of revelation, coupled with a turn to empirical science as the source for arriving at truth, undermines the foundations of religious tradition for Christians and Jews alike.

The rise of nation-states and civil power in the "long eighteenth century" of the Enlightenment (1685–1815) and the simultaneous decline of church control over political and economic institutions fosters a clearly articulated theory of religious tolerance for the very

first time. Although I am arguing that tolerance is a poor sub-
stitute for deep equality, in the long run of history, it is a great
advance over discrimination, oppression, and violence. All of these
factors—secularization, tolerance, Christian Hebraism, empirical
science—help set the stage for the emancipation of the Jews in the
eighteenth and nineteenth centuries. Emancipation recognizes the
civil and legal rights to which Jews are entitled in the countries in
which they live, freeing them from circumscribed lives in ghettos
to enter more fully into the wider society. Aided by their Christian
allies and by nonreligious advocates for basic human rights, Jews
press hard for equality.

In 1791, the United States becomes the first country to explicitly
acknowledge religious rights, with the U.S. Constitution's rejection of religious tests for public office and the ratification of the
First Amendment's protection of religious freedom. By the 1860s,
most European nations provide some measure of political fairness,
if not actual acceptance, for Jews. In France, Abbé Henri Grégoire (1750–1831) spearheads the campaign for civic emancipation
of French Jews. Like other Christians discussed in this chapter,
the Roman Catholic abbot believes Jews are to play a key role in
the coming millennium. But legal equality does not impart social
equality, and Jews continue to be seen as foreigners in their home
countries. Non-Jews expect Jews to abandon their traditional practices in order to assimilate as Europeans. In fact, Abbé Grégoire
initially gains attention by winning first prize in an essay contest
on the question "Are there possibilities of making the Jews more
useful and happier in France?" The presupposition underlying the
question is that social encapsulation and discrimination have created moral and social shortcomings in Jews. By integrating them
fully into civic life, they will become happy and productive members of society.

The Haskalah, or Jewish Enlightenment, that sweeps across Europe between 1770 and 1880 counters the pressure to conform. It is
true that Jewish intellectuals—the Maskilim (wise ones)—of this
period promote assimilation and encourage the study of worldly

subjects. At the same time, they develop a vibrant Jewish culture out of which pour poetry, literature, drama, and a rededication to Hebrew as a spoken, rather than religious, language. The pioneer of the Haskalah is Moses Mendelssohn (1729–1786), who "renewed the possibility of dialogue with Christianity."[3] The artist Moritz Daniel Oppenheim immortalizes Mendelssohn's friendship with Christian intellectual Gotthold Ephraim Lessing (1729–1781) in a painting titled "Lavater and Lessing Visit Moses Mendelssohn" (1856).[4] Mendelssohn maintains a correspondence and engages in conversation with prominent Christian intellectuals, arguing on the basis of rationalism for religious tolerance. Why should anyone in the world be excluded from salvation, he wonders, when everyone can attain it on the basis of their own religion and ethics? An Orthodox Jew, Mendelssohn proposes the notion of an "invisible church," comprising the purest ethics, which includes Christians, Jews, Muslims, Confucianists, and even ancient Greeks and Romans.

The unity of Judaism itself is threatened in the drive for assimilation. Reform, or Liberal, Judaism arises as a result of the entry of Jews into the broader non-Jewish society. It offers a middle course between following rabbinic law as a strict Orthodox Jew and converting to Christianity. Reform Jews believe that since societies evolve over time, religion should make appropriate modifications to meet those changes. The changes that Reform Jews make in Europe are largely liturgical and cosmetic—at least at first—with synagogue services being held in the vernacular, prayers being added or dropped, an organ being used, and mixed male and female choirs being organized. Abraham Geiger, considered the founder of Reform Judaism, believes that Judaism's gift to humanity is its ethical monotheism—the system of morality revealed by the one God. While the German rabbi and scholar does not see the point of dietary laws, believing that they separated Jew from non-Jew, he accepts circumcision.

Although Reform Judaism begins on the European continent and becomes popular in England, it really takes off with the immigration of Jews to the United States in the nineteenth century. The

adoption of the Pittsburgh Platform in 1885—a statement that outlines the beliefs of Reform Jews—marks it as distinctly different.
While accepting the Bible as an instrument of religious and moral
instruction, the signatories hold that Mosaic and rabbinical laws
are products of their time and no longer binding. Further, they
declare, "We consider ourselves no longer a nation, but a religious
community, and therefore expect neither a return to Palestine, nor
sacrificial worship under the sons of Aaron, nor the restoration of
any of the laws concerning the Jewish state."[5] Rather than an individual Messiah, the document articulates hope for a messianic age
in which a kingdom of truth, justice, and peace among all will be
established. It is important to point out that modern Reform Jews
do not share all the views contained in the Pittsburgh Platform,
and that it remains a radical document even today.

In reaction to what are seen as the excesses of Reform Judaism,
counter movements emerge. Thanks to continuing immigration,
America sees yet another development within Judaism. Conservative Judaism arises with the establishment of the Jewish Theological
Seminary in America in 1887. On the one hand, Conservative Jews
are more observant of halakhah than Reform Jews; on the other,
they accept the findings of critical biblical studies and are willing
to compromise with some of the demands of the secular world. But
even Orthodox Judaism changes in the nineteenth century with
the development of what is called Modern Orthodoxy. Strictly observant yet open to contemporary thinking, Orthodox Jews in the
modern camp are willing to interact with non-Jews—unlike ultra-
Orthodox Jews, who tend to live and work in their own enclaves.

There are other branches of Judaism—for example, Reconstructionist, Humanistic, and Hasidic—but in the United States,
Reform Judaism is the largest "denomination," at 35 percent, with
Conservative next at 18 percent, and other denominations or Jews
without affiliation making up the balance. Orthodox Jews make
up only 10 percent of American Jews. These figures may change
in the future, given the high birth rate within the Orthodox community. In contrast, Reform and Conservative Jews make up only

a tiny percentage of Jews in Israel, with almost 50 percent of Israel's Jews saying they are secular, 30 percent saying they are "Masorti," or traditional—roughly equivalent to the American Conservative Branch of Judaism—and about 10 percent seeing themselves as Orthodox or ultra-Orthodox.[6]

Just as Judaism consists of three major branches growing from a single root, so also does Christianity, whose three major limbs—Catholicism, Protestantism, and Orthodoxy—stem from one trunk. Thus, neither Judaism nor Christianity is monolithic. Not all Jews, historically or today, support founding a secular nation-state called Israel, believing instead that it will happen through the will of God rather than humankind. Similarly, not all Christians necessarily interpret biblical prophecy as describing current events, particularly as they pertain to Jews and the nation of Israel. Yet the convergence of Jews and Christians who, for widely differing reasons, support a Jewish state, has profoundly altered world history. The yearning of the Jewish people for a permanent home is called Zionism, a nationalist movement for self-determination and self-governance. It takes an affirmative and even militant stance toward Jewish survival in the here and now. Christian Zionism, however, supports creating a Jewish state as part of a larger eschatological vision. The return of Jews to biblical Zion, along with the restoration of the temple and the priesthood in Jerusalem, serves as preparation for the second advent of the Messiah, that is, Jesus Christ. (Jewish Zionism and contemporary Christian Zionism are considered in greater detail in Chapter 11.)

The millenarian expectations that Christians hold during the Reformation and Renaissance wane in the eighteenth century but come roaring back in the nineteenth. A fascination with biblical prophecy and a concomitant desire to proselytize coalesce to animate Christian Zionists who see Jews as an indispensable component of God's Endtime plan. Part of this involves encouraging Jewish settlement in Palestine, while another part seeks conversion of Jews to Christianity. Yet these same ardent missionaries become fervent defenders of Jews and Judaism in the face of rising antisemitism in the nineteenth century. Jews respond to Christian evangelism and Christian Zionism in a number of different ways. We can see the continuation of complex identity, with its accompanying ambivalence, as an explanation for the dynamism that characterizes nineteenth-century Jewish and Christian relations.

Eschatology and Zionism

The expectation that the world as we know it will end in the near future, with violence and terror preceding an era of peace on earth, destabilizes the status quo. For that reason, institutional Christianity postpones the radical upsets promised in the New Testament book of Revelation and relocates the kingdom of God from earth to heaven. Yet, at certain moments in history, individual Christians act on the belief that heavenly salvation is imminent on earth. The medieval era is one such moment, as is the period of the Reformation. In the nineteenth century, Protestant Christians also experience eagerness for Christ's return and his inauguration of God's rule on earth. They believe that Jews will play a key role in the upcoming eschatological drama.

Commitment to evangelization is high on the agenda for Protestant Christians who see great opportunities in European imperialistic expansion for bringing the world to Christ. Coupled with a fervent belief in the coming millennium and the thousand-year reign of Christ, Christians turn to Jews to realize their Endtime dreams of Jesus's return. Their work embraces two goals: the first is to convert Jews to Christianity; the second is to restore the Jewish people to Palestine. Energetic programs to encourage Jews to move to Palestine accompany missionary activity. New readings of the Bible, especially the Christian Old Testament, justify these moves.

An emphasis on the authority of scripture arises during the sixteenth-century Reformation and leads Protestant Christians in succeeding centuries to assiduously study the Bible. This includes learning Hebrew and Greek to understand the Old Testament and

New Testament, respectively. By the nineteenth century, two divergent paths emerge. One is centered in Germany and emphasizes the historical study of the Bible, asking questions about authorship, dating, provenance, and context. The other, primarily located in England and the United States, stresses the prophetic reading of the Bible, with a focus on what texts have to say about the present and the future.

America's successful war of independence against England in the late eighteenth century also boosts interest in biblical prophecy. Political and religious leaders see this victory as the result of God's providence and interpret the new nation as the New Israel, over and against the Old Israel of Europe. The Second Great Awakening—an outpouring of religious energy that occurs in the first decade of the nineteenth century—spurs the study of the Bible, especially its prophetic writings. Millennial feeling runs high, and two new religious groups, Mormons and Adventists, preach that Jesus Christ will return to earth very soon.

In the British Isles, a member of a small Protestant sect called the Plymouth Brethren introduces a reading of scripture that divides time into dispensations—eras in which God works through different instruments to bring about salvation.[7] Jews and Christians alike have long divided history into specific epochs of salvation. What is new is the role that Jews will play in God's ultimate plans for all humanity. John Nelson Darby (1800–1882) is behind dispensationalism, arguing that God designed seven distinct time periods, beginning with creation (the Dispensation of Innocence) and ending with the Millennial Kingdom of Christ. Between those bookends, dispensationalists find room for Jews and their ancestors, the Israelites, until the time of Jesus and the Church, the penultimate dispensation. Prior to the final dispensation, God will fulfill the promises to the Jews: they will return to their own land in order to welcome the Messiah, who will bring about final redemption for the entire planet. Christians believe this Messiah is Jesus, who will come again. Jews are dubious. "Either the Messiah of the Jews has come, or he is yet to come," prominent Jewish

American diplomat Mordecai Manuel Noah (1785–1851) tells an audience of Christians in 1844.[8] If he has not yet appeared, it is appropriate for Jews to return to Palestine to await his arrival. Noah respectfully dismisses proselytization efforts: first pragmatically, noting their lack of success, and then theologically, reminding his listeners of the biblical promises—"they shall occupy their own land *as Jews*" (italics in original).[9] And, in case Christians have forgotten, Noah adds that Jesus himself said, "Salvation is of the Jews" (John 4:22).

Dispensationalism introduces a new wrinkle into the premillennialist and postmillennialist divide among Protestant Christians. Postmillennialist Christians believe that their efforts to christianize the globe will bring about Christ's return at the end of the thousand years predicted in Revelation 20. They must therefore engage aggressively and swiftly to bring about Christ's presence by improving conditions on earth with which to welcome him. Premillennialist Christians, in contrast, think that Jesus will come at the beginning of the millennium, as the world declines further into chaos and disruption. Dispensationalist Christians are premillennialist in the sense that they believe things on earth are bad and will get worse in a Great Tribulation. But they differ in that they see the Bible as prophesying what is to come, not what has already happened, as the premillennialists read it.

Rather than viewing the church as the New Israel, dispensationalists are literalists: Israel means Israel, not the church. As a result, they have "consistently and explicitly assigned the utmost importance to the Jewish people in their understanding of the course of human history and in their eschatological hopes."[10] The promises made to Israel through Abraham and David are eternal, even though Israel lost its earlier glory in its rejection of Christ. There are a number of theories about what happens during the Great Tribulation and when that will occur: unconverted Jews will return to the land, establish a nation, and rebuild the temple in Jerusalem. A Jewish Antichrist, however, will arise and require obeisance. A lot of blood will be shed in wars, plagues, and disasters, but some Jews who have heard the gospel will turn to Jesus, and this remnant will survive the turmoil. Another eschatological teaching has it that Jesus will become judge of the world and will carry out judgment based on how nations have treated the Jews.[11] Still another is that the remnant of Jews who accept Christ as Lord and Savior will administer Christ's millennial kingdom under his rule, rebuilding the temple at that time and reinstituting the sacrificial system.

The presence of Jews in the Land of Israel is crucial to dispensationalist eschatologies. Although there is debate in the past as to whether Jews should be converted prior to settlement, most dispensationalists resolve that question by the start of the twentieth century: residence first, conversion later. (There are still a number of Christian missionary societies that direct their efforts primarily, or solely, to Jews, however). The centrality of a Jewish state and of a Jewish role in Endtime helps to explain contemporary conservative Christian support for Israel. At the same time, it is clear that everything that might be recognizably Jewish—such as Torah observance—will eventually pass away in the embrace of Jesus. Thus, dispensationalism is "good for the Jews" up to a point, but in the end it still requires conversion to Christianity and abandonment of the people Israel.

Evangelism and Zionism

Regardless of their mixed motives, Christians actively support Jewish settlement of Palestine throughout the nineteenth and twentieth centuries. Some Christian pioneers also establish utopian communes in Palestine, but these are exceptions since Christians are expected to be raptured into the air wherever they are when Christ comes. (The Rapture is an Endtime belief that good Christians will be transported to heaven with the return of Christ; everyone else, including bad Christians, will be left behind.) In the meantime, Israel must first be restored. Myriad missionary societies, prophecy conferences, symposiums on Israel (the people), and Bible study groups devote hours, days, and months to preparing for the end by deconstructing the messages found in scripture. Contributing to this process is Cyrus I. Scofield (1843–1921), who devises the Scofield Reference Bible in 1909. His King James Version provides notes and commentaries that outline and cross-reference key passages predicting the ways and means to the Last Judgment. Scofield's commentaries introduce readers to terminology such as Great Tribulation, time of Jacob's trouble, time of the gentiles, and pretribulation rapture. Dispensationalism thus makes it into the homes of American Protestants through the Scofield Bible.[12]

Christian plans for the Jewish return from dispersion predate Jewish political Zionism. Many Americans are caught up in this hope, seeing it as preliminary to Christ's return. William E. Blackstone (1841–1935), for example, spends a lifetime advocating for Jewish restoration to Palestine. From his Chicago Hebrew Mission, he edits *The Jewish Era: A Christian Magazine on Behalf of Israel,* which publishes articles on Jewish settlements in Palestine, the Zionist movement, developments in world Jewry, and Jewish holidays and rituals.[13] In 1891 he presents a petition to President Benjamin Harrison signed by more than four hundred dignitaries calling for an international agreement to give Palestine to the Jews. The Blackstone Memorial, as the petition is called, is noteworthy in that it anticipates much of Theodor Herzl's program of Jewish political Zionism.[14] Blackstone later writes to President Grover Cleveland to remind him of the Memorial, and in 1903 a group of Methodist preachers in Chicago endorses the Memorial and sends it to President Theodore Roosevelt. The petition calls for an international conference to address the plight of Jews in Russia and to consider relocating them to Palestine. (Eastern Europe and Russia have become the home of Ashkenazi Jews who settle in Europe but are pushed eastward by continuous expulsions. Although they develop a vibrant culture, they come under increasing persecution during the nineteenth century.) Blackstone works closely with American Zionists such as Nathan Straus and Louis D. Brandeis on a similar petition submitted to President Woodrow Wilson in 1916. Yet ambiguity and ambivalence mark the work of the Methodist minister. Blackstone believes in the ultimate conversion of the Jews, and at times his outlook appears outright antisemitic. He has no love for Judaism, which he predicts will disappear in the coming millennium. Yet before his death, he funds programs to help Jewish refugees, and in the end he leaves his estate to the Zionist movement.[15]

Belief in the divine plan to restore Israel to the Jews, at least for a time, is not unique to North American Christians. Victorian England also proves to be fertile ground for a burgeoning Christian Zionism, although it remains a fringe movement throughout the century, despite the prominent names behind it. The missionary movement in the British Isles grows rapidly under the assumption that "Christianity had an exclusive claim to be the highest truth revealed to mankind."[16] In England and Scotland alone, more than twenty societies are established for the conversion of Jews.[17] Prominent among these is the London Society for Promoting Christianity Amongst the Jews. Established in 1809, it is active throughout Europe (including Russia), North Africa, and the Middle East. The society finds Catholic Poland to be especially fruitful, thanks to the fact that the society takes a special interest in the vast Jewish population living in the former Polish-Lithuanian Commonwealth.[18] In addition to publishing traditional Jewish and Christian texts in Hebrew translation, the society produces a Yiddish version of the New Testament. Not only does the society work for the conversion of individual Jews, it also hopes to restore the Jewish people to Palestine "as a sign of the eventual millennium to come."[19] Yet the society publishes anti-Jewish tracts as well, such as an attack on the Talmud, which appears in German, French, Italian, and Yiddish translations in 1837. The society's most controversial action is to establish the office of an Anglican bishop in Jerusalem in 1841, consecrating Michael Solomon Alexander, a Jewish convert to Christianity, whose explicit mission as bishop is to convert other Jews.

Anthony Ashley-Cooper, the Seventh Lord Shaftesbury (1801–1885), is among those promoting the Anglican bishop in the expectation that a nation of converted Anglican Jews will welcome Jesus on his imminent return. A social progressive who fosters legislative protections for the poor, Lord Shaftesbury is also convinced that "the Jews were destined by God to return to their own land as part of the fulfillment of biblical prophecy."[20] Leading British citizens and the cultured class endorse Christian Zionist ideas throughout the nineteenth century. Although their advocacy of Jewish restoration falls outside the mainstream, their views are nonetheless well-known and quite influential.[21] Lord Shaftesbury makes his own theological convictions more palatable to policy makers by pointing out the advantages for British imperial interests in the Middle East. In September 1840, when he presents a plan for Jewish settlement of Palestine to Lord Palmerston, the British Foreign Minister, he makes no mention of God, the Bible, or the Second Coming. Rather, he merely reminds Palmerston that resettling Jews in Palestine is "the cheapest and safest mode of supplying the wastes of those depopulated regions."[22]

Converts, Rabbis, and Missionaries

While Christian support for Zionism and resettlement of Palestine stimulates amicable relations between Jews and Christians, missionary endeavors directed at Jewish conversion prove divisive. But the issue is even more complicated than that. Jews entering gentile society are under tremendous pressure to relinquish their ethnicity—in dress, habits, language, and beliefs. They face a range of possibilities. They can abandon Europe and head for Palestine, where they might be Jewish on their own terms. They can stay in Europe and remain Orthodox, living in a parallel world that has its own laws, customs, and practices, and occasionally intersecting with the non-Jewish world. They can turn to Reform Judaism, which offers one way to remain Jewish and still assimilate into the wider society. This is the path many Jews take upon immigrating to the United States. Or they can convert to Christianity, which opens wide the doors of acceptance and worldly success, but at a price.

How do nineteenth-century Jews respond to Christian missionary outreach? In his account of "radical assimilation," which he characterizes as "the history of Jews who did not want to be Jews," Todd Endelman analyzes the various ways individuals shed the "burden" of Jewishness.[23] According to the Judaic Studies professor, those who convert do so primarily out of convenience rather than conviction, that is, for nonspiritual reasons.[24] A collection of essays entitled *Converts of Conviction* challenges Endelman's perspective.[25] While contributors to that volume agree that the majority of converts do so for economic, social, or political reasons, they also argue that those who convert for spiritual reasons are worth investigating. Some move from Judaism to Christianity out of conviction, some question the foundations of both religions after their conversion, and "some even returned to Judaism or adopted a hybrid faith consisting of elements of both religions."[26] Thus, the spiritual journeys of converts illuminate modern Jewish identity formation and Jewish and Christian relations.

There is yet another course for Jews to take: reconciliation. This is the approach of Rabbi Elijah Zvi Soloveitchik (1805–1881), who pens a Hebrew translation of the New Testament Synoptic Gospels in the 1860s but first publishes it in French, German, and Polish editions before putting out Hebrew and English versions.[27] Probably relying upon a Christian translation of the New Testament into Hebrew, Soloveitchik analyzes the gospels in light of Maimonides' "Thirteen Principles of the Jewish Faith" and the Talmud. The rabbi's purpose is to demonstrate that there is nothing in the Christian Gospels at odds with either Jewish belief or rabbinic teachings. Undoubtedly aware of missionary interests, Jewish conversions, and escalating antisemitism, Soloveitchik proposes a way out, namely, to recognize that there is nothing dividing Christians and Jews. This means there is no need for conversion in either direction. Soloveitchik never claims to be objective but rather seeks "to prove the symmetry of Judaism and Christian on theological grounds that he hoped would diminish anti-Semitism."[28]

It is unclear whether Soloveitchik is writing for Christians, in an attempt to dissuade them from proselytization, or for Jews, in the hope of preventing conversions. The fact that he writes in the first person plural (we), as though he were a Christian, leads some to speculate that he himself is a convert, but this is rather unlikely. For Rabbi Soloveitchik, Christianity is simply another form of Judaism. And, unlike Reform Jews, who see Jesus as a reformer (like themselves), Soloveitchik perceives him as "a normative teacher of the Mosaic message."[29] Thus, with a single stroke, Rabbi Elijah Zvi Soloveitchik wipes out both Christian triumphalist claims and Jewish assertions of religious superiority.

But the rabbi's program of reconciliation is lost in the fires of anti-Jewish campaigns sweeping across Europe in the 1870s. A growing eugenics movement, spurred in part by Charles Darwin's findings on natural selection, coupled with a belief that different (superior and inferior) races explain cultural variation, solidifies prejudice against Jews. A short pamphlet titled *The Victory of Judaism over Germandom* capitalizes on the new "science" of race. Published in 1879, *Victory* quickly goes through twelve editions and spawns the formation of the League of Antisemites in Germany. Wilhelm Marr, the author, claims that he writes "without a trace of religious prejudice" and presents the future as if it has arrived. With Germany supposedly under the heel of "this Semitic people," his pamphlet rouses German passions against the so-called alien race.

A few decades later, another pamphlet reinforces Marr's assertions that Jewish bankers and financiers are attempting to control the world, if they haven't gained control already. Agents of the czar's secret police fabricate *The Protocols of the Elders of Zion* from two nineteenth-century antisemitic sources, and it first appears in Russia in 1905.[30] The *Protocols* purport to be the conversations of a council of Jewish elders who plan to rule the world. Twenty-four short statements outline their conspiracy to undermine government and business institutions. They depict Jews as having greater power, wealth, and population than is actually the case. Although exposed as a forgery by 1921, the *Protocols* are republished in English by automaker Henry Ford in his newspaper the *Dearborn Independent*. The antisemitic tract is long-lived—in 2021, a tattered copy is found at the workstation of a member of the U.S. Capitol Police.

Two German historians and biblicists, Franz Delitzsch (1813–1890) and Hermann Strack (1848–1922), challenge this proliferation of antisemitism despite their commitment to *Judenmission,* that is, missions to Jews. Their evangelizing enterprise leads both scholars to specialize in the Hebrew language and postbiblical literature, and ultimately to defend Jews and their sacred texts from antisemitic attacks. Indeed, using his competence in rabbinics, Strack writes one of the first comprehensive histories of the blood libel—the false accusation that Jews kill Christians, especially children, to use their blood in religious rituals. *Das Blut im Glauben und Aberglauben der Menschheit* (Blood in Humankind's Beliefs and Superstitions, published in English as The Jew and Human Sacrifice) goes through nine editions before World War I, becoming "the definitive scholarly defense of the Jews."[31] Demonstrating their ambivalence at the same time, both men also denigrate Judaism in harsh language, arguing for the surpassing excellence of Christianity.

A staunch Lutheran, Delitzsch founds the Institutum Judaicum (Jewish Studies Institute) in Leipzig in 1880 to foster accurate knowledge of Judaism by Christians preparing to become missionaries. (Now called the Institutum Judaicum Delitzschianum, or simply the Delitzschianum, it serves only scholarly purposes today.) Few who study there become active missionaries, concentrating instead on the new field of Jewish Studies. Delitzsch collaborates with leading Jewish scholars, developing and maintaining friendships and professional associations throughout his life. He writes the first comprehensive history of Hebrew poetry, edits at least two volumes of Jewish writings, assists in developing a Jewish edition of the Hebrew Bible, and translates the New Testament into Hebrew—the translation that Rabbi Soloveitchik probably utilized for his own version. Delitzsch's book *Jüdisches Handwerkerleben zur Zeit Jesu* (Jewish Artisan Life in the Time of Jesus) praises first-century Jewish culture and presents Jews as hardworking and industrious, "implicitly holding them up as models of contemporary German youth."[32] Delitzsch also publishes a challenge to, and correction of, the misrepresentation of the Talmud published by an antisemitic polemicist, though his own plea shares some of the same criticisms of contemporary Jews.[33] Yet his vicious criticism of Abraham Geiger's comparison of Jesus with Rabbi Hillel convinces modern Jews to look upon Delitzsch with disapprobation.[34]

Hermann Strack is equally supersessionist in outlook, believing that Christianity is superior to Judaism. Nevertheless, the Institutum Judaicum that he founds in Berlin in 1883 lacks the missionary orientation of the Delitzschianum, and Hebrew language and literature are the focus. Jewish scholars give guest lectures, and theological exchange is encouraged. Strack is a leading non-Jewish scholar in Bible and Talmud, Hebrew and Aramaic, and the Masorah.[35] (The Masorah, developed between the seventh and tenth centuries CE, standardizes spelling and grammar in the Hebrew Bible.) Unlike Delitzsch, who takes to pamphleteering to counter the growth of antisemitism, Strack takes to the courts and universities. "From 1880 [to] 1992, no voice in Germany spoke out against the defamation of Judaism so consistently or with such authority."[36] He acknowledges his debt to numerous Jewish colleagues in writing the *Introduction to the Talmud and Midrash,* which remains a standard reference work even today. Its publication in English in 1931 is sponsored by the Central Conference of American Rabbis. He is best known for a commentary on the New Testament, coauthored with Paul Billerbeck (1853–1932), which integrates Talmud and Midrash to show the Jewish origins of Jesus's sayings and the connections between Judaism and Christianity—with the latter transcending the former. Despite its considerable critics and its supersessionist approach, the Strack-Billerbeck commentary continues to be used by Christians, and even by Jews.

The Puzzle of Christian Zionism

With its emphasis on an eschatological outcome, Christian Zionism is in many ways the opposite of Jewish Zionism.[37] Christian Zionists do support an independent nation, but in the expectation that Judaism and Jews will disappear. For this reason, the Christian Zionist position, especially the evangelistic thrust of nineteenth-century missionary societies, is marked by a deep ambivalence toward Jews and Judaism. The pro-Jewish, pro-conversion stance of Victorian-era defenders of Jews exemplifies complex identity. For the most part, the veneration of Jews and Jewish culture comes at the expense of respect for Judaism, the religion.

At the same time, it is clear that people frequently do the right thing for the wrong reasons. By today's standards, the *Judenmission* of Christians to Jews is generally deemed antisemitic. Ironically, however, the *Judenmission* causes the evangelizing, and even colonizing, of Christian consciousness by Jewish culture. The major—and Jews may say only—benefit of this mission is the development of friendship with, and sympathy for, Jews as colleagues and neighbors worthy of protection. The conversion of Christians to philosemitic activism is helpful, perhaps even commendable, despite its contamination by missionary goals. The alternative, the conversion to antisemitic action, which comes to fulfillment in the twentieth century, is unbearable.

In 1923, Alexander Marx writes on the occasion of Hermann Strack's death that "Strack's name will forever remain connected with Jewish learning." After listing the Christian talmudist's many contributions to Jewish culture, the professor at the Jewish Theological Seminary of America adds, "To him we are even more indebted for his brave defence of Judaism against the many aspersions by its unscrupulous opponents."[38] Millions more brave defenders of Judaism would be needed for the coming storm in Europe.

Part III

TRANSFORMATIONS AFTER
THE HOLOCAUST

Chapter 7

THE RIGHTEOUS
AND THE REPROBATE

A single man was created in the world, to teach that if any man has caused a single soul to perish from Israel Scripture imputes it to him as though he had caused a whole world to perish; and if any man saves alive a single soul from Israel Scripture imputes it to him as though he had saved alive a whole world.
—MISHNAH SANHEDRIN 4.5, DANBY

"Lord, when was it that we saw you hungry or thirsty or a stranger or naked or sick or in prison, and did not take care of you?" Then he will answer them, "Truly I tell you, just as you did not do it to one of the least of these, you did not do it to me."
—MATTHEW 25:44–45, NRSV

Both Jews and Christians perform countless acts of heroism during World War II, but neither group is as courageous as we'd like to think. Stories of Jewish resistance emerge in the 1960s to refute assertions of Jewish passivity, and though armed defiance exists, it is by far the exception rather than the rule. Although extolled for their antipathy to Adolf Hitler and totalitarianism, the Protestant pastors Dietrich Bonhoeffer (1906–1945) and Martin Niemöller (1892–1984) have little affection for Jews. Individuals aid Jews for a variety of reasons—national pride and patriotism, humanitarian sensibility, antipathy to Nazism—and not just religious ethics that mandated kindness. "The picture is neither completely black, nor purely white," writes the author of *The Grey Book,* a catalog of Christian statements of support for Jews before, during, and after World War II—entitled grey because "white and black are mingled."[1] Yet the Holocaust is so monumentally horrific that stories of good deeds and deep equality almost seem trivial.[2] (While many Jews and most Israelis prefer the term *Shoah*—catastrophe— to *Holocaust*—whole burnt offering—to describe the genocide of European Jews, I am using *Holocaust* because it is most familiar to readers in the United States.)

Nevertheless, Christian culpability for the events leading up to the Holocaust is undeniable. The antisemitism prevalent in two thousand years of Christian teaching could be marshaled relatively quickly against Jews. This is especially true in Germany during the interwar period. Many have documented in great detail the dejudaization of Jesus in the German churches at this time, and even "non-Aryan" converts to Christianity are eventually expelled.[3] After World War II, when German political, educational, and military institutions are denazified, the German Christian Movement (GCM) is not. Pastors who had been leaders of the GCM— which supported Hitler's policies and introduced them into the churches—are briefly shunned before being readmitted to state-funded Protestant churches.[4]

There are other ways to consider the tragedy of Christian complicity, however. We might look at the Christians before the war who try to warn others of the rising tide of hatred, along with Jews who attempt to raise awareness of the gravity of the events unfolding. Both groups work together to persuade government actors to open the doors of America and England to refugees, only to be turned away. There are innumerable rescuers during the war. One little-known story is the way that Jews and Christians collaborate on rescue efforts, not only individually but, more importantly, through cooperative agencies. Jewish organizations rely heavily on Christian institutions in occupied and bordering countries to feed, house, clothe, hide, and smuggle Jews to safety. Meanwhile, Christian groups arrange for these services to be provided and remain in close contact with Jewish agencies. Churches and synagogues alike finance the Jewish rescue groups that play a role in saving thousands.

The number of rescuers, Jewish and Christian, is vastly undercounted. In 1953, the Israeli Parliament establishes Yad Vashem, the Martyrs and Heroes Remembrance Authority, to memorialize Jews who died in the destruction. At the same time, the Knesset legally defines the "Righteous of the Nations" as "high minded gentiles who risked their lives to save Jews." The first "righteous" are recognized in 1962, when eleven trees are planted at a memorial site in Jerusalem. The four criteria for nomination are strict: actual rescue of a Jew from threat of death or deportation, high risk of endangerment, motivation (that is, not for money, proselytization, or other consideration), and testimony from the survivors with documentation.[5] As of January 2020, only 27,712 people from 51 nations have been awarded the honor of Righteous, and it is fairly certain that many more rescuers have simply not been accounted for.[6] For example, thousands of citizens of Norway, Finland, Denmark, and Sweden who transport more than 7,000 Jews to safety by boat are not honored. Nor is Angelo Roncalli, the future Pope John XXIII, who facilitates the escape of thousands of Jews in Bulgaria, Slovakia, Hungary, Romania, and Greece. Excluded as well are Jewish rescuers, because Jews are not eligible for this honor.

The story of the righteous must be told in tandem with that of the reprobate—those who turn a blind eye to the horrors escalating around them. In addition, it is clear that a number of non-Jewish rescuers have mixed motives, most importantly that of wanting to convert Jews to Christianity. Saul Friedländer's expression "the ambiguity of good" (*die Zwiespältigkeit des Guten*) captures the mixture of impulses and personalities that characterizes concerned Christians.[7] The Hungarian-born Jewish historian utilizes this as the subtitle of his 1969 biography of Kurt Gerstein, the Waffen SS member who engineers the administration of Zyklon-B gas for the death camps but who simultaneously destroys vast stores of that same gas. Gerstein repeatedly alerts religious and political leaders throughout Europe to what is happening to Jews, to no avail.

There are countless Christians who resist Nazism before and during the war in a variety of different ways, large and small. With few resources other than their own quick wits and the deep conviction that mass murder is wrong, rescuers resist the war by myriad means. The most successful efforts unite Christians and Jews, working together in secret organizations. It is easy to see why most people are unwilling to take risks; more puzzling is why so many choose to face extreme hazards. One reason may be the fact that rescuers see their neighbors in the face of the persecuted. Sometimes they are literal neighbors; at other times they are the neighbors shared by a common humanity. This quality of neighborliness— such a tiny thing to challenge the Nazi war machine—indicates yet another facet of the deep equality I am exploring in this book.

Before the War

Outside of Germany, the rest of the world closely watches events unfold in the Third Reich—the ascent of Chancellor Adolf Hitler in early 1933, the promulgation of the Nuremberg Laws in 1935, and the Kristallnacht pogrom of 1938. Shortly after Hitler assumes power, Jews begin to be dismissed from civil service jobs and excluded from various professions, though not until the summer of 1933 does the Reichstag strip naturalized Jews of their citizenship. The Nuremberg Laws then revoke citizenship of all Jews in 1935. On 30 September 1938, England and Germany sign the Munich Agreement, which cedes the Sudetenland in Czechoslovakia to Germany. In effect, this curtails England's ability to officially criticize Hitler or Nazism, a policy that lasts until Germany invades Poland on 1 September 1939. Finally, the Kristallnacht pogrom of 9–10 November 1938, that occurs in Germany, Austria, and the Sudetenland brings the National Socialist agenda regarding Jews to the world's attention. More than 7,000 Jewish shops are looted, hundreds of synagogues are burned or destroyed, and 30,000 Jewish men are arrested.

The German Christian Movement—a Protestant organization—largely capitulates to the demands of Nazis. Its members fail to protest the "Aryan Paragraph" instituted in 1933, which requires a purge of all non-Aryan leaders, and eventually includes converts to Christianity. The GCM (known as *Deutsche Christen*) glorifies Hitler and sees him as a prophet. Some churches in the Reformed and Lutheran traditions do protest, however. Called the Confessing Church, its members agree to the Barmen Declaration in 1934. But the declaration never censures persecution of the Jews, only the idolatry of Hitler (and not even by name); it rejects the "false doctrine" that the church can give ruling authority to vested leaders (*Führer*) and asserts that God's dominion (*Reich*) is composed of justice. Regional Protestant synods do warn against National Socialism more explicitly, and five hundred pastors are arrested in 1935 after reading a statement from their pulpits that condemns the idolatry of blood, race, nationality, honor, and freedom.[8] Not until 1943, however, does the Confessing Church explicitly denounce antisemitism. (Only the Jehovah's Witnesses refuse to compromise with the Third Reich—by not serving in the military and not swearing to serve the state—and pay the price with about 1,900 murdered.)

The record for Catholics is equally mixed. Although some historians do not see the Roman Catholic Church as offering much early opposition to National Socialism, others claim it is initially an instrument of resistance.[9] By 1930, Catholics make up about 35 percent of the German population, and their Center Party, working in coalition governments with the Social Democrats, is a vital force in the Weimar Republic after World War I. In fact, in the early 1930s, "Catholic criticism of the National Socialists was vehement and sustained in the press and from the pulpits."[10] In 1930, when a priest prohibits church members in his parish from joining the Nazi Party and denies the sacrament of communion to Nazi Catholics, his bishop supports him. The next year, bishops in Bavaria, Cologne, Paderborn, and the upper Rhine declare that National Socialism is incompatible with Catholic teachings.[11] Until 1933, most church leaders remain steadfast in their condemnation of National Socialism.[12]

What happens in 1933 to change that? That is the year the Vatican Secretary of State, Eugenio Pacelli, signs a concordat (agreement) with Hitler to gain certain privileges for the Catholic Church in Germany. Clergy are now forbidden to take political stands, and bishops must swear allegiance to the Reich. In return, the state will fund Catholic schools, allow for Catholic appointment of clergy, and stay out of internal church affairs. The anti-Nazi sentiment expressed in German Catholicism in the 1920s collapses when the church's ban on Nazi party membership is withdrawn as a result of the concordat. To be sure, there are already Catholic clergy and laity who support National Socialism and applaud Hitler's successes, but with the concordat, all challenges to Nazism are officially suppressed.

The only Catholic priest in Germany to publicly protest Nazism after the concordat is Bernhard Lichtenberg (1875–1943). The rector at St. Hedwig's Cathedral in Berlin denounces Kristallnacht in 1938 and prays daily for Jews, Jewish Christians, and other victims of the regime. When the Nazis issue an edict stating that it is treason to help a Jew, Lichtenberg drafts a statement he plans to read from the pulpit: "Let us not be misled by this un-Christian way of thinking but follow the strict command of Jesus Christ: 'You shall love your neighbor as you love yourself.'"[13] He is denounced to the Gestapo, arrested, and interrogated before he can read the proclamation. Sentenced to two years in Tegel prison, he is told he can remain free upon release if he promises not to preach politics from the pulpit. In failing health, the priest refuses and asks to be sent to serve as a pastoral minister in one of the camps. En route to Dachau, he falls gravely ill and dies in 1943. In 2004, more than 60 years later, Yad Vashem declares Bernhard Lichtenberg as one of the righteous.

While the churches in Germany are largely silent about the crimes perpetrated against Jews, most throughout Europe, the British Isles, and the United States vigorously condemn the actions of the National Socialists. A number of factors prompt religious bodies to protest the persecution of Jews. While some speak out of concern for Jewish converts to Christianity or from missionary motives, most, like Father Lichtenberg, point to biblical texts enjoining kindness and compassion for all people. Some note that Jesus himself is Jewish. Those who have close contacts with Jewish leaders tend to be the most vocal.

Even before the rise of Nazism, Christians and Jews outside of Germany work to halt the expansion of antisemitism. For example, in 1927, members of the two faiths found the National Conference of Christians and Jews for the Advancement of Justice, Amity and Peace. It is the first interreligious national organization in the United States developed to counter discrimination against Catholics and Jews. With its name shortened to National Conference of Christians and Jews, the NCCJ hopes to analyze and allay religious prejudice, establish the basis of cooperation for common ends, and "immunize the public mind and emotions" against misinformation, propaganda, and hatred by encouraging mutual respect and appreciation.[14] NCCJ wins Jewish support in response to Christian goodwill and as a move to forestall missionary outreach.[15] The group's "Tolerance Trio" may have sparked the opening line of many jokes. During the 1930s and 1940s, a priest, a rabbi, and a minister travel around the country making joint appearances to dispel religious stereotypes. As hard it is to believe today, many who come to watch the entertaining presentations have never before seen a person of a different faith, let alone a Jew, a Catholic, and a Protestant together on a single stage.

It is an English clergyman who does more than any other Christian before the war to call attention to the growing threat of antisemitism. James Parkes (1896–1981) publishes his first book, *The Jew and His Neighbor,* in 1930, after working for two student Christian organizations in continental Europe and witnessing antisemitism firsthand.[16] Even before Hitler assumes power in Germany, "Parkes was responding to appeals for help from Jewish students suffering discrimination."[17] He returns to England to study at Oxford and writes a dissertation, later published in 1934 as *The Conflict of the Church and the Synagogue,* that makes him a recognized authority on the "Jewish Question."[18] Convinced that the position of Jews in Europe is precarious, Parkes works with Jewish and Christian organizations in England to rescue Jewish refugees, even taking Jews from Germany into his home.

One rescue program is the Movement for the Care of Children from Germany, which begins under the leadership of Cosmo Gordon Lang, the Archbishop of Canterbury. English families take in almost ten thousand children between 1939 and 1945, the vast majority of refugees being Jews rather than Christians or non-Aryan Christians. Foster parents are enjoined from proselytizing their Jewish wards and are asked to ensure that Jewish teachers or rabbis visit regularly.[19] When Parkes learns that one boy has been placed with a zealous missionary family, he sees to his rescue and that of twenty-eight other boys similarly "kidnapped."[20] (The English *Kindertransport* prompts similar relocation efforts by the U.S. Congress, but due to a lack of popular support, the proposed legislation is withdrawn.)

Christian voices are raised immediately after Kristallnacht, expressing outrage and harshly denouncing the violence. Just a few days following the pogrom, the Church Council of Canton Zurich publicly declares, "We must not be silent. We must consider it a Christian obligation to cry out against it, not only within our church walls but to the world at large."[21] Catholic bishops in Milan, Belgium, Paris, and Lisbon decry Kristallnacht.[22] The Church of England protests as well, to the embarrassment of the British government, which has just signed away the sovereignty of Czechoslovakia to Hitler. In the United States, Protestant, Catholic, and Jewish groups organize a national day of prayer for refugees on 20 November 1938. In addition, the Executive Committee of the Federal Council of Churches of Christ—an interdenominational group that represented churches with a membership totaling 25,551,560—issues an appeal to all people to fund Protestant, Catholic, and Jewish relief efforts directed at Jewish refugees.[23]

Throughout this time, numerous Jewish relief organizations and advocacy groups seek to aid the embattled Jews of Europe, providing food, shelter, and immigration services, and financing other programs. American Jewish groups found the German Jewish Children's Aid in 1934 in an effort to place children sixteen or younger with foster families or relatives in the United States.[24] The American Jewish Joint Distribution Committee, the Hebrew Immigrant Aid Society, and countless other groups and individuals work within the Jewish community and with Christian organizations to mobilize resources and change public opinion. In Europe a number of Jewish groups, including the Women's International Zionist Organization, marshal the resources of Jews and Christians alike. Interreligious opposition to National Socialism is high outside of Central Europe.

During the War

It is readily apparent that location, time, and circumstances make resistance to Germany and Nazism not just dangerous but suicidal once World War II starts. The response of non-Jews to the perilous position of Jews during the war depends upon where they live. Those in the Axis countries—Germany, Italy, and Spain—and in occupied nations such as Belgium, France, and the Netherlands, take risks different from those living in countries that are neutral or those at war with the Axis nations. Moreover, places like Austria and Poland, with a legacy of antisemitism, seem much more willing to submit to Nazi imperatives. German commandos also find eager assassins among people living in Ukraine, along with collaborators in other Soviet republics who blame Jews, rather than Communists, for their lack of freedom. In the 1930s, the threat of Communism under Joseph Stalin appears greater than the threat of fascism under Adolf Hitler, Francisco Franco, and Benito Mussolini, especially as far as Catholic Christians are concerned. Bavarian Catholics in southern Germany, as well as

Spanish and Italian Catholics, actually hope that Hitler might freeze the advance of Communism by expanding the war to the eastern front.

The extent of Christian complicity in the crimes of Hitler explodes into public awareness in 1963 when Rolf Hochhuth (1931–2020) castigates the wartime role played by the Roman Catholic Church in his drama *The Deputy*. The German Protestant author takes particular aim at Pope Pius XII (p. 1939–1958), depicting the pontiff as a man indifferent to the fate of the Jews and more concerned about the fortunes, both literal and metaphorical, of the Vatican. The complete seven-act work presents a more complex portrayal of the pope than the show that runs on Broadway in 1964, which theater critics pronounce "grossly edited" and "butchered." The reaction among theatergoers varies: horror on the part of non-Christians, shame on the part of Protestants, and outrage and indignation on the part of Catholics.

A debate has raged ever since over the pope's silence concerning the Holocaust. Jewish writers and religious figures have come to the pope's defense, Christian writers and religious figures have bitterly attacked him, and the opposite is true as well. The Vatican Archives' release of more than a million digitized documents from the papers of Pius XII in 2020 may resolve the debate one way or the other. One historian promises that "the new discoveries [from the archives] provide ample grounds to believe that the story of Pius XII and the Jews remains to be written."[25] Regardless of what the documents reveal, it is clear that Pius XII has come to symbolize the failure of all Christians who were confronted with the Final Solution and had the ability—and responsibility—to do something about it. Just as Adolf Eichmann (1906–1962) becomes the face of Nazi malevolence during his 1961 trial for war crimes, Pope Pius XII becomes the face of Christian indifference. And yet, "to hold that the pope always acted negatively toward Jews is to close one's eyes to the historical record."[26]

Pius XII's predecessor, Ambrogio Damiano Achille Ratti—Pope Pius XI (p. 1922–1939)—orchestrates a chorus of protests against racial legislation promoted by the Axis nations.[27] Although Ratti retains traditional Christian views about the Jews—that they are no longer the chosen people, that they crucified Christ, and so on—his opposition to antisemitism and fascism is loud and clear. This is not the case with Ratti's successor, Eugenio Pacelli.

Christened "Hitler's Pope" by one author, Pius XII seems to view his first duty as maintaining and protecting the neutrality of Vatican City.[28] The Vatican finds fascist regimes congenial in their rejection of Communism and their support of conservative values. But when it comes to trespassing on ecclesiastical turf, especially regarding who can and cannot be considered a Christian, church prelates resist. Unlike his predecessor, Pacelli takes a less vocal approach. Preferring to avoid an open breach with the Axis nations, he refuses to condemn war crimes of which he is well aware.

In fact, Jews are not the only victims whom the Vatican ignores. Atrocities in Poland against Catholics, euthanasia programs in Germany, the murder of some 700,000 Orthodox Serbs, Italy's aggression against Greece—all of these happen with little dissent from the Holy See.[29] Instead, Pacelli preserves a faith in diplomatic neutrality, seeing that as the means by which the church might continue to operate freely. "Still, what the Vatican did during the war years, when the Pope was the only man in Europe free from any taint of propaganda, was considerably more than nothing," remarks Hannah Arendt (1906–1975). The Jewish intellectual says it would have been enough but for the fact that the pope is the "Vicar of Christ."[30]

The silence of Pius XII must be measured against the silence of the Allies. Countries that could have accepted Jewish refugees, including the United States, turn them away. Diplomatic papers released in 1963 show that the British are more afraid of "extrusion"—that is, of Jews being forced off the continent and into England—than of extermination.[31] Moreover, the U.S. State Department, with the secret support of President Franklin Roosevelt, blocks congressional efforts to help Jewish refugees relocate to Palestine. Proposals to "ransom" Jews by paying off Hitler are also rejected. Jewish parachutists from Palestine are not allowed to drop into Hungary when the predicament is most desperate, although they are permitted to parachute in at the end of the war.[32] Perhaps the most notable instance of the Allies' silence is the refusal to bomb the railroad lines leading to Auschwitz, a proposal made by Rabbi Michael Dov Weissmandl (1903–1957), an ultra-Orthodox rabbi and one of the leaders of the Jewish underground in Slovakia.[33]

Rescue as Resistance

The judgment regarding silence falls upon all Christians of that era. Basically the individual churchgoer is faced with the same choices that confront church leaders.[34] While keeping the focus on Pope Pius XII highlights the fact that "the church had the potential to develop large-scale rescue operations," it also diverts attention from the actions of ordinary Catholics—and thousands of Jews and Christians—who did step up to help their Jewish neighbors.[35] That they could not save more does not diminish the integrity or value of what they do working together. "The importance of the rescue action lay not only in the actual salvation of thousands," according to one account of Jewish resistance. "It consisted also in the heightened morale of the individuals who had participated in it. They had not submitted passively to the decrees of the Nazis."[36]

A spate of books describing armed resistance emerges in the 1960s in response to assertions of Jewish "passivity" during the war made by Jewish writers like Raul Hilberg, Bruno Bettelheim, and Hannah Arendt. These books catalog specific uprisings, rebellions, and attacks that involve combat. They describe the actions of a Jewish underground that operates in nearly every ghetto and labor/concentration camp. This underground raises spirits, reduces physical suffering, and plans and executes armed revolts.[37] If the Nazis' objective is the elimination of all Jews, then any effort to thwart that goal might be seen as resistance—from secreting papers out of ghettos to smuggling people to sanctuary. Thus, by an expansive definition, the work to rescue Jews can be seen as any concrete attempt to resist the Nazi extermination machine.

It is somewhat ironic that Jewish rescuers have received so little attention. They are not recognized at the Yad Vashem memorial, which focuses on those who die (the martyrs), those who physically resist (the heroes), and non-Jewish rescuers (the righteous). It seems to be expected that Jews should help other Jews, as members of the same faith and the same people. Yet large-scale Christian rescue efforts would not have been possible without the cooperation and coordination of Jewish individuals and organizations.

With persecution occurring in Germany in the 1930s, thousands of Jews look for safety in the Netherlands. Although initially silent about National Socialism, the Dutch become some of the more resistant of all western Europe with the German invasion in May 1940 and the subsequent occupation.[38] When deportations begin to occur in 1942, a general strike is declared in Amsterdam and surrounding cities. Nevertheless, approximately 107,000 Jews are sent to the Auschwitz and Sobibor death camps from the Netherlands, and only a few thousand survive. But about 25,000 to 30,000 Jews go into hiding.[39] A Jewish underground, primarily members of *Hechalutz Holland*—young adults who are in training to move to Palestine—works with Christian families to find shelter for those in hiding.

Among the leaders is Joachim Shimon (d. 1943), who flees from Germany to Holland in 1938. The vast open expanses of Holland, however, coupled with the country's own bureaucratic efficiency at maintaining records of Jewish residents, make hiding a last resort. Shimon and his wife Adina have already been smuggling children into Switzerland with the assistance of a Jewish rescue organization in Geneva, before he decides to devise an escape route through Belgium and France and across the Pyrenees into Spain.[40] The Jews who travel with Shimon would first gather at the home of Jasper Daams and his wife Wip and spend the night with the Christian couple before their departure. Daams has identified a place for Jews to cross the border into Belgium. Yad Vashem declares Jasper

Daams one of the righteous in 1990, although his wife Wip, who helps hide Jews, is not yet recognized.

Shimon and his associate Menachem Pinkhof later join forces with another Protestant couple, Johan (Joop) Westerweel and his wife Wilhelmina Dora Bosdriesz. Yad Vashem considers Joop one of "the most daring and successful leaders of the Dutch resistance leaders." He is a pacifist and an activist who is earlier imprisoned for refusing the draft. Even before connecting with the Dutch Zionist organizers, he and his wife shelter Jewish refugees. What becomes known as the Westerweel group teams up with *Hechalutz* young adults to smuggle Jews out of Holland. Shimon personally leads three groups across the border, but when the Gestapo captures him in 1943, he kills himself before revealing the names of his associates. After Shimon dies, Joop takes over leading groups to the Pyrenees. Meanwhile, Joop's wife Wil is arrested while attempting to free an active *Hechalutz* member from a prison. She is taken to the Vught concentration camp, where she witnesses her husband's execution in August 1944. She is then transferred to Ravensbrück but allowed to go to Sweden on a prisoner exchange due to her ill health. Yad Vashem declares both Johan and Wilhelmina Westerweel righteous in 1963.

Gertrud Luckner (1900–1995), a Protestant convert to Catholicism, works for Caritas, a Catholic relief organization in Freiburg, Germany, when the Nuremberg Laws begin to isolate Jewish citizens from other Germans. Luckner is a bit of a loner, working through private and personal contacts to get Jews to safety in Switzerland. Much of her work consists of doing "small things" to make life easier for Jews—shopping for groceries when they are at work, accompanying those wearing the yellow badge, reposting packages from Vienna in Freiburg so they will get through to family members in Poland, and other mundane tasks. But she also works with the local Catholic archdiocese, obtaining official credentials from the archbishop of Freiburg that allow her to travel throughout Germany to lobby Catholic groups to aid "non-Aryans." She remains in close contact with Leo Baeck (1873–1956), a renowned Jewish intellectual and leader of the Reich Union of Jews, headquartered in Berlin. The two establish coded language that gives Luckner entrée into Jewish groups in cities where she is unknown; she would ascertain needs and attempt to secure assistance through her contacts.[41] The Gestapo arrests her while she is en route to Berlin in March 1943 to give Baeck 5,000 Reichsmarks (about $1,000) in aid for the Jews of the city. But Baeck has already been sent to the Theresienstadt concentration camp. Luckner is reported as saying to her captors, "If you are sending me to a concentration camp, send me to Theresienstadt where Leo Baeck is."[42] The Nazis send her to Ravensbrück instead. (The Russian Army liberates Theresienstadt the day before Baeck is scheduled to be executed.) After the war, Luckner goes on to become a leading advocate for restitution and reparation for the victims of the Nazis, and for Jewish and Christian dialogue.[43] She visits Israel in 1951, one of the first Germans to do so, and Yad Vashem awards her the title of righteous in 1966 for smuggling Jews to Switzerland.

What prompts individuals to risk death? In her study of Polish rescuers, Nechama Tec says that most aid is unplanned and spur of the moment, and that it almost always is solicited by Jews rather than offered, unprompted, by Christians.[44] The Holocaust scholar examines the reasons non-Jewish rescuers give in order to come up with a typology. "Without exception and regardless of the country they came from," she writes, "helpers insisted that for them saving Jews was a natural duty. In the overwhelming majority of cases, their protection of Jews fit into an already established pattern of helping the needy."[45] That pattern included a sense of individuality, independence and self-reliance, and a tendency to provide help as a matter of fact rather than as heroics.

The Good Neighbor

One of the hallmarks of deep equality is neighborliness, that is, doing the duty that lies nearest to you, in the words of essayist

Thomas Carlyle. This is not an ethic that exists outside human consciousness or in a utopian future, but rather one always present and daily acted upon in many small ways. Moreover, both Judaism and Christianity explicitly lift up the virtue of being a good neighbor. The Tanakh states that the Lord commands the people Israel to "Love your fellow as yourself" (Leviticus 19:18b NJPS). Jesus quotes this same scripture when asked what the greatest commandment is. The first commandment is to love God, Jesus says, repeating the Shema, the Jewish statement of faith: "Hear, O Israel: the Lord our God, the Lord is one." Then he adds a second: "You shall love your neighbor as yourself" (Mark 12:29, 31 NRSV).

Neighborliness encompasses concern, love, friendship, protection, and assistance. It frequently becomes most visible in times of natural disasters, when communities and individuals come together to provide mutual aid. This simple feature of deep equality seems miniscule, almost absurd, when compared to the enormity of the Holocaust. Yet uncounted small acts of neighborliness occur during World War II—misdirecting an enemy, feigning ignorance, offering a bit of bread, lying about a friend's whereabouts—that are life-saving.

The journalist Rebecca Solnit documents post-disaster responses in her book *A Paradise Built in Hell*.[46] The account shows that in times of stress, people reach out and help each other across traditional boundaries of race, class, and religion. Differences fade away as people face a common enemy. Clearly the circumstances of war differ from those of natural disasters. It is also true that extraordinary events are as likely to pull people apart as to bring them together. Yet one of the conditions for deep equality is the respect and caring that neighbors have for each other.

The record from World War II shows that thousands of individuals act to save their neighbors even when it means imprisonment, torture, and death—but millions of rescuers are needed. The overwhelming evidence indicates that most neighbors looked the other way as they saw their friends and associates suddenly disappear. It is an exaggeration, however, to say that no one did anything. There are numerous cases of ordinary people doing extraordinary things. "They were peasants, housewives, factory workers, teachers, professional men, and clergy of all faiths, who fought with bare hands against the mightiest military juggernaut in modern times."[47]

Chapter 8

REPENTANCE
AND FORGIVENESS

We realize that the mark of Cain stands upon our foreheads. Across the centuries our brother Abel has lain in the blood which we drew or shed the tears we caused by forgetting Thy Love. Forgive us for the curse we falsely attached to their name as Jews. Forgive us for crucifying Thee a second time in their flesh. For we knew not what we did.

—ATTRIBUTED TO POPE JOHN XXIII[1]

The collusion of German Protestants and Catholics with the rise of National Socialism and the oppression of Jews, both institutionally and individually, is well documented. Ordinary Christians do not believe that collaboration with Nazism violated the tenets of their faith. Most Germans welcome the expulsion of Jews from public life in the early years of the Third Reich. With the defeat of Germany and the Axis powers, however, a myth develops "of Christian resistance to Hitler and of Nazi persecution of the churches."[2]

It takes more than two decades after the war ends for Christian denominational bodies to begin to recognize, and then to admit, that church teachings somehow shape believers' attitudes toward Jews. This is due, in part, to a lack of knowledge of the full extent of the mass murder that had occurred. In the twenty-first century, it seems incredible that after the war no one knew exactly how many people had been killed in the 1930s and 1940s. The political scientist Raul Hilberg had great difficulty finding a publisher willing to print his documentation of the Nazi bureaucracy that created the annihilation factories. In the 1940s and 1950s, when Hilberg works on his project, "the academic world was oblivious to the subject and publishers found it unwelcome."[3] *The Destruction of the European Jews* is finally published in 1961, thanks to the financial patronage of a Czech Jew who survives the Holocaust. This information gap explains why not a single doctoral dissertation is written in the United States on the Holocaust prior to 1970.[4]

And yet, in the three decades following World War II, Catholic and Protestant bodies issue more than 40 official statements on Christian and Jewish relations, demonstrating "a renewed and renewing attitude on the part of the Church toward the Jewish people."[5] The deliberations that lead to these statements acknowledge responsibility for the deaths of millions of Jews. Although Protestant and Orthodox churches had already expressed repentance in joint declarations, it is the Second Vatican Council held by the Roman Catholic Church that serves as a major pivot point in the history of Christian and Jewish relations. Jews contribute to all of these achievements in concrete ways. Through a variety of means, Christians express repentance and Jews offer forgiveness for the terrible tragedy of the Shoah.

French philosopher Jacques Derrida (1930–2004) asserts that living together requires something more than legal rights and political equality. He notes the importance of repentance and forgiveness for creating a world in which all may live well together.[6] To receive forgiveness requires acknowledging wrongdoing and repenting of it. Hannah Arendt describes forgiveness as a public rather than a religious virtue. She links the idea of forgiveness to the concept of promise in a dynamic process that recognizes human frailty. People need forgiving and the dismissal of guilt "in order to make it possible for life to go on by constantly releasing men from what they have done unknowingly."[7] Arendt's generous forgiving and dismissing seems inadequate to describe responses to the Holocaust, but on the smaller scale of interreligious communication they are a good start.

Simon Wiesenthal's book *The Sunflower* presents a different perspective on forgiveness. He describes his encounter with a dying Nazi who confesses to a terrible crime and asks Wiesenthal, a Jew working in a forced labor camp in Poland, to forgive him. Wiesenthal remains silent, but the event sticks with him and leads to his recounting the incident and asking, "What should I have done?" The famed Nazi hunter organizes a symposium of theologians, novelists, lawyers and others, and first publishes the results in 1976.[8] His depiction of the atrocity is harrowing, and as many contributors note, only the person injured can offer forgiveness. Yet in the post-Holocaust environment, Christians and institutional church bodies do sincerely repent of their sins of commission and omission and do seek forgiveness from the Jewish community. And many Jews do extend, if not forgiveness, acceptance of the sincerity of those who are penitent and, in turn, the willingness to engage in dialogue. Christians, however, have to take the first step to acknowledge their guilt. Only with this recognition can the processes of deep equality be set in motion.

The Earliest Protestant and Orthodox Responses

German churches are under pressure during the Allied Occupation to come to terms with their complicity with Hitlerism and their role in the war. The Stuttgart Confession of Guilt of October 1945 is a halfhearted declaration that avoids mentioning either war crimes or Jews, while the 1947 Darmstadt Statement confesses to Christian antisemitism, but then advocates missions to Jews so as not to continue to be antisemitic!

Christian members of the International Council of Christians and Jews issue a much stronger statement that frames a new era in Jewish-Christian relations. Founded in 1946, the council organizes an Emergency Conference on Anti-Semitism that meets in Seelisberg, Switzerland, the next year. In cooperation with their Jewish colleagues, Christians develop "An Address to the Churches," or what comes to be known as the Ten Points of Seelisberg. The preamble begins by explicitly mentioning the persecution and murder of millions of Jews, then goes on to address Christian antisemitism directly.[9]

The Ten Points of Seelisberg are drawn from a larger list initially proposed by the Jewish historian Jules Isaac (1877–1963) in his book *Jesus and Israel.* The 647-page volume, which he writes while in hiding during World War II, compares texts of the gospels with Catholic and Protestant commentaries. (A French Catholic woman shelters Isaac from 1943 to the end of the war, telling inquirers that he is her uncle.) Isaac demonstrates "how these inaccurate commentaries—found in books, footnotes, sermons, or catechism lessons—are largely responsible for the Christian's anti-Semitic conditioning.[10] After publishing *Jesus and Israel* in 1947, Isaac forms a Jewish and Christian interfaith group to work together to "purify" Christian teachings about Jews—or, rather, to purge them of their anti-Judaic assumptions.

Isaac's most influential book, however, is *The Teaching of Contempt: Christian Roots of Anti-Semitism*, published in 1964, the year after he dies. The book identifies three main themes found in Christian traditions. First, God disperses the Jews as a punishment for the crucifixion of Jesus. Second, the Judaism of Jesus's day is "degenerate," that is, mere legalism without a soul. Finally, Jews then and now are guilty of the crime of deicide—they are "Christ killers." Isaac urges Christians to eradicate these unofficial doctrines from church teachings. Many church bodies take up his challenge in succeeding decades.

In the meantime, Protestant Christians continue to issue statements that acknowledge the Holocaust (six million Jews were murdered) and diagnose the problem (antisemitism) but see the solution as evangelization (increased missionary efforts to Jews). For example, the World Council of Churches (WCC) 1948 report on "The Christian Approach to the Jews" exhibits a somewhat schizophrenic style. (Protestant and Orthodox denominations are members of the WCC, but the Roman Catholic Church is not.) It begins with an introduction that declares that God has bound Jews and Christians together in special solidarity, "linking our destinies together in His design."[11] The very next article concerns "The Church's commission to preach the Gospel to all men." This is followed by praise for the inheritance that Christians have received from Israel—the covenant, the prophets, the promise, and the Messiah. The report then goes on to state that "the Church has received this spiritual heritage from Israel and is therefore in honour bound to render it back in the light of the Cross"—in other words, it must evangelize Jews in gratitude for the spiritual gifts Christians have appropriated. Next comes the confession "that too often we have failed to manifest Christian love towards our Jewish neighbours," and that Christians did not fight antisemitism with all their strength. The statement thus calls upon all churches to denounce antisemitism, a sin "against God and man." But it then concludes with renewed emphasis on "the Christian witness to the Jewish people."

The first "theologically sophisticated declaration" does not emerge until 1950, when the Berlin-Weissensee Synod of the Evangelical Church in Germany expresses guilt and calls for change in long-held anti-Jewish doctrines.[12] The synod affirms—or rather reaffirms—that Jesus is Jewish, that God's covenant with Israel remains in effect after the crucifixion of Jesus, that by neglect and silence the churches are guilty of crimes committed against the Jews, and that God's judgment has fallen upon Germans for what was done to the Jews. The statement asks all Christians to renounce antisemitism and "to resist it vigorously," including protecting Jewish cemeteries that may be untended. These statements repudiate previous Christian teachings about Jews and their relationship to Christianity. One Christian tradition not renounced, however, is proselytizing Jews. The declaration ends by requesting God's compassion "to bring about the day of fulfillment, when we, with the rescued Israel, will sing praises of the victory of Jesus Christ."[13]

Throughout this period, Jules Isaac continues to appeal to churches in lectures and publications for an end to Christian antisemitism and teaching of contempt for Jews. His influence is visible in the 1961 statement issued by the World Council of Churches in its Third Assembly, held in New Delhi. The sentiments are a far cry from the 1948 WCC reassertion of the need for ongoing proselytizing of Jews. The "Resolution on Anti-Semitism" in 1961 calls upon its member churches to denounce antisemitism as "absolutely irreconcilable with the profession and practice of the Christian faith."[14] But the assembly goes further by urging Christian resistance to every form of antisemitism and the abandonment of anti-Jewish elements in its tradition.

While these statements reveal the thinking of official church bodies, individual Christians are active in a different way. One of the most unusual instances of Christian repentance is the establishment of a Protestant order of women religious in Germany—the Ecumenical Sisterhood of Mary (which becomes the *Evangelische,* or Protestant, Sisterhood in 1963). Mother Basilea Schlink (1905–2001, b. Klara Schlink) and Mother Martyria (1904–1999, b. Erika Madauss) cofound the order in 1947, adopting traditional monastic vows of poverty, celibacy, and obedience. Their primary task is "intercessory repentance" for the sins of the German people against the Jews. Mother Basilea sees the sin of the Holocaust as so heinous that perpetual repentance is demanded of all guilty parties, "including all of Germany's Gentile Christians."[15] Only through interceding on behalf of those for whom they are repenting could the German people atone for their guilt and forestall God's coming judgment.[16] Mother Basilea's ministry of reconciliation extends to the state of Israel, "our older brother," which she fervently supports. She and Mother Martyria travel to Israel in 1955, long before West Germany has normalized relations with the young nation. They discover that the sisters are needed there, and in 1957 two members of their order come to volunteer as hospital assistants.

At the same time, Mother Basilea believes that God has dispersed Jews because they have not recognized Jesus as their Messiah. But now that suffering is over, and Jews can return home to the land of Israel. In 1961 the order establishes a free, kosher guesthouse for Holocaust survivors to visit Israel. Beit Avraham (House of Abraham) operates in the Talpiot neighborhood of Jerusalem until 2014, when it closes because survivors are so elderly and frail they can no longer make the trip to Israel. The order also raises funds for Israeli charities, campaigns for Jewish civil rights internationally, and cares for Jewish graves in Germany.[17] But members of the order still live in the hope that one day Israel will accept Jesus as the promised Messiah.

It is apparent that Protestant and Orthodox Christians slowly recognize their guilt for not resisting antisemitism—though not for their failure to protest the Holocaust while it is happening. At the same time, their own desire for Jewish conversion to Christianity could lead to the eradication of Jews as surely as Hitler's final solution. Repudiation of proselytizing Jews will come only in the twenty-first century.

Roman Catholic Responses

Like their Protestant counterparts, German Catholics issue statements concerning the role that the church and individuals play in the Third Reich. Unlike Protestants, however, Catholic lay members feel that official statements do not go far enough and that the hierarchy has failed them. Other critics note that priests and ministers risked their lives speaking out, while Catholic bishops remained silent. Later on, the bishops speak up for convicted war criminals, pleading for leniency and even amnesty during the Nuremberg Trials. An exasperated high commissioner for the trials tells one bishop that "sympathy should be not so much for the perpetrators of the deeds as for their victims."[18] But the bishops see themselves as victims who opt for the silence of Jesus before Pilate rather than speaking out and facing certain death under Hitler.

By far the most significant step any Christian group takes toward transforming Christian understanding of Jews and Judaism is the document on non-Christian religions adopted at the Second Vatican Council and promulgated in 1965 by Pope Paul VI (p. 1963–1978). Pope John XXIII (p. 1958–1963) convenes Vatican Council II a year after he becomes pontiff, and sessions are held between 1960 and 1965. Born Angelo Roncalli, the new pope wants to update church teachings and bring them into the modern world. If Roncalli's predecessor Pius XII is criticized for his want of compassion for the Jews of Europe, Roncalli is celebrated for his rescue of more than 60,000 Jews when he is Papal Nuncio to Turkey. Although Yad Vashem does not list John XXIII among the righteous, when the Catholic Church canonizes him in 2014, the Israeli Knesset holds a special session to honor the pope's saving thousands of Jewish lives and opening the door to a new epoch in Jewish and Christian relations.

Jules Isaac plays an important role in Rome, just as he does at Seelisberg and New Delhi. He personally meets with Pius XII in 1949 to ask the pontiff to eliminate the prayer *pro perfidis Judaeis* ("for the unfaithful Jews") from the Good Friday liturgy. He also asks that the congregation kneel for the Jews during that liturgy. Pius softens the translation a bit and re-establishes the practice of kneeling for Jews on Good Friday.[19] When Angelo Roncalli becomes Pope John XXIII in 1958, he goes still further, eliminating the word *perfidis* from the Good Friday prayer entirely. According to a dramatic and perhaps apocryphal story, when he hears the offensive words sung during the Good Friday liturgy in the Sistine Chapel, he stops the service and asks the choir to sing the prayer again without the language about the Jews. The next year the pope expunges two additional prejudicial sentences from Catholic liturgies. In 1960, Isaac has a private audience with Pope John, in response to his call for an ecumenical council of the Catholic Church. As a result of that discussion, the pope asks Cardinal Augustin Bea (1881–1961) to address issues concerning Jews in the meetings of the Secretariat for the Promotion of Christian Unity. "Had it not been for this initiative, the Jewish question may not have been addressed at all."[20]

Most importantly, the influence of Isaac can be seen in the document on non-Christian relations that emerges from the council and its partial amelioration of the teaching of contempt. *Nostra Aetate* (In Our Age) is a groundbreaking statement. Vatican officials want to get input from Jews during its writing, but various Jewish leaders are divided on whether to participate as advisers or to comment on draft documents. On the one hand, there is the belief that friendship between Jews and Christians might prevent antisemitism in the future. A number of Jews advocate for changes, not only in Catholic teaching materials but even in Catholic theology. On the other hand, some argue that Jews should steer clear of any involvement with church reform, refusing to participate in development of a Jewish statement or to comment publicly on Vatican efforts. This derives in part from the conviction that the ultimate motivation in extending the olive branch is conversion of Jews to Christianity. "Furthermore, if the Jews advocated change in Church theology, the Church might expect theological reciprocity from the Jews."[21] It is a reasonable concern based on past history.

In 1961, Cardinal Bea invites the American Jewish Committee (AJC) to conduct research into anti-Jewish elements of Catholic teaching and liturgy, and to suggest steps for making changes.[22] AJC officers and scholars who enlist in the project enthusiastically respond by providing two memoranda: "The Image of the Jew in Catholic Teaching," which provides vivid evidence of the teaching of contempt in pedagogical materials, and "Anti-Jewish Elements in Catholic Liturgy," which shows how worship language presents "the Jews collectively as bloodthirsty killers of Jesus."[23] The AJC recommends further discussions concerning its findings, and Cardinal Bea and Rabbi Abraham Joshua Heschel (1907–1972), one of the members of AJC's advisory committee, meet together at the end of the year. The AJC then organizes a group of six European and American Jews to advise the Vatican.[24]

In 1962 Heschel submits a memorandum to Bea "On Improving Catholic-Jewish Relations."[25] The fourteen-page document spends the first three and a half pages reflecting on the demands of God, the sinfulness of hatred, and the role of the prophets, which is to shed light on the current situation. Only after that does Heschel recommend "the Church's vigorous repudiation of anti-semitism" and "authoritative clarification" on anti-Jewish religious teachings.

Heschel sees Vatican Council II as having the unique opportunity
to "reject and condemn those who assert that the Jews as a people
are responsible for the Crucifixion of Christ." The rabbi also asks
the council to acknowledge "the integrity and permanent precious-
ness of Jews and Judaism." By observing that "genuine love implies
that Jews be accepted as Jews," he implicitly counsels a repudiation
of missionary outreach to Jews. A final recommendation is that the
Vatican establish a high-level commission to oversee Catholic and
Jewish relations.

Resistance to a proposed statement about Jews, however, comes
from several directions. First, some delegates argue that the statement contradicts the Bible and Church teachings. Second, others
believe that any positive statement about Jews will be interpreted
as support for Israel, which might affect Catholic Christians living
in Arab states. Moreover, Catholics living outside of Europe have
little interest or stake in revisiting the Holocaust, as it is remote in
time and place. Finally, it is undeniable that some of the prelates
at the council are antisemitic.[26] Anti-Jewish articles and books are
distributed openly or clandestinely among clergy at the council.[27] A
few days after the first session of the Council closes, every delegate
receives a 900-page, privately printed copy of *Complotto contro la
Chiesa* (Plot Against the Church), which accuses Jews of supporting Communism and Freemasonry, and of infiltrating the Church
in order to overrun it. "The tract even justified Hitler and the Nazis' killing of the Jews."[28]

Both Pope John XXIII and Cardinal Bea want to develop a
statement that focuses directly on Christian antisemitism, the Holocaust, and the theological relationship between Christianity and
Judaism. One early draft of the statement, printed in the 7 October 1963 edition of *The New York Times,* acknowledges the Jewish
roots of the church, rejects the idea that all Jews are to blame for
the death of Christ, and robustly repudiates antisemitism. However, a watered-down draft is revealed in 1964, shortly before the
third session of the council opens. It lacks the condemnation of
antisemitism and the denial of Jewish guilt and looks forward to

the "eventual union of the Jewish people with the Church"—a statement the church does not make regarding Muslims or other non-Catholic Christians.

Rabbi Heschel expresses outrage over the revisions, especially the call for conversion, which he sees as spiritual fratricide. "As I have repeatedly stated to the leading personalities at the Vatican, I am ready to go to Auschwitz any time, if faced with the alternative of conversion or death."[29] The new pope, Paul VI, holds a personal audience with Heschel and explains that he considers the document friendly to Jews and based on biblical teachings. According to Rabbi Heschel, the pope says that Jews are not obliged to accept the teachings of the Church. In his memorandum concerning the meeting, which he submits to the pope and to Cardinal Bea, Heschel writes that Jews do not need Vatican approval to exist as Jews—"nearly every chapter in the Bible expresses the promise of God's fidelity to His Covenant with our people." In apparent exasperation, the rabbi states, "It is not gratitude that we ask for: it is the cure of a disease affecting so many minds that we pray for."[30]

Liberals at the council fight for the earlier version and try to strengthen it as well. According to one Jewish observer, American Catholic bishops play an exemplary role.[31] They are among the most vocal sponsors of a strong statement repudiating antisemitism and renouncing the deicide charge. While the final draft does include some of Cardinal Bea's proposals, the end product is not a statement about Jewish and Christian relations, but rather a *Declaration on the Relation of the Church to Non-Christian Religions*.[32] Only after dealing with Hinduism, Buddhism, and Islam does *Nostra Aetate* address Judaism in Section 4.

There is much in *Nostra Aetate* for a Jew, or any non-Christian, to object to. While not rejecting anything true or holy in other religions, the church "is in duty bound to proclaim without fail, Christ who is the way, the truth and the life," and it is in Christ where "men find the [fullness] of their religious life."[33] In addition, although the Church encourages Christians to acknowledge and preserve the spiritual and moral truths found in other religions, ultimately they must bear witness to their own faith and way of life. Finally, a theology of replacement is clearly stated: "It is true that the Church is the new people of God."

At the same time, there is much to applaud in *Nostra Aetate,* including the strong statement of the irrevocability of God's promises to the Israelites and to their descendants the Jews, taken from the apostle Paul's letter to the Romans (9–11). The influence of Jules Isaac, of the Ten Points of Seelisberg, and of Jewish advisers to conciliar committees is apparent throughout the document. For example, the fact that Jesus and the disciples are Jewish is explicitly affirmed, the shared spiritual heritage of Jews and Christians is lifted up, and the deicide charge is condemned, as is language suggesting that Jews are rejected or accursed. The statement concludes by saying that the Church "reproves every form of persecution against whomsoever it may be directed ... [and] deplores all hatreds, persecutions, displays of antisemitism leveled at any time or from any source against the Jews."

Jewish Responses to Vatican II

Jewish reaction to *Nostra Aetate* is understandably mixed, with some praising the document for officially condemning antisemitism and others criticizing it for its failure to mention the Holocaust or historical Christian anti-Judaism. The Jewish theologian Eliezer Berkovits (1908–1992) asserts that rejecting the long-held claim that Jews are collectively responsible for the crucifixion of Jesus is not particularly inspiring. "Having persecuted them for centuries, the Church is now kind enough to say that the Jews are not altogether guilty," he observes. "It is difficult to have much respect for such a declaration."[34]

Samuel Sandmel develops an ingenious response to *Nostra Aetate* by devising his own statement titled "The Synagogue and the Christian People."[35] By closely following the content of *Nostra Aetate,* Sandmel's proposed declaration deftly reveals how Nostra

Aetate might strike Jewish readers. Where the Catholic statement opens by recalling the "spiritual bond linking the people of the new covenant with Abraham's stock," Sandmel's statement bluntly begins, "The Synagogue views the Christian people as among its offspring." Where the Catholic statement absolves Jews of killing Christ, Sandmel's statement absolves Christians of killing Jews. "The Synagogue cannot, and does not, hold innocent Christians of our day responsible for the persecutions of the past, nor all Christians responsible, in the present or the future, for the misdeeds which may come from some." And where *Nostra Aetate* concludes with the affirmation of Christian preaching as a duty of the Church, Sandmel declares that the Synagogue neither seeks the dissolution of its offspring nor asks Christians to abandon Christianity. "Rather, it desires that its offspring attain and maintain the spiritual heights which they often nobly expressed."

The most thorough examination of all of the documents that emerge from Vatican II comes from Ben Zion Bokser (1907–1984), a leading figure in Conservative Judaism in the United States. Rabbi Bokser calls the council "a great milestone" in the history of the Church, and of importance to the Jewish people. While he expresses admiration for the Church's support of welfare state legislation, as affirmed in the Pastoral Constitution on the Church in the Modern World, he also indicates his disappointment that the constitution seems to see Christianity as the only solution to the world's problems. Perhaps most disappointing to the rabbi is the continual sectarian outlook that permeates the council's declarations, including the Constitution on Religious Freedom. Even though the documents acknowledge that truth exists in other religions, they continually claim that the Church is the sole custodian of "the full and final truth," and that the Church anticipates converting all peoples to Christianity.[36]

Rabbi Bokser finally addresses the specifics of *Nostra Aetate*, namely, the statement about Jews. He concedes that any change in Catholic attitudes toward Jews and Judaism is an important step, no matter how small. He is grateful that the deicide charge against

Jews and the claim of inherited guilt for Jesus's death are rejected, although there is no acknowledgment of the fact that Christian teaching has contributed to antisemitism.[37] Moreover, the document does state that some Jewish authorities "pressed for the death of Christ." Rabbi Bokser admits that Christianity is beginning to ameliorate the teachings of contempt, but that much more is needed. Because he finds "much that is noble in Christianity," he also finds it "unworthy of a great religious tradition to seek its own enhancement by degrading another faith."

A more sympathetic account comes from Rabbi Arthur Gilbert (d. 1976), one of the Jewish advisers to the church leaders who meet over the four-year convocation. *The Vatican Council and the Jews* analyzes each version of the document that the council considers and then presents the last two drafts in side-by-side comparison, along with a detailed timeline of events. Gilbert, a founder of the very first Reconstructionist Seminary in the United States and a lifelong advocate for interreligious dialogue, sees *Nostra Aetate* as a significant move forward. He notes the deep rift within the Catholic Church between the progressives, who are open to dialogue and transformation, and the conservatives, who feel that the church, "pure and without blemish," contains all truth.[38] "But by the time of its conclusion the Vatican Council had spoken words more profound than most Catholics will be able to comprehend, interpret, and put into effect for years to come."[39] Gilbert's words turn out to be prophetic.

Chapter 9

DARING TO ENGAGE

If Jew and Christian are both witnesses, they must speak from
where they are. But unless they presume to be on the throne
of divine judgment, they must listen as well as speak, risking
self-exposure just because they are witnesses.

—EMIL FACKENHEIM[1]

Vatican II and *Nostra Aetate* are important not so much for what
they officially state but for the doors that open as a result, inaugu-
rating what is called the "golden age" of Christian-Jewish relations
in the late 1960s and 1970s.[2] The Vatican establishes a high-level
Commission for Religious Relations with the Jews in 1974, just as
Abraham Joshua Heschel had recommended in 1962. The commission issues a set of "Guidelines" the same year that propose
a number of practical changes concerning liturgy, teaching, and
education, and include a call for joint social action.[3] The commission goes still further in 1985, with its "Notes on the Correct Way
to Present the Jews and Judaism in Preaching and Catechesis in
the Roman Catholic Church." The document introduces radical
departures from traditional teachings with its implicit repudiation
of replacement theology and its explicit assertion that some of the
controversies that Jesus has with Jewish authorities depicted in the
New Testament are not historical.[4]

Protestant and Orthodox Christians also begin concerted efforts to revise teaching curricula and reform liturgy. In 1977, the
Consultation on the Church and the Jewish People of the World

Council of Churches issues plans and recommendations regarding Jewish and Christian relations that parallel those introduced by the Vatican "Guidelines" of 1974. The report acknowledges problems with the traditional Christian approach of proselytizing, before turning to the problem of antisemitism and specifically mentioning the teaching of contempt. It continues that "Christians should be aware of the vibrant and continuing development of Judaism in post-Biblical times." It advises letting dialogue partners "define their religious identity in terms of their own self-understanding."[5] In other words, Christians must allow Jews to state what Judaism is rather than operate under their own assumptions. The document bluntly asserts that "the Jewish revelation … does not need Christianity at all for its self-definition."[6] The concluding section on Christian teaching, preaching, and liturgy confesses that negative views of Jews and Judaism persist in the hymns and services of the church, and refers Christians to the Ten Points of Seelisberg for guidance in enacting concrete modifications.

In addition to Christian organizations taking tangible steps to alter worship and education, a flourishing interfaith movement facilitates dialogue and cooperation by coordinating lectures, conferences, and research. An alphabet soup of associations emerges to facilitate this process—ICCJ (International Council of Christians and Jews), CSG (Christian Scholars Group), and CCJR (Council of Centers on Jewish-Christian Relations), to name just a few. Colleges and universities establish formal programs in Jewish and Christian Studies. Academic journals—such as *The Ecumenist* (the first to commence publication, in 1962), the *Journal of Ecumenical Studies* (the longest running), *The Ecumenical Review* (initially focused on Christianity but now broadened to interreligious questions), and *Studies in Jewish-Christian Relations* (the most recent)—appear and publish the results of studies aimed at promoting knowledge and understanding between Christians and Jews. In the late 1970s, the Stimulus Foundation begins to fund publication of studies in Judaism and Christianity through Paulist Press, the publishing arm of the Paulist Fathers. If Rabbi Marc Tanenbaum is correct when he writes that the core problem among Christians is the "immense ignorance, if not illiteracy, regarding Judaism," a growing number of people are working on a variety of fronts to ameliorate it.[7]

Radical changes occur thanks to the commitment of individuals and groups to listen sincerely and act accordingly. The most notable transformations are visible in materials routinely used for Christian education and liturgy. It is remarkable that Jewish organizations finance Christian self-studies into the antisemitic stereotypes that appear in worship and instruction. More surprising is that the studies result in the actual improvement of liturgies and teaching materials through the elimination of antisemitic elements.

These joint efforts require great courage, especially on the part of Jews, who have the most to lose by engaging in dialogue, given the history of disputations and debate. In some respects, however, they have the most to gain, if Christians take their comments and recommendations seriously. Christians also have a lot to lose by making significant alterations in traditional practices. They, too, demonstrate courage in maintaining respect for Jewish truths, recognizing that Jews do not share their deeply held convictions. "Agonistic respect" is the term used to describe the process of admitting the existence of different faith commitments and beliefs about ultimate truth. It requires a willingness to live within a sort of indeterminacy, a waiting between now and a future disclosure of ultimate truth. As the twentieth-century Jewish philosopher Emil Fackenheim observes, unless Jews and Christians currently sit on the throne of divine judgment, they must listen as well as speak.

In the dialogical endeavor, both Jews and Christians manifest a willingness to give up, or at least temporarily set aside, their competing claims to possess absolute truth. Agonistic respect moves beyond mere politeness and involves recognizing and honoring the inherent value in the other side's view.[8] This does not mean giving up beliefs and commitments, or compromising with an understanding of truth or Truth. Rather, it implies listening with respect to another's convictions and using imagination to walk in someone else's spiritual shoes. This takes courage.

The Question of Dialogue

Christians seek dialogue with Jews for many reasons: atonement for the Holocaust, repentance for historical violence, knowledge of Judaism and the Bible, cultivating friendships, and deepening of their own faith. Scholars, clerics, and ordinary laypersons initiate groups and institutes committed to interreligious understanding at a deep level in the decades following the 1950s. Yet Jews are wary of engagement. Even before World War II, when the National Conference of Christians and Jews emphasizes shared religious values that contribute to the American way of life, some Jews feel compelled to highlight their differences. Writing in 1943, the Jewish editor and scholar Trude Weiss-Rosmarin (1908–1989) stresses "the eternal and fundamental differences between Judaism and Christianity," adding that goodwill between Jews and Christians should not obliterate distinctions.[9] Her popular book *Judaism and Christianity: The Differences* goes through multiple editions to the end of the twentieth century.

An interfaith consciousness nevertheless seems the order of the day in postwar America. The Second World War, the Korean War, and the newly emerging Cold War bring service members of all faiths together and undermine, though do not eradicate, the dominance of white Anglo-Saxon Protestant norms. The Jewish philosopher and sociologist Will Herberg (1901–1977) discusses the new dynamic in his book *Protestant–Catholic–Jew*, in which he analyzes the upsurge of religiosity in the 1950s. He describes the elements of a "Jewish-Christian faith," which he identifies as God-centered. This faith, shared by Jews, Catholics, and Protestants, is based upon the revelation of God in the Bible and is expressed through community: "the Jew or Christian finds access to his God from within the People of God."[10]

It is true that "country club" antisemitism continues to exist after the war. Laura Z. Hobson exposes the problem in her bestselling novel *Gentleman's Agreement* (1947), which is made into a movie starring Gregory Peck as a journalist posing as a Jew to investigate the reality of antisemitism. Nevertheless, the threat of "godless" Communism unites all "godly" Americans against a common enemy. Presidents from Dwight D. Eisenhower to George W. Bush employ the concept of a "Judeo-Christian tradition" to score political rather than religious points. Although Europeans in the twentieth century tend to eschew the Judeo-Christian label, by the twenty-first, "the term 'Judeo-Christian tradition' is central to the debates about the EU Constitution between 2003 and 2005." Politicians from across the ideological spectrum use it, as do religious leaders from all denominations.[11]

Not all Jews welcome this truncated form of Judaism. The strongest critique comes from American Jewish intellectual Arthur Cohen (1928–1986) in a series of essays collected in a book titled *The Myth of the Judeo-Christian Tradition*. In bitter terms, Cohen declares that "we can learn much from the history of Jewish-Christian relations, but the one thing we cannot make of it is a discourse of community, fellowship, and understanding. How, then, do we make of it a tradition?"[12] For Cohen, the myth of the Judeo-Christian tradition obscures the "authentic, meaningful, and irrevocable" division between the two faiths. Although he admits that Jews and Christians believe in the same God, the same creation, and the same sacred history (up to a point), he concludes that they must remain eternally in opposition, given that "Israel makes Torah the Way and Christianity makes Jesus Christ the companion of the passage." Indeed, "the one thing that unites us in the order of faith is theological enmity."[13] Contemporary historical exigencies, however, have brought adherents of the two faiths together to attack a common enemy, which Cohen identifies as secularism and Will Herberg sees as a kind of "American culture-religion" that embraces Americanism with religious fervor.[14]

It is not entirely surprising, therefore, when Rabbi Joseph B. Soloveitchik (1903–1993) emphatically rejects most forms of interreligious dialogue in several speeches and articles in the 1960s. (Joseph B. Soloveitchik is a descendant of Rabbi Elijah Zvi Soloveitchik, discussed in Chapter 7.) Soloveitchik is one of a half dozen Jewish consultants working with Cardinal Augustin Bea on the Vatican's statement about Jewish and Christian relations. Both publicly and privately, however, the leader of Modern Orthodoxy in the United States has serious doubts about the wisdom of working with Christians.[15] He does not object to cooperating on social programs through secular organizations, but he draws the line at theological discussions. Convinced that the underlying agenda for dialogue is conversion and that participation in Vatican II deliberations would give the impression of Jewish endorsement of its positions, Soloveitchik expresses his reservations behind the scenes to Conservative and Reform Jews.[16] He is most concerned that if the Catholic Church changes its own dogmatic positions, reciprocal modifications in Jewish theology would be expected.

In a lengthy article bearing the clarion title "Confrontation," Rabbi Soloveitchik presents four conditions he believes are required for genuine dialogue.[17] First, Judaism is a completely independent religion, free of any other religion (i.e., Christianity). Second, religious experience does not lend itself to standardization or universalism, but rather is intimate, linking each individual with God. Thus, "the confrontation should occur not at a theological, but at a mundane human level." The rabbi's third condition is that "the community of the few," by which he means Judaism, should refrain from suggesting any changes in ritual or sacred texts. Rather, if liberal-minded Christians think modifications are advisable, they should act on their own convictions, without prompting from Jews. Finally, given the history of the two faiths over two millennia, Jews are not ready to revise or reverse historical attitudes "to trade favors pertaining to fundamental matters of faith, and to reconcile 'some' differences." This would essentially betray the faith of Jewish martyrs to persecution over the centuries.

Clearly, the rabbi views contemporary dialogue through the lenses of coercive medieval disputations over theology. Dialogue is not possible in situations of asymmetrical power such as existed the Middle Ages. King James of Aragon, for instance, orders a "disputation" in Barcelona in 1263 in which a Jewish convert to Christianity, Pablo Christiani, debates Nachmanides—Moses ben Nachman (1194–1270). Certain issues are off limits, however, such as faith in Jesus Christ, which "cannot, because of its certainty, be placed under dispute."[18] The king commends Nachmanides when it appears that the Jew wins the day. But when his Dominican opponents claim victory, Nachmanides publishes a text of the debate that leads to charges of blasphemy, although the pamphlet includes only what he had said in the king's presence. Recognizing the validity of Nachmanides' defense, but bowing to pressure from church prelates, King James sentences Nachmanides to two years' exile. The sage dies in Jerusalem, after establishing a synagogue that still exists in the Old City.

The medieval disputations include discussions of whether Jesus is the Messiah, whether the Messiah is human or divine, whether Mary is a virgin, whether God is three-in-one, and whether Christianity is the true faith. These doctrinal questions seem to have been in Rabbi Soloveitchik's mind in an "Addendum" he writes to "Confrontation." In the Addendum he makes a list of topics off-limits for discussion, including "Judaic monotheism and the Christian idea of Trinity; The Messianic idea in Judaism and Christianity; The Jewish attitude on Jesus," and more.[19] It would be impossible to achieve mutual understanding, Soloveitchik writes, since Jews and Christians start from different frames of reference and use different categories.[20] But he is more than willing to talk with Christians about humanitarian endeavors such as war and peace, poverty, civil rights, and other subjects of common concern. In short, Soloveitchik envisions theological dialogue as a grave threat to a minority community, the Jewish people.

In an influential address given at Union Theological Seminary in 1965, Rabbi Abraham Joshua Heschel offers a rebuttal to his Orthodox colleague. The first rabbi ever appointed to the Protestant faculty, Heschel declares that "no religion is an island," arguing that in the wake of the Holocaust, Jews and Christians—and members of all of the world's religions, for that matter—can no

longer afford to be parochial.[21] Heschel enumerates all of the things
that unite the two faiths:

> A commitment to the Hebrew Bible as Holy Scripture.
> Faith in the Creator, the God of Abraham, commitment
> to many of His commandments, to justice and mercy, a
> sense of contrition, sensitivity to the sanctity of life and
> to the involvement of God in history, the conviction that
> without the holy the good will be defeated, prayer that
> history may not end before the end of days, and so much
> more.[22]

In a model of the dilemma posed by agonistic respect, Heschel also
remarks on the existence of different truth claims and notes that
every religion believes it has the truth, even though truth is exclusive. He encourages an attitude of humility, since ultimate truth
cannot be expressed in words or concepts, and concludes that "one
truth comes to expression in many ways of understanding."[23]

Anticipating Heschel's claim that no religion is an island, Martin Buber (1878–1965) develops a philosophy of dialogue in the early
twentieth century that centers on relationship between subjects as
opposed to relationship between subjects and objects. Although
readers frequently view his short but profound book *I and Thou*
as a prescription for the human approach to God, Buber himself
emphasizes the centrality of human connections as the way to
encounter the divine "Thou."[24] No isolated "I" exists apart from relationship with others and thus each individual has inherent worth
and must recognize that fact in order to live authentically. Indeed,
says Buber, one can be in relation with a tree: "What I encounter
is neither the soul of a tree nor a dryad, but the tree itself."[25] The
Jewish philosopher promotes dialogue throughout his life, encouraging relationship between Jews and Christians, Palestinians and
Israelis, and others at a deep level.

Daring to Engage

Despite apparent differences between and among Jews, a common anxiety over Christian proselytizing characterizes the concerns of those contemplating dialogue. Although papal edicts throughout history prohibit forced conversions, Christians attempt to evangelize Jews by forcing them to listen to sermons, limiting Jewish access to their own services, destroying Jewish holy books, and threatening death if Jews do not submit to baptism. In the practice of *kiddush ha-shem*, many Jews choose death over baptism. (Literally meaning sanctification of the Name, *kiddush ha-shem* refers to acts of martyrdom that Jews voluntarily undertake.) Even after World War II, some Christians believe that interfaith dialogue is merely a new and improved means of evangelization. This history is not easily set aside in the cause of dialogue.

Aware of the risks of being proselytized, many Jews nonetheless welcome the opportunity to talk frankly with Christians. Not only do they help shape some of the documents of Vatican II, but they continue to suggest changes in liturgical and educational materials for Protestants and Catholics and to engage in joint examinations of many of the topics that Rabbi Soloveitchik deems off limits. They are encouraged by the remarkable shift in attitudes they see occurring—from the abandonment of missionary enterprises to Jews by the Catholic Church and mainline Protestant churches, to an emerging post-Holocaust Christian theology, primarily in the United States and Canada, that seeks to return Jews to their rightful place as God's first covenantal people. This new climate fosters "a greater degree of mutual recognition and legitimacy" and motivates Christians to eliminate their own anti-Jewish prejudices.[26] Jewish scholars begin to study the New Testament and other Christian texts, bringing the knowledge of Hebrew language and Jewish history to their research. They learn, to their surprise, that early Christian literature offers a number of insights into nascent Judaism. Meanwhile, Christian scholars begin to study first-century Judaic religions, along with the Talmud and other postbiblical Jewish literature, in order to understand the life and times of Jesus and the early church. The scholarship concerning Late Antiquity and the early Middle Ages is enriched for everyone as a result.

Three examples illustrate the giant strides that Jews take toward interreligious understanding at the end of the twentieth century. The Theology Committee of the International Council of Christians and Jews (ICCJ) issues a statement in 1993 on "Jews and Christians in Search of a Common Religious Basis for Contributing to a Better World."[27] The ICCJ is the same group that produces the pivotal Ten Points of Seelisberg in 1947. "Better World" includes a section devoted to Jewish perspectives on cooperation and communication with Christians. The writers assert that all humanity is included in God's covenant with Noah and thus has a share in God's ultimate redemption. Moreover, they acknowledge that by sharing a common agenda that encompasses serving God the Creator, a special relationship exists between Judaism and Christianity. "Better World" anticipates subsequent Jewish declarations, but does not receive as much publicity because it comes out of Europe and because at that time public interest in Jewish and Christian dialogue is waning.

"A Jewish Statement on Christians and Christianity" receives great attention in 2000, however, due to its appearance as a full-page ad in *The New York Times*.[28] More than 200 predominantly liberal rabbis and academics primarily from the United States endorse *Dabru Emet* (Speak the Truth). Another reason for its wide reception is that *Dabru Emet* explicitly addresses theological issues within Judaism. One illustration concerns differences relating to scripture, where the declaration proclaims:

> Christians know and serve God through Jesus Christ and the Christian tradition. Jews know and serve God through Torah and the Jewish tradition. That difference will not be settled by one community insisting that it has interpreted Scripture more accurately than the other.

In other words, neither Jews nor Christians have a monopoly on interpreting shared scriptures. *Dabru Emet* also exculpates Christianity the religion, though not individual Christians, for the rise of Nazism—a contention that meets with criticism from other Jews but is appreciated by Christians. And, in an implicit dismissal of Rabbi Soloveitchik's position, the signatories assert that "A new relationship between Jews and Christians will not weaken Jewish practice." On the contrary, "Only if we cherish our own traditions can we pursue this relationship with integrity."

While Christians welcome the statement—and, indeed, for decades have encouraged Jews to develop such a document—Jews have mixed reactions. While many Jews find the statement groundbreaking and significant, Jon D. Levenson, in contrast, publishes a caustic critique, faulting the declaration for skating over real differences between the two faiths, such as the nature of God or the composition and authority of the Bible. The Jewish Studies professor faults the statement's depiction of "the two disputants ... as simply different," observing that everything that is of vital importance vanishes in this assumption.[29] Levenson points out that the risks of losing the identity found in religious practice are much higher for Jews than for Christians in the interreligious concord posited by *Dabru Emet*.

Of equal or perhaps even more consequence than *Dabru Emet* is the statement Orthodox rabbis adopt in 2015.[30] *To Do the Will of Our Father in Heaven* is initially signed by twenty-five Orthodox rabbis from Israel, the United States, and Europe, with more than fifty additional signatories from around the globe. The statement asserts that the emergence of Christianity is neither an accident nor an error, but God's gift to humanity. "In separating Judaism and Christianity, G-d willed a separation between partners with significant theological differences, not a separation between enemies." (Some Jews do not spell out the sacred name of God.) Although Jews and Christians have more in common than what divides them, substantial differences remain between the two communities. Still, God employs many messengers and methods to realize the divine plan. Called a breakthrough in Orthodox thinking about Judaism, the proclamation "acknowledged that Christianity and Judaism are no longer engaged in a theological duel to the death," says one signatory. "Given our toxic history, this is unprecedented in Orthodoxy."[31] Although hostility toward Christianity continues to run high among some Orthodox Jews, other Jews, particularly in the United States, are working to mitigate or abandon the antagonism.[32]

Educational Reform

Formal statements of goodwill are a good start, but change would not have occurred had not individuals, as well as institutions, been highly motivated to consider substantive modifications in educational materials. These adjustments occur primarily within the Catholic community, but also within some Protestant denominations, as a direct result of encounters with Jewish organizations that provide input and feedback. One of the most important factors is the financial support that Jewish and interfaith groups give to underwrite studies, reviews, and consultations that reveal the extent of antisemitic sentiment in Christian worship and teaching.

The American Jewish Committee (AJC) plays an extraordinary role in facilitating the transformation of pedagogical materials. AJC stimulates a series of textbook self-studies by Christian and Jewish scholars in the United States and Europe in the 1960s and 1970s, with the objective of analyzing intergroup relations based on race, religion, and ethnicity. The organization sponsors investigations of resources used in Catholic schools, along with studies of beliefs that different Protestant groups hold about Jews. The AJC reports furnish sufficient evidence to lend credence to Jewish concerns about the extent of antisemitism present in educational materials.[33]

A decade after its Protestant study, AJC commissions yet another report to see if any changes have occurred in Protestant textbooks as a result of the first analysis. Parallel studies of Catholic religious education texts in France, Spain, and Italy (not sponsored by AJC) have similar results, although the French texts seem principally free from the deicide charge.[34] But, somewhat disturbingly, the European studies disclose "a total absence of any mention of the Shoah, and hardly any reference to the State of Israel."[35] The good news is that nearly fifteen years after the first investigation in 1961, a new study finds that Catholic teaching materials have improved significantly since Vatican II.[36] At the same time, traditional and nonhistorical depictions of Jesus and the Jews, the Pharisees, the crucifixion, and the covenant remain troublesome, such as Jewish leaders plotting against Jesus or the Roman procurator Pilate appearing to be an impartial administrator.

Like the AJC, the Anti-Defamation League (ADL) of B'nai B'rith is at the forefront of supporting the restructuring of Christian education at all levels. In 1970, ADL publishes a *Teachers' Guide to Jews and Their Religion* written for Catholic high school teachers and featuring lectures from a group of American Jewish leaders. The book, which goes through several editions, features sections on American Judaism, Jewish beliefs, Jewish worship and observances throughout the year, and the lifeways of the Jewish people, along with suggested classroom activities and discussion topics. A foreword to the book recommends that Catholic religion teachers get acquainted with some actual Jews to make the teaching manual more effective.[37]

The teaching of contempt is not limited to elementary and secondary religious education, however. In 1965, the ADL convenes a conference of Catholic and Protestant educators on the treatment of Jews and the Jewish faith in Christian seminaries. Subsequently published as *Judaism and the Christian Seminary Curriculum*, conference papers focus on the ways that Christian education in the seminaries might lead to antisemitism in courses on biblical studies, the early church, ethics, and Israel.[38] The truly noteworthy thing about the conference and the book that follows is not only that a Jewish group organizes them, but that Catholic and Protestant scholars engage in a joint discussion of advanced theological studies.

Just as Christians are reconsidering and revising their educational materials, Jews—with the encouragement of the AJC—are reviewing their own educational materials about Christians. The 1965 Dropsie College study of Jewish textbooks identifies a *Leidensgeschichte* (history of suffering) motif in which persecution of Jews is frequently emphasized, as are Jewish contributions and uniqueness.[39] The report summarizes the differences between material emanating from Orthodox, Conservative, and Reform traditions—with Orthodox textbooks generally arguing for the superiority of Judaism over Christianity, Conservative texts seeing Jesus as a "great teacher" but not significantly discussing Christianity, and Reform books seeing Christianity as an advance over polytheism but also an adulterated form of Judaism. The authors conclude that Jewish religious education, which generally occurs as a supplement to public schooling, focuses on prayer, ritual, and ceremonies, with references to outside groups in textbooks limited to discussions of history.

A different perspective comes from Israeli historian Pinchas Lapide (1922–1997), who surveys the depiction of Jesus in ten history textbooks used in Israeli schools in 1973.[40] Noting the centuries-old tradition among Jews of not speaking the name of Jesus, Lapide notes the progress made—from a minimum of two lines to a full chapter of four pages. He also examines a thirty-five-page book about early Christianity published by the Israel Ministry of Education for use by twelve- and thirteen-year-olds. He notes that Jesus is not "saddled" with responsibility for Christian hatred of Jews, that the Jewishness of Jesus is taken for granted, and that Jesus is presented as faithful to the Torah.[41] "The present-day schoolbooks of Israel contain what is undoubtedly the most sympathetic picture of Jesus ever offered to a generation of Jewish children by their teachers."[42]

Liturgical Reform

Even the best-intentioned educational efforts have little impact if antisemitic elements remain part of weekly worship services. Special seasons and holidays, such as Advent leading to Christmas and Holy Week leading to Easter, are especially problematic. Jews are distinctly depicted as the enemies of Jesus in the centuries-old passion play produced every ten years at Oberammergau in Germany and in Mel Gibson's film *The Passion of the Christ* (2004). An additional complication today is that some Christians celebrate a Seder during Holy Week, imbuing it with Christian rather than Jewish significance. All too often, Christians "baptize" the Seder by incorporating it into New Testament accounts of the Last Supper or making it the prologue to the sacrament of communion.[43] Nevertheless, efforts to mitigate triumphalist messages in worship are in fact being made. Again, Jewish cooperation with Christians has a strong impact.

In response to a request made by Cardinal Bea, the American Jewish Committee provides a report to the Vatican's Secretariat for Christian Unity on "Anti-Jewish Elements in Catholic Liturgy" in the fall of 1961.[44] (AJC had already submitted an evaluation of the image of Jews in Catholic education that summer.) The report acknowledges changes that have been made to the Good Friday liturgy but notes that problems remain in the missal (the book containing texts used throughout the year in the Catholic Church), homilies, commentaries, and the breviary (the book used in religious communities containing texts for daily services). Focusing on the public worship of the church, the study points out that many troublesome passages come directly from the New Testament. For example, the words "They will hand you over in meetings and in their synagogues they will whip you" (Mark 13:9, Matthew 10:17 NRSV) are read on the memorial day of every apostle and gospel writer. The AJC writers admit that including certain scripture readings is a "venerable tradition," but add that other, less controversial texts are available. Unfortunately, the liturgies in use in 1961 incorporate age-old antisemitic accusations. The depiction of the Jews as a people is uniformly negative, and they are held collectively responsible for the crucifixion.[45]

At least one of the prayers said during Holy Week, notes the AJC report, is particularly offensive because it deliberately inverts a well-known Jewish prayer of thanksgiving to God into an accusation Jesus makes against God's people, the Jews. In the Christian Good Friday *Improperia*, the Solemn Reproaches, Jesus addresses people who have harmed him. The ninth-century text has a long history of stirring up resentment against Jews. Christians would say or sing the *Improperia* responsively. "Then they'd leave the church, form a mob, and attack Jewish communities."[46] The 2006 book of *Evangelical Lutheran Worship* includes a new version of the Reproaches, adding the word "church" to make it clear whom exactly Jesus criticizes, and explicitly condemning the church's history of antisemitism:

> O my people, O my church, what more could I have done for you?
> Answer me.
> I grafted you into my people Israel,
> but you made them scapegoats for your own guilt,
> and you have prepared a cross for your Savior.[47]

While an improvement over earlier Solemn Reproaches, the problem of twisting a prayer of thanksgiving into a series of reproofs remains.

Recognizing that later conflicts between Jews and early Christians are retrojected into the passion narratives, American Catholic bishops in 1988 adopt clear guidelines for avoiding antisemitic representations.[48] The inclination to heighten opposition in dramatic productions is natural but leads to erroneous conclusions. The bishops advise avoiding anything that suggests that Jesus opposes Torah or that his teachings oppose the Pharisees as a group. With the exception of the Gospel of Luke (13:31), the Pharisees are not even mentioned in accounts of Jesus's passion. And in Luke, they attempt to warn Jesus of a plot against him.[49] The bishops also note that historical accounts of Pilate describe him as a cruel and ruthless tyrant, rather than as a sympathetic character, as some gospels do.[50] They conclude that it is possible to remain faithful to the biblical witness and not create an antisemitic liturgy.

Ordinary Christians and Jews have begun to engage in dialogue through shared liturgy, holding joint services on Holocaust Remembrance Day (Yom HaShoah).[51] Christians on their own or in consultation with Jews develop liturgies of repentance and remembrance in the early 1970s. One of the first such services is conducted in the chapel at Queens College in Charlotte, North Carolina.[52] Since that pioneering effort, annual observances held in synagogues, temples, churches, museums, art galleries, community centers, and public buildings mark the occasion. Services may include talks given by Holocaust survivors, poetry written and found in concentration camps, readings from *The Diary of Anne Frank*, statements of confession and repentance, music, sermons, candle lighting, and more. An interfaith anthology of *Liturgies on the Holocaust* provides a wealth of sample programs from the United States and Canada.[53]

Perhaps one of the most important developments is the practice of visiting synagogues, temples, churches, and cathedrals by adherents of the two faiths. "Until the 1960s, synagogues had been exclusive Jewish territories, with non-Jews showing little interest in visiting Jewish houses of worship."[54] Pulpit exchanges, shared worship services on Thanksgiving, interfaith gatherings on Holocaust Remembrance Day, joint study of sacred texts, and adult education programs on interreligious topics are now well-established practices for both Christians and Jews. In addition, college courses in religion studies today often require a site visit to services held by one of the religions being studied.

We take most of the changes discussed in this chapter for granted, forgetting the courage required to get Jews and Christians to collaborate on projects of mutual concern. This is especially true when the projects touch on religious commitments and discussions center on questions of the deepest meaning. Agonistic respect does not come cheaply, but its rewards are great. The lives of Christians and Jews are being enriched and challenged, as individuals meet, talk, and listen to each other speaking of deepest commitments and meaning.

Chapter 10

RETHINKING THEOLOGY

If the renunciation of supersessionism now enables Jews and Christians to talk theology with one another, then we should understand why we need to talk theology with one another.

—DAVID NOVAK[1]

Dialogue demands reconstruction of Christian self-understanding precisely because so much of how we think about Christianity is built upon a distorted portrait of Judaism.

—MARY C. BOYS[2]

While Jews and Christians disagree on many issues, they do agree that the Holocaust is a world-changing experience—or, in the words of Rabbi Irving Greenberg, an "orienting event."[3] Just as the Exodus and the revelation at Mount Sinai give the Israelites and their descendants, the Jews, a new understanding and relationship with God, and the life, death, and resurrection of Jesus opens the way for non-Jews to have a relationship with the one God, so too does the Holocaust alter human conceptions of the divine. Greenberg identifies a second orienting event for Jews and Judaism: the "recreation" of the state of Israel in the twentieth century. While the Orthodox rabbi and educator goes on to say that the destruction of the temple in Jerusalem in 70 CE also shapes subsequent Jewish understanding of God, no similarly traumatic incident threatens the foundations of Christianity until the twentieth century. The

Reformation of the sixteenth century certainly shakes up church organization and structures, but it does not challenge or collapse the faith of millions. But the Holocaust demands a repudiation of the ancient assumptions that teach that Christianity superseded or replaced Judaism, and is the New Israel. The mass murder of Jews demands a new Christian theology of Judaism, a new examination of the ties between God's chosen people and Abraham's children by adoption. Jewish theologians face a different set of problems for understanding, or redefining, Israel's relationship with God. They have to ask themselves if, after two thousand years and millions of deaths, Judaism needs a theology of Christianity.

A number of theologians have grappled with the antisemitism and supersessionism that seems endemic to many Christian teachings. Christian post-Holocaust theologians propose interpreting the givens of their religious tradition in new and constructive ways, fashioning new Christologies that do not put Jesus at odds with Judaism. Jewish scholars are engaged in a similar task in terms of forging a Jewish theology of Christianity. The practice of avoiding discussions with or about the "idolators" no longer seems to serve many Jews after the Holocaust.

But the remarkable theologizing that Jews conduct can occur only with the radical theologizing of Christians attempting to revisit and revise the historic teachings of contempt after the Holocaust, and these transformations require mutually reinforcing generosity and unselfishness. Generosity implies a willingness to forgo competition and to abandon the conflict over who is "right." In this regard, it is a bit like agonistic respect, since it allows the other person to speak and be heard. Yet generosity is no guarantee of equality since there is always the chance that the giver can withhold or rescind the gift.[4]

It is up to Christians to take the first step to demonstrate to their Jewish counterparts that they are both serious and sincere in their repudiation of supersessionism and their affirmation that God's promises are eternal—including the covenant made with Israel at Mount Sinai. A contrite spirit is required to admit that some

Christian dogma itself is inherently antisemitic. A generous spirit is needed to make changes to remedy the problem. This happens between individuals and at institutional and formal levels, although it has yet to appear in many churches.

Jews manifest generosity as well in their acceptance of Christian determination to eliminate all vestiges of antisemitism. Although initially suspicious, those with the courage and desire to participate in dialogue understand that their Christian interlocutors are eager to listen to what Jews have to say. This gives Jews the freedom to reimagine their own traditions apart from Christian speculation over the meaning of Judaism.

Abandoning Supersessionism

Knowledge and understanding, friendship and feasting do not eradicate antisemitism if the fundamental belief system of Christianity presupposes ascendancy over Judaism. A number of theologians wrestle with doctrinal issues as a result of dialogue with Jews as well as individual and collective soul-searching amongst themselves. They wonder whether antisemitism is intrinsic to Christian faith. "Is it possible," asks Catholic theologian Gregory Baum (1923–2017), "that the anti-Jewish virus is an integral part of the Christian message so that by removing the virus we destroy the message?"[5] Baum and other scholars want to discern the essence of Christianity in the conviction that, at its core, their faith is not inherently antisemitic. But the difficulty they face is enormous "as long as the Christian Church regards itself as the successor of Israel."[6] If Jesus is the one and only way to salvation, there is no theological space for any other religion, not least Judaism.

There are at least four elements in the Christian faith that contribute to the triumphalist posture known as supersessionism. They include the belief that a new covenant inaugurated by Jesus replaces the original covenant God made with the Israelites; the belief that, as a result, the Jews are no longer God's chosen people and thus the

Torah has been abrogated; the belief that Christians alone have the correct interpretation of Jewish scripture, that is, the Old Testament; and the belief that Jesus is the Messiah foretold in scripture and the fulfillment of God's promises. Theologians in the early church define Christianity over and against Judaism. They make the mystical dualities found in the apostle Paul's writings—Law–Gospel, flesh–spirit, death–life—into the hard-and-fast categories of Judaism–Christianity. Thus, antisemitism in the first centuries of Christianity "was an expression of Christian self-affirmation," neither secondary nor superficial.[7] This historical and ongoing denigration of the Jews and their religion is the exact issue that post-Holocaust theologians want to address.

The post-Holocaust scholars A. Roy and Alice L. Eckardt would devote fifty years to articulating a nonsupersessionist Christian theology. In *Elder and Younger Brothers,* Roy Eckardt (1918–1998) differentiates between theories of discontinuity (the elements that divide Christians and Jews) and those of continuity (the elements that unite people of the two faiths).[8] Christians who emphasize discontinuity stress the uniqueness and finality of Christianity, believing that the election of Israel is ended and that Christianity fulfills the promises of biblical faith and is the successor to Judaism. In contrast, those who accentuate continuity highlight the sacred history of the original people of God, which Christianity continues. For these Christians, Jesus opens up God's everlasting covenant with Israel to gentiles. Indeed, Eckardt identifies a single covenant that has two sides—one for the people Israel and the other for pagans, as he calls non-Jews. For him, Judaism remains a living and vital faith "in the only real God as King and Redeemer."[9]

The theory of continuity takes two approaches: single-covenant and double-covenant theology. According to single-covenant theology, as exemplified by Roy Eckardt and others, there is one basic covenant that is extended from Jews to the non-Jewish world through Jesus. Catholic theologian Monika Hellwig (1929–2005), for example, sees the two faiths as complementary aspects of the same "eschatological reality," which exists in the future rather than in the present. But Jews and Christians have a foretaste of that reality in their respective practices. The "new covenant" in Jesus is in continuity with Israel's covenant because it allows non-Jews to share the election that is first bestowed upon the people Israel. Hellwig adds that this does not retire or displace Israel, but simply brings gentiles into the knowledge and worship of the one God of Israel and extends God's promises with Israel to them.[10] Another proponent of single-covenant theology is Paul van Buren (1924–1998), an Episcopal priest and scholar. His trilogy *A Theology of the Jewish-Christian Reality* outlines his conviction that Israel has two fundamental and essential branches: Judaism and Christianity. Neither is superfluous or irrelevant. The single-covenant perspective sees Christians as participating within the Jewish covenant— "Judaism for gentiles," as Christianity is sometimes called.

The clearest and most recent example of single-covenant theology comes from the Vatican's Commission for Religious Relations with the Jews.[11] Writing in 2015 on the fiftieth anniversary of *Nostra Aetate*, the commission reaffirms and strengthens a number of points made in 1965, most especially the renunciation and condemnation of replacement theology, which asserts that Christianity supplants Judaism. The statement (I am shortening the title to "Gifts and Calling") reiterates Paul's declaration in his letter to the Romans that "the gifts and the calling of God are irrevocable" (Romans 11:29), an important element of *Nostra Aetate*. "Gifts and Calling" stresses the continuity that exists between the people Israel and the Church, who share the one God of the Covenant in addition to scriptures, promises, and hopes. It maintains that the Christian Old Testament is open to both, adding that "a response to God's word of salvation that accords with one or the other tradition can thus open up access to God, even if it is left up to his counsel of salvation to determine in what way he may intend to save mankind in each instance." But since God wills universal salvation, and since the Church sees Christ as the sole mediator of that salvation, there cannot be two paths, such as "Jews hold to the Torah, Christians hold to Christ." This is because "the Church is the definitive and unsurpassable locus of the salvific action of God." So, on the one hand, the Sinai covenant is eternal and remains in force; on the other, the new covenant in Christ is added to this original covenant. The commission resolves the dilemma of Jewish salvation "without confessing Christ explicitly" the same way Paul does: by declaring ultimate reconciliation of the covenantal issue to be "an unfathomable divine mystery."

It is clear that the Commission for Religious Relations with the Jews strongly rejects the other model of continuity—namely, double-covenant theology—which posits two distinct but equally valid covenants—one for Jews and one for everyone else. The first modern proponent of double-covenant theology comes from the early twentieth-century Jewish philosopher Franz Rosenzweig (1886–1929). Two events transform Rosenzweig's life and thought. The first is his 1913 meeting with Eugen Rosenstock-Huessy (1888–1973), a Jewish convert to Christianity, with whom he has intense discussions about the two religions. Rosenzweig nearly converts to Christianity himself before he has what might be characterized as a mystical experience during a Yom Kippur service, the second event. He recommits himself to Judaism and establishes a center for Jewish adult learning in Frankfurt, Germany. But his preparation for conversion gives him a profound understanding of Christianity, deeper than that of most Christian or Jewish contemporaries.

While corresponding with Rosenstock-Huessy as they both serve on the front in World War I, Rosenzweig also drafts his magnum opus, *The Star of Redemption*.[12] A massive and complex work of philosophy, history, and linguistics, its first two-thirds are devoted to philosophical issues. Only in the last third does Rosenzweig tackle the role and purpose of Judaism and Christianity. He uses the symbol of Judaism, the star of David, to explain his philosophy. According to Rosenzweig, one of the triangles in the star of David symbolizes God, Humanity ("Man," in his terminology), and World, while the overlapping triangle signifies Creation, Revelation, and Redemption. Both religions incorporate all of these elements, but in different ways. For Jews, their election requires a turn inward to maintain community and faithfulness to God. Observing the commandments creates boundaries and cohesion for this community. But God's plan is to redeem all people, so Christians turn outward to bring gentiles to the Savior and thereby to God. In Rosenzweig's vision, missionary activity is an essential part of Christianity, since the church must first win the world before the "eternal end." Therefore, rays emanate out from the star, refracting "the fire that glows inwardly" in order to guide pagans into the One.[13]

It is fair to say that Rosenzweig privileges Judaism over Christianity, writing that the star of redemption already shines in the "innermost narrows of the Jewish heart," whereas the hope of Christians lies in the future.[14] Moreover, Christians would be lost without Jews, whose very existence demonstrates the continuing presence of God. Yet Jews need Christians—or, at any rate, God does, from Rosenzweig's perspective—since both are working on the same task. "To us, he gave eternal life by igniting in our heart the fire of the Star of his truth. He placed the Christians on the eternal way by making them hasten after the rays of the Star of his truth into all time until the eternal end." Rosenzweig concludes, "The truth, the whole truth, belongs therefore neither to them nor to us."[15] Both Judaism and Christianity connect humans to eternity by establishing communal institutions. By following their respective liturgical calendars, in effect, they are engaged in "mutual walking, mutual doing, mutual becoming."[16] Ultimate redemption, however, exists only in the future.

A Christian proponent of double-covenant theology is James Parkes, whose historical studies persuade him that Judaism and Christianity are two distinct religions; neither is an incomplete form of the other. On the contrary, history has demonstrated that both faiths have validity by a number of criteria—vitality, creativity, and holiness, to list just three. Parkes argues that the revelation of God at Mount Sinai exhibits God to humans at their most basic level, that is, as social beings living in community. The revelation at Calvary addresses humanity at another level, namely, the human being as an individual in a personal relationship with God. Both revelations are identical expressions of the infinite in the finite, existing together in creative tension. Parkes goes further, however, and introduces scientific humanism and the quest for truth as a third revelation of the divine. In this way, he reconceptualizes the Christian doctrine of the Trinity, replacing the three persons, Father-Son-Spirit, with the three channels Judaism-Christianity-Humanism.[17] While Parkes's unorthodox Trinitarian doctrine gains no adherents, his purpose is to shift the focus from Christ to God, thereby creating a theocentric rather than christocentric faith to allow for additional revelations of the divine.[18]

The subtitle of E.P. Sanders's masterwork on *Paul and Palestinian Judaism* hints at his outlook: *A Comparison of Patterns of Religion*.[19] Sanders argues that the "covenantal nomism" of first-century Judaism differs markedly from Paul's "participationist eschatology." Covenantal nomism, on the one hand, describes the relationship that Israel, and Jews, have with God. God has graciously invited Israel into a covenant. In response, the Israelites and their descendants observe the "Law," *nomos* in Greek, *torah* in Hebrew.[20] On the other hand, participationist eschatology requires a transformation that involves "becoming one person with Christ, dying with him to sin, and sharing the promise of his resurrection."[21] By transferring one's loyalties from worldly and otherworldly powers to the Lord Jesus Christ, one is freed from enslavement to the powers of sin and death. Because Paul's pattern of religion is not covenantal nomism, Sanders concludes that "Paul presents an *essentially different type of religiousness from any found in Palestinian Jewish literature*" (italics in original).[22]

Technically speaking, Sanders does not argue for a second or double covenant but rather for two entirely different types of religion. He grants legitimacy to both types, taking pains to affirm that there is no reason to think that one religious pattern—covenantal nomism or participationist eschatology—is superior or inferior to another. Yet Sanders also observes that Paul rejects equality between the two faiths since, in effect, the apostle denies Jewish privilege as the elect of God who receive the gift of Torah.[23] "Since salvation is only by Christ, the following of *any other path is wrong*" (italics in original).[24] Pauline scholars have challenged Sanders in the decades since he first made his assessment, arguing that the New Testament scholar has overdrawn the differences between Paul and his opponents. But at the time he is writing, Sanders's theory dismantles centuries of anti-Jewish traditions about Paul's teachings.

The Jewish talmudist and historian Jacob Neusner (1932–2016) would agree with Sanders that Judaism and Christianity are two entirely distinct and separate religions. Christianity is discontinuous with Judaism and is instead "a divine intervention into history," thus making it autonomous, absolute, unique, and in no way indebted or connected to Judaism.[25] Somewhat like Sanders and his "pattern of religion," Neusner identifies "religious systems" that encompass social life, customs, worldviews, self-definition, and ethics.[26] Judaism and Christianity are therefore completely different religious systems, not different versions of a single faith. Neusner frequently characterizes Jewish and Christian relations both historically and in the present by invoking the expression "different people talking about different things to different people." On at least one occasion, he adds to his signature statement, "with no possibility of mutual comprehension, let alone dialogue."[27] Despite his bleak assessment, this influential Jewish intellectual does, in fact, engage in interfaith dialogue and coauthors several books with Christians that address issues of mutual concern.

Single- and double-covenant theologies attempt to sustain the legitimacy of both Judaism and Christianity, maintaining the status of the original covenant and conferring validity on the new covenant. In 1965, *Nostra Aetate* confesses this more or less explicitly when the document states that "God does not take back the gifts he bestowed or the choice he made."[28] Roy Eckardt broaches the issue bluntly when he asks Christians if they believe God is true to God's word: "Do we or do we not believe that the Lord remains faithful to his Covenant with original Israel?" Certainly Israel deserves praise for "undeviating fealty to its recognition of the divine promises."[29]

Although existing Christian liturgies may not yet fully adopt the view that the original covenant with Israel remains in effect, denominational and scholarly statements do. For example, the 2002 statement *A Sacred Obligation*, from the Christian Scholars Group, declares in Article 1: "God's covenant with the Jewish people endures forever."[30] The Presbyterian Church (USA) makes a similar statement in its study guide for local congregations, which presents seven theological affirmations that attempt to lay the foundation for "a new and better relationship under God between Christians and Jews." They include the assertion that "Christians have not replaced Jews" and the avowal that God has called both the church and the Jewish people for witness to the world. "The relationship of the church to contemporary Jews is based on that gracious and irrevocable election of both."[31] The United Methodist Church's Social Principles statement, adopted in 2016, elaborates on Guiding Principles for Christian-Jewish Relations. Article 4 states, "Christians and Jews are bound to God through biblical covenants that are eternally valid."[32]

In addition, both Christian and Jewish groups make numerous formal statements that accept, or at least acknowledge, diverse readings of shared scripture, thus abandoning supersessionism in yet another way. The Pontifical Biblical Commission issues a major study in 2001 titled *The Jewish People and Their Sacred Scriptures in the Christian Bible,* which breaks from the longstanding tradition of denigrating rabbinic, or Jewish, readings of the Old Testament. On the practical level of understanding scripture, Christians can "learn much from Jewish exegesis practised for more than two thousand years, and, in fact, they have learned much in the course of history."[33] *Dabru Emet*, the 2002 statement issued by Jewish scholars, notes that members of both faiths seek authority from the same holy book, taking away similar lessons, such as God's creation of the universe, God's establishment of a covenant with the people Israel, and God's promise of redemption. "Yet," it adds, "Jews and

Christians interpret the Bible differently on many points. Such differences must always be respected."[34] The authors of *The Bible With and Without Jesus* presuppose such differences and actually celebrate them, writing that "The Old Testament, the Tanakh, the Hebrew Bible—whatever we call it—is too complex to hold only one meaning and too theologically relevant to both Jews and Christians to be the property of only one community."[35]

Rethinking Christology

By the twenty-first century, some churches reduce or even purge at least three elements of Christian supersessionism from instructional materials. They disavow belief in the annulment of God's covenant, the replacement of Israel by the church, and Christian "rights" to Jewish scriptures. But Christology—that is, the identity of Jesus, whether as Messiah or as the Incarnation of God—remains divisive. Christians believe that with the life, death, and resurrection of Jesus (the "Christ event"), God redeems the world, fulfilling the promises made to the Israelites through the Old Testament prophets. Jews counter by saying that the world is not yet redeemed. Christians developing a post-Holocaust theology make the same observation. Moreover, the anticipation of a "second" coming by the Messiah reveals that Paul and the first apostles know that the world has not yet changed in the way they expected.

Two thousand years later, Christians take up this same problem in light of an awareness of the problem of supersessionism. Rosemary Radford Ruether, a Catholic feminist theologian, inaugurates her scholarly career with a scathing critique of the triumphalist posture, explaining in stark language why "the Jewish rejection of the Christian interpretation [of prophetic Judaism] is substantially justified."[36] If the biblical idea of the Kingdom of God is that in which the lion lies down with the lamb and swords become ploughshares, then "it is quite meaningless to speak of the Messiah as having come when the Kingdom has not come."[37] But since

Christ did not return, and since the early church is unwilling or unable to admit it had been mistaken, the work of reinterpreting messiahship begins.

Ruether proposes that Christians consider the Resurrection the way Jews consider the Exodus—an experience of salvation that is remembered by heirs of the community that experience it.[38] These events form the ground of ultimate hope, a preview of the goal of history when God's will is done on earth. But final redemption remains in the future, for Christians as much as for Jews.[39] Christians can experience God's kingdom in Christ in the present, but this is not the complete or last word. For the church, the reign of God is both here and not yet here.[40] This is true for Jews as well, since on Shabbat, "Jews act *as if the Messiah has come,*" resting once each week in what seems to be a perfect world (italics in original).[41] This both/and viewpoint offers Christians a new way of relating to members of other religions. It leaves room in world history for other means of grace—that is, other religions—since divine redemption is not yet complete.[42]

What makes Christianity unique, then? The person of Jesus may hold the key, according to Father John Pawlikowski, a four-time presidential appointee to the U.S. Holocaust Memorial Museum. After many years of leading interfaith dialogue, he concludes that "no lasting resolution of the historic Christian-Jewish tension is possible unless the Church is ready to significantly rethink its traditional interpretation of Christology."[43] Influenced by the Jewish theologian Ellis Rivkin (1918–2010), Pawlikowski places Jesus within the tradition of the Pharisees, who had already begun a "revolution" that shifts the emphasis from God-and-nation to God-and-individual in early Judaism. This move encourages the internalization of faith within each person.[44] Although Jesus also departs from the Pharisees, the ultimate break comes not from Jesus but from his followers, who attribute divinity to him in their liturgy. Pawlikowski explains that the theology of Incarnation is a later development.[45] When early Christians come to see that humanity itself is central to the self-definition of God, they infer that each individual is somehow divine, sharing in God's nature. "Thus in a very real sense one can say that God did not become man in Jesus. God always was man; humanity was an integral part of the Godhead from the beginning."[46] It is simply the Christ event that makes this fact evident to the world, just as the revelation at Mount Sinai demonstrates God's presence in history.

Jewish Theologies of Christianity

Formal and informal dialogues between Jews and Christians lead some churches to revise and even repudiate what once seemed to be eternal concepts. They develop new theologies of Judaism that see Jews and Christians working together as a single people of God. Do Jews need a theology of Christianity as well? Many are skeptical, given the background of Jewish and Christian relations. "Jews come to the dialogue with a different agenda than do Christians; for us, the problem is history—specifically, Christian persecution of Jews."[47] Some Jews are offended by statements and declarations affirming the legitimacy of God's covenant with Israel. "It is not a matter of whether Christianity acknowledges fragmentary truths in Judaism," cries Rabbi Eliezer Berkovits. "All we want of Christians is that they keep their hands off us and our children!"[48] Centuries of persecution create an instinctive anti-Christianity that still exists for many Jews today. But a few think the time has come to go beyond habitual attitudes of evading Christianity entirely or degrading it polemically or academically.[49] Although Emil Fackenheim does not agree with Rosenzweig's double-covenant approach, he does admit the necessity of a Jewish doctrine of Christianity.[50] In the 1970s and 1980s, a number of Jewish scholars try to "argue Jewishly" for the special status of Christians.[51]

A first step toward this is to emphasize the Noachide Commandments as a way to recognize Christians as worthy of "associate membership" in the House of Israel.[52] As noted in Chapter 6, the Noachide Laws are seven moral precepts the entire human race is obliged to observe. While Jews are enjoined to keep all of the biblical commandments, non-Jews need follow only seven in order for God to consider them righteous and thereby secure a place in the "world to come." These seven are prohibitions against idolatry, blasphemy, bloodshed, sexual sins, theft, and eating from a living animal (that is, a prohibition on cruelty to animals). The New Testament book of Acts alludes to several of these prohibitions (15:28–29) in its requirements for non-Jewish believers in Christ. A final instruction is to establish a legal system that would presumably enforce the prohibitions. The medieval philosopher Maimonides adds that people must not only observe these edicts but that they must accept them as divinely revealed, that is, from God rather than natural law or reason. Jews do not require conversion to Judaism for an individual to be deemed righteous in the sight of God, only the practice of basic ethics. This means that God accepts Hindus, Buddhists, Muslims, and others as "good people," without their being Jewish. But Christians, with their incorporation of the entire Tanakh into their self-understanding, do not fall neatly into this category.

Michael Wyschogrod (1928–2015) considers this problem by reading Paul's letter to the Galatians anew. The Jewish philosopher argues that Paul sees the church as composed of Jewish and gentile believers in Christ, who live according to two sets of commandments—the complete Torah for Jews and the seven Noachide commandments for gentiles. This explains why Paul vociferously rejects Torah observance for non-Jews: conversion to Judaism is not necessary to be part of the people of God. Wyschogrod points to the debate in the church in Jerusalem described in Acts 15 about this very issue. On the one hand, Jews maintain their observance of the whole law of Moses. On the other, gentiles are instructed only to follow the minimal Noachide Law. All, however, believe in Jesus the Messiah.

But further, writes Wyschogrod on a number of occasions, Jewish converts to Christianity ought to remain observant Jews, even as they profess faith in Jesus. This is the practice of the early church

(Acts 21:20) and should be part of Christianity today. In return, Jews should clearly articulate the Noachide election of all gentiles and provide a place in the synagogue for Noachide converts—"not as Jews, but as gentiles who love and are obedient to the God of Israel who is also the God of all humankind."[33] The truth of Paul, remarks Wyschogrod, is that "the non-election of the gentiles cannot be as deep and permanent as Judaism has often assumed."[34] In other words, gentiles have a place in God's plan for Israel.

Greatly influenced by the Christian theologian Karl Barth, Wyschogrod develops a Jewish theology of Christian and Jewish relations grounded in scripture. Another Jewish scholar, David Novak—like Wyschogrod, very committed to, and influenced by, the dialogical project—justifies discourse with Christians on the basis of philosophy and postbiblical Jewish tradition.[35] Both Judaism and Christianity are based on revelatory events leading to truth claims that "are not only different but mutually exclusive."[36] In Novak's view, one worships God either by Torah or by Christ. Novak compares two philosophical orientations: that of Aristotle and that of Maimonides. The logic of Aristotle, called "potency-act," explains ordinary issues, while the logic of Maimonides, called "possibility-realization," illuminates significant metaphysical questions. With potency-act, potential events inevitably happen, whereas with possibility-realization, events may or may not occur. Novak concludes that the possibility-realization model offers "a greater role for God's direct and free action and a greater number of imaginable outcomes."[37] In plain language, the divine freedom to create whatever and whenever correlates with the human pluralism found in dialogue. According to Novak, acknowledging the autonomy of God allows members of different faith communities to understand, but not judge, each other.

Like Novak and Wyschogrod, Irving Greenberg (b. 1933) develops a positive Jewish theology of Christianity.[38] The longtime participant in interreligious dialogue sees God's will for perfecting and repairing the world with a second covenant in the rise of Christianity as a religion apart from Judaism. Both Judaism and

Christianity are outgrowths of the original biblical covenant, each interpreting it in their own way. But "only a religion less ethnically Jewish and with less distinctive observances could have spread so far," concludes the Orthodox rabbi.[59] Rather than seeing the emergence of Christianity as a mistake, Jews should see it as bringing the message of faith and ethics to those who would never have met a Jew or heard of the God of Israel. "Jews should bless God every day that Christianity existed and exists," he writes. Judaism has become a blessing to the nations through Christianity and its extension of the message of God's love to hundreds of millions. But, adds Greenberg, the accomplishments of Christianity are only made possible through the insights of Judaism. Therefore, "Christians should bless God every day that Judaism existed, and exists."[60]

Post-Holocaust Christian theologians and contemporary Jewish thinkers share the spirit of generosity and goodwill evident in Rabbi Greenberg's comments. There are many synonyms for generosity—kindness, unselfishness, graciousness, decency, and affection, to note just a few. Perhaps the word that best expresses the work of reconstructing theology is *grace*, which suggests freely given and quite possibly unmerited gifts. This grace is seen in the way that all parties, Christian and Jewish, relinquish destructive beliefs. Grace itself is a blessing to those engaged in dialogue. By sharing their views, they extend it to all Jews and Christians, who may then have a taste of deep equality in the present.

Part IV

PRESENT PROSPECTS

Chapter 11

ZIONISM AND EVANGELISM

The nation of Israel cannot be ignored; we see the Jews as a miracle of history.... What other people can trace their continuous unity back nearly 4,000 years?

—HAL LINDSEY[1]

Don't we American Jews experience a sense of heroic loneliness and alienation from the general society, whenever the problem of Israel comes up in a conversation, and we recognize the incommensurability of our viewpoint with that of the international political community?

—JOSEPH B. SOLOVEITCHIK[2]

Zionism and evangelism are two similar religious impulses driving in opposite directions. The desire to fulfill the will of God inspires Jews and Christians to action. But that will seems to lead to radically different places.

At its heart a nationalist movement, Zionism is the inward turn of the Jewish people to a permanent home—physically, emotionally, culturally, ethnically, spiritually, and in every other possible way. The notion of a return to the land "became a basic element of Jewish self-understanding and of the interpretation of their existence in exile."[3] It is an expectation grounded in the future rather than in the past.

In contrast, evangelism is the outward propulsion for Christians to go into the world to preach the gospel to all nations. "The world is my parish," proclaims John Wesley (1703–1791), the founder of Methodism. "In whatever part of it I am, I judge it meet, right, and my bounden duty to declare unto all that are willing to hear, the glad tidings of salvation."[4] In this regard, Franz Rosenzweig's symbol of the star of redemption, which depicts rays emanating from a central star, aptly symbolizes the movement of adherents of both faiths—toward the deepest center for Jews and toward the furthest periphery for Christians, both dwelling within God's kingdom according to their calling.

While it seems obvious that an ethnic group would want to claim its own territory—Kurdistan for Kurds, Tibet for Tibetans, Palestine for Palestinians, and Israel for the Jewish people—what is less obvious is why Christians would so strongly favor a Jewish homeland. Historical and geopolitical reasons provide part of the answer, but theological motivations, especially the missionary impulse, seem primary. Somewhat paradoxically, conversionary and triumphalistic incentives foster support for an independent Jewish state. The "Holy Land" for Christians signifies the biblical home of the Israelites, the physical home of Jesus's life, death, and resurrection, and, for prophecy-minded believers, the future site of Jesus's return. Messianic expectations merge in Jerusalem, creating a robust bond between Jewish and Christian Zionists.

Five positions within Christianity toward Israel seem to have emerged since the founding of the state of Israel in 1948. Post-Holocaust theologians offer unqualified affirmation of Israel and its policies, renouncing all missionary endeavors directed at Jews. Evangelical Christians deliver unreserved and generally uncritical loyalty, but it is in anticipation of the ultimate conversion of Jews. Liberal Protestants relinquish any attempts at proselytizing Jews but provide qualified endorsement, backing both Israeli and Palestinian claims. Vatican policies demonstrate the changing positions of the Roman Catholic Church—from refusing to recognize the state of Israel in 1948, to maintaining diplomatic relations beginning in the

1970s, to offering formal recognition in 1993. Finally, Orthodox Christians focus on the fact that their roots go back to first-century Palestine, and so their concern is for the protection of the centuries-old church and its adherents.

Christians have worked with Jews in the realization of a Jewish homeland for almost two hundred years, beginning in the early nineteenth century. While events of the twentieth and twenty-first centuries are not without controversy, they nevertheless contribute to the process of deep equality, although many—if not most—Palestinians would disagree. Christians continue to cooperate with Jews in supporting the state of Israel, although today that work does not seem sufficient to overcome the divisions between Israelis and Palestinians. This points to the fact that deep equality with peace and justice may well lie in the cooperation of Israelis and Palestinians, and not primarily in engagement between Jews and Christians.

The Jewish State and Its Early Supporters

In the twentieth century, Christians and Jews agitate for statehood on many fronts—religious, political, and popular. England is the prime target of activism, with its colonial interests in the Middle East and, after World War I, control of Palestine. The British elite, which includes wealthy Jews and Christians, influences Prime Minister David Lloyd George and his cabinet to take a sympathetic stance toward "Jewish Zionist aspirations." The famous Balfour Declaration of 1917—a short letter that Arthur James Balfour, the British Foreign Secretary, writes to Lord Lionel Walter Rothschild—simply states:

> His Majesty's Government view with favour the establishment in Palestine of a national home for the Jewish people, and will use their best endeavors to facilitate the achievement of this object, it being clearly understood

that nothing shall be done which may prejudice the civil and religious rights of existing non-Jewish communities in Palestine or the rights and political status enjoyed by Jews in any other country.[5]

The Balfour Declaration is the first of many official documents in which Jewish interests are pitted against those of the majority population living in Palestine.[6] A Palestine Mandate issued by the League of Nations in 1922 gives England official control of Palestine (thus, the British Mandate). A British white paper of 1939 clarifies what a "national home for the Jewish people" might actually mean. And in 1947, United Nations General Assembly Resolution 181 partitions the land of Palestine into two areas that are intended to become two separate nations: an "Arab State" and a "Jewish State." Although Israel accepts the terms of the U.N. resolution, Palestinians do not, and a civil war ensues, with Arab nations backing Palestinians. As a result, Jewish militants bypass the steps to statehood outlined in the resolution and declare an independent Israel on 14 May 1948, the day the British Mandate expires. The next day, a coalition of Arab forces enters Palestinian territory, and the first Arab-Israeli war begins. It concludes in 1949 with the signing of armistice agreements between Israel and its opponents—Egypt, Transjordan, Lebanon, and Syria. The war for independence displaces 700,000 Palestinians from their homes, and Arab nations expel 200,000 Jewish citizens in retaliation.

With independence, both Jews and Christians have to face the fact that others are already living in the Promised Land. The rallying cry "a land without a nation for a nation without a land," is more frequently expressed as "a land without a people for a people without a land," even though the land already has people living on it. A few Christian and Jewish visitors to Palestine, including the founder of Jewish Zionism Theodor Herzl (1860–1904), do recognize the fact that the land is inhabited, but it is not to their Eurocentric standards. "European and American travelers during the nineteenth century ... described the Holy Land in terms of a profound fall from grace."[7] Only a handful of early Zionists acknowledge the potential for conflict between new Jewish settlers and established Arab residents. Ahad Ha'am (Asher Ginzberg, 1856–1927) prophetically warns after his visit to Palestine in 1891 that "if the time comes when the life of our people in Eretz Israel develops to the point of encroaching upon the native population, they will not easily yield their place."[8]

Statehood for Israel brings the conflict between Jews and Palestinians to a head, and Christian support for Israel, if not for Jews, wavers as a result. While evangelizing the Jews has largely been a failure, missions to Arabs are much more successful. Protestant missionaries establish well-respected universities and schools throughout the Arab world. Although they are a minority within the Muslim Middle East, Arab Christians become important leaders in their communities. In fact, Arab nationalism has its roots in Christian missions, in part the result of increased opportunities for literacy and advanced education. All of these factors bolster Christian concern about Palestinians.

Not until World War II breaks out in 1939 do liberal Protestants, along with some Catholics, actively organize to ameliorate the threat that Nazism poses to Jews by encouraging unrestricted immigration to Palestine and to the United States. Under the leadership of prominent Protestant theologian Reinhold Niebuhr (1892–1971), the American Palestine Committee (APC) lobbies for the Zionist cause throughout the 1940s. Unique in that the group comprises liberal Protestant, rather than fundamentalist or dispensationalist Christians, the APC "endorsed Zionism for very different reasons: Christian guilt, humanitarian concern, and political pragmatism."[9] Although most Americans focus on winning the war, the APC continues to concentrate on relocating Jews to Palestine, with Niebuhr concluding that "a refuge, later a homeland, should be supported by Christians as a moral obligation due to the centuries of Jewish suffering at the hands of Christians."[10] In 1946, APC unites with another group to form the American Christian Palestine Committee (ACPC) and continues to press the Zionist cause. ACPC hails independence as a victory, noting at the same time "the coming Palestinian refugee problem would prevent some from offering their wholesale support to Israel."[11] Nevertheless, it is powerful Protestant and Jewish support that leads President Harry S Truman to make the United States the first nation in the world to grant de facto, or informal, recognition of Israeli statehood. The Soviet Union is the first to grant de jure, or legal, recognition.

Thus when war erupts again in 1967, Christian responses are mixed, ranging from condemnation of Israel's preemptive strike against its enemies to denunciation of the Arab League's threats "to wipe Israel off the face of the map."[12] The victory exhilarates Jews around the globe, who view Israel's situation as a potential second Holocaust. Israel's massive and decisive blitz in the Six-Day War in 1967 demonstrates that the little David can again defeat the giant Goliath. But for many Christians, the Six-Day War and the Yom Kippur War in 1973 reveal that Israel is no longer an idealized utopia ruled by King David, but rather an independent political entity operating in its own self-interest, just like any other country in the world. The neutral, or even antagonistic, position many churches take on the wars creates tensions in the blossoming interfaith discussions then occurring between Jews and Christians.

In November 1975, the United Nations General Assembly adopts Resolution 3379, which states that "Zionism is a form of racism and racial discrimination." (The U.N. General Assembly revokes Resolution 3379 in 1991.[13]) The response from churches is swift, with the U.N. vote evoking "a near unanimity of criticism from Christian spokesmen."[14] An American Jewish Committee survey shows not only the broad extent of outrage that American Christians express, but also indicates that Christians see the resolution as an articulation of antisemitism. "The leadership and masses of the Christian world ... have understood the terrifying seriousness of this massive, systematic campaign of Arab leadership to try to dehumanize Israel and the Jewish people," observes one Jewish leader in interfaith dialogue.[15] The responses come swiftly and spontaneously from denominational leadership, church bodies, local churches, campus ministries, individual clergy, academics, and religion journalists. Although some statements combine support for Israel's safety and security with recognition of Palestinian rights, the vast majority unambiguously denounce the U.N. resolution.

The Moral Necessity of Israel

Christian post-Holocaust theologians undoubtedly hold views about Israel that come closest to those of Jews. Disavowing all attempts at proselytizing, these theologians understand the political, social, and religious significance of Israel. Shortly after the 1967 war, Roy and Alice Eckardt (1923–2020) make "the case for Israel" in sympathetic terms, criticizing the silence of the churches in the face of the possible extermination of Israel.[16] The points in their case for Israel parallel those that Jewish and Israeli leaders make. They assert that "Palestine/Israel" is the original homeland of Jews and that the maintenance of a sovereign state "is morally justified by the countless years of oppression of the Jews."[17] In a follow-up article, the Eckardts argue for the "moral necessity" of Christians casting their lot publicly with Israel "in opposition to unceasing Arab exterminationism." Such support is required to atone for the historic crimes Christians have committed against the people Israel.[18]

Few post-Holocaust theologians, let alone mainstream Christians, are as supportive of Israel as the Eckardts. Nevertheless, their accusation of the silence of the churches in 1967 is only mildly overstated. Numerous clergy and other church leaders do issue statements of conscience in support of Israel prior to the armed conflict, but for the most part, church establishments remain ambivalent or silent.[19] An executive committee of the National Council of Churches (NCC), for example, adopts a six-point resolution that appears to be neutral but uses unmistakably pro-Arab rhetoric.[20]

The NCC inaugurates a group in 1969 to examine Jewish and Christian relations. First called the Israel Study Group, it eventually becomes known by the shorthand Christian Scholars Group (CSG).

Roman Catholic scholars join the discussions, and the National Conference of Catholic Bishops (NCCB) becomes a cosponsor with the NCC. The first topic on the agenda is "Israel: People, Land, State." When the NCC and NCCB can no longer fund the organization, the National Conference of Christians and Jews and the Daughters of Sion—a Catholic women's religious order devoted to promoting interreligious dialogue—pick up the tab for meetings and publications. The Center for Christian-Jewish Learning at Boston College hosts the CSG today. After the Yom Kippur War in 1973, the CSG issues a formal statement urging the churches to focus on questions concerning "the legitimacy of the Jewish state, the rights of the Palestinians, and the problem of the refugees—Jewish as well as Arab."[21] It goes on to affirm that the validity of Israel rests upon moral and legal grounds, yet it admits that many Christians understand Israel on theological, rather than political, bases.

JerUSAlem[22]

The position of evangelical Christians differs markedly from that of post-Holocaust theologians. If the 1967 war engenders a lukewarm response from mainstream churches, it electrifies conservative Christians. With Israel's capture of all of Jerusalem, the second step in a countdown to Armageddon has occurred.

Three key events involve Jews in the dispensationalist march to the Endtime.[23] The first is the rebirth of the Jewish nation in Palestine, which will trigger hostility and lead to an attack that sets the stage for the final world war. That rebirth occurs in 1948 with Israel's independence. The second is the possession of Jerusalem and its sacred sites in 1967. This is a necessary transition to the third and final event—rebuilding the temple. Hal Lindsey, one of the most influential of the dispensationalists, does admit that the Dome of the Rock on the Temple Mount presents a problem for this last step. "Obstacle or no obstacle, it is certain that the Temple will be rebuilt. Prophecy demands it."[24]

Lindsey and other evangelicals have no sympathy for Palestinians, whom they lump with Communists during the Cold War and link with terrorists today. With little understanding of Islam, they feel more affinity with Jews than with Muslims—religiously (seeing Muslims as idolators), culturally (seeing them as radically Other), and politically (believing that Muslims will play a destructive role in the Endtime scenario). "According to the Bible," writes Lindsey, "the Middle East crisis will continue to escalate until it threatens the peace of the whole world."[25]

In the dispensationalist worldview, Iran displaces Russia as the major threat to Israel's survival. This is the belief of Christians United for Israel (CUFI), begun in 2006 under the leadership of televangelist Rev. John Hagee. Claiming eight million members, CUFI's stated mission is to defend Israel and fight antisemitism. CUFI has many programs, including a weekly television show that airs on Fox Business News and Trinity Broadcasting Network, a film production company, financial support for student organizations on campuses to speak up for Israel, and sponsored trips for pastors to Israel. The organization is frequently described as the gentile arm of the American Israel Public Affairs Committee, a staunchly pro-Israel lobbying group.[26]

Once situated on the fringes of Evangelical Christianity, dispensationalist views such as Hagee's become popularized in the United States after the 1967 and 1973 wars, when Israel's existence is threatened. In the 1990s and early 2000s, the best-selling *Left Behind* series introduces millions of readers to the dispensationalist calendar and its vocabulary through its depictions of the Rapture, the Tribulation, Antichrist, and the Mark of the Beast.[27] Big-screen movies, paperback fiction, Christian radio and television broadcasting, and social media extend dispensationalist views far beyond their nineteenth-century beginnings and put Israel firmly on the eschatological map.

Christian Zionists who move to Israel go even further, living out their beliefs in the place where the Endtime begin. In 1970, for example, pietist and Reformed Christians from Europe create the

International Christian Embassy Jerusalem (ICEJ). When Israel passes the Jerusalem Law, which claims control of the entire city, most nations move their diplomatic facilities to Tel Aviv in protest. But ICEJ is created as "an act of sympathy and support for Israel on the part of true Christians at a time when even friendly or neutral countries betrayed her."[28] ICEJ abstains from proselytizing Jews and financially supports Israeli business initiatives and settlement of occupied territories—though the ICEJ and other Christians would not call it an occupation. "The notion that Israel is 'occupying' the West Bank and Gaza is anathema to today's evangelical Christian Zionists."[29] They believe in a Greater Israel that enlarges the Israeli state beyond the Green Line and into territories captured in the 1967 war.

Government officials welcome Christian Zionists to Israel. Then-Prime Minister Benjamin Netanyahu sends greetings on the thirtieth annual Feast of Tabernacles observance organized by ICEJ. U.S. House Republican leader Tom DeLay, an unwavering supporter of Israel, sings the national anthem of Israel at a Christian Coalition Rally in 2002, addresses the Knesset in 2003, and recites the Kaddish after an Israeli astronaut dies in the explosion on the space shuttle Columbia, also in 2003. Christian Zionists are dependable allies in a world full of antagonists. In the end, however, Jews, Judaism, and Israel will disappear for these Christians. "Despite professing such great love for Israel, dispensationalists embrace a story that leads to the destruction of Jews."[30] For now, Israelis seem disposed to accept that bargain. In the short term, they have vocal allies. They leave the long term up to God.

As part of their conversionist agenda, conservative Christians today nurture Messianic Jews. They see in Jewish acceptance of Yeshua (or Yahshua) as the promised Messiah a sign of the coming advent. Primarily shepherded by Protestant congregations, Messianic Jews are generally Jewish by birth, maintain Jewish practices such as rituals and holidays, utilize Jewish symbols such as the Star of David and the menorah, and see themselves as faithful Jews. These Jews continue to be observant, with the primary difference from their contemporaries being the conviction that Jesus is the promised Davidic king. Jews who adopt Jesus as the Messiah say they feel that they have "completed" or "fulfilled" their Judaism. A few Messianic Jews are Christian converts to Judaism who retain a commitment to Jesus as they practice Jewish traditions. Conservatives believe that the rise of a "Jewish church" is evidence of the approaching Endtime.

Messianic Jews differ from Jews for Jesus, a movement that emerges in the 1970s along with other new religions. Jews for Jesus appeals primarily to middle-class Jewish young adults who, like their non-Jewish peers, are seeking alternatives to their parents' religion. Liberal Protestants, as well as all kinds of Jews, do not favor this development. For liberals, it jeopardizes the newly emergent climate that fosters dialogue rather than conversion. For Jews, it signals yet another assimilationist project and thus annihilation of Judaism. A wave of anticonversionist pamphlets and books comes out, warning Jewish parents and their children of the danger. One advisory cautions against Christian missionaries in the starkest terms: "As vultures hovering and circling over thirsting bodies in the desert, they come with their tracts to the spiritual wastelands of suburbia, patiently waiting for the opportunity to snare yet another Jewish soul thirsting for Divinity."[31] The initial impetus of Jews for Jesus is indeed conversionary, but the movement of Messianic Jews changes considerably over the decades, with its members becoming less Christian in belief and more Jewish in practice.

Some Jewish scholars are advocating a new understanding of Messianic Jews, seeing Messianic Judaism as one among many expressions of Judaism. "Alongside Hasidim, Orthodox Judaism, Conservative Judaism, Reform Judaism, Reconstructionist Judaism, and Humanistic Judaism, Messianic Judaism offers a pathway through the Jewish heritage."[32] In the twenty-first century, Messianic Jews begin a process of disengagement from their evangelical patrons. A number of Messianic Jewish leaders assume the following core values at an annual theological conference at the end of the twentieth century:

The Jewish people are "us," not "them."

The richness of the rabbinic tradition is a valuable part of our heritage as Jewish people.

Messianic Judaism is a Judaism and not a cosmetically altered "Jewish style" version of what is extant in the wider Christianity community.[33]

Intense debate follows, both within the Messianic Jewish community and with evangelical benefactors. The current evangelical-messianic controversies seem to function as a type of family dispute, with Messianic Jews breaking away from their parents (Christian and Jewish) in new and unexpected ways.[34] Yet their belief in the divinity of Christ continues to put Messianic Jews outside the bounds of Judaism.[35]

What About Palestine?

While dispensationalists and Messianic Jews are problematic, apart from their support of Zionism, the most disquieting Christian friends of Israel—for Jews—remain mainline Protestants, Orthodox Christians, and, to a lesser extent, Catholics. Ironically, these are the people most likely to work professionally with Jews, to socialize with Jews, and to accept Judaism as a legitimate faith on its own terms. Church bodies have affirmed again and again the legitimacy of the state of Israel and have explicitly repudiated conversionary efforts. At the same time, they demand justice, including statehood, for Palestinians. A few denominations and organizations go so far as to endorse the Palestine Liberation Organization (PLO), chiefly in statements encouraging officials from Israel to negotiate with the PLO. Fewer still back the movement to boycott, divest, and sanction Israel (BDS), although national church councils have heated debates over BDS. Yet by far the majority of formal and informal declarations regarding the Israeli-Palestinian conflict feature a both/and position. Two paragraphs in a statement made by the Union of Evangelical Churches in Switzerland in 1979 make this clear:

> 6. We consider it the duty of the Christian Churches and all Christians to intervene in defence of the right to existence of the Jewish people, which is especially linked with us ... and to stand by Israel in her growing isolation.

> 7. We regard it also as a duty for Christian Churches and all Christians to intervene so that the right to live and the conditions of life of Palestinian Arabs be appreciated. In this connection we regard it as an urgent task to work out a clarification of the concept of "Palestinian" and to examine their possibility of self-determination.[36]

Missionary success in reaching the Arab world accounts, in part, for the pro-Palestinian tilt in many denominations, as does the influence of Arab Christians. In 1979, the American Jewish Committee analyzes anti-Israel influences in U.S. churches and finds four factors at work: missionary and relief programs directed at Arabs, the theology of liberation prevalent in the 1960s and 1970s, Eastern Rite Catholic and Orthodox churches that are primarily Arab in ethnicity, and institutional ties between denominations in the United States and the Arab churches.[37] In addition, sympathy for nationalist movements and for oppressed peoples marks the 1960s political counterculture—from the plight of African Americans in the United States to local populations in Asia, particularly Vietnam, and in Palestine, especially after the 1967 war. Mainline Protestant organizations, which believe engagement with the world on behalf of social justice is biblically mandated, tend to support progressive—and even radical—causes, which includes espousing a theology of the poor. Although Martin Luther King, Jr., is a vocal supporter of Israel, most African Americans come to identify with Palestinians—as people of color, as people they believe are dispossessed and, to some extent, as a result of antisemitic feelings.

The World Council of Churches, whose membership includes Eastern Rite Catholic and Eastern Orthodox churches in Arab countries, has taken the most provocative positions. Almost from its inception, the WCC has espoused a pro-Palestinian stance. The organization condemns violence, "whether perpetrated by the State of Israel inside the Occupied Palestinian Territories or by Palestinian armed groups inside the State of Israel."[38] Yet an examination of its official statements reveals Israeli aggression is condemned far more often than that of Palestinians. In a 2001 statement, the Central Committee of the WCC defends the second Intifada, declaring that "it is the right as much as the duty of an occupied people to struggle against injustice in order to gain freedom," adding, however, that nonviolent resistance is stronger and more efficient.[39] Yet the interdenominational body also advocates for international control of Jerusalem. When the Donald Trump administration recognizes Jerusalem as the capital of Israel in 2017, the WCC general secretary disapprovingly says that the step breaks with almost seventy years of U.S. policy.[40]

The status of Jerusalem is one of the sticking points that the Vatican has in its initial refusal to recognize Israel's independent status in 1948. Jews are disappointed that *Nostra Aetate* fails to mention the state of Israel. Nevertheless, de facto diplomatic relations exist between the Vatican and Israel beginning in the 1970s. In 1974, Pope Paul VI becomes the first pope to visit Jerusalem. But he adopts a distinctly nonpolitical stance in his trip, billing it simply as a visit to the Holy Land rather than a diplomatic mission. Meanwhile, Lebanese Catholic bishops seek the intervention of the world's Catholic bishops in 1974 on behalf of the Palestinian refugees living in Lebanon, and Maronite Catholics repeatedly pressure the Holy See to intervene in the Lebanese civil war (1975–1990).

The Vatican's approach to Israel in particular, and Jews and Judaism in general, improves dramatically under the papacy of John Paul II (p. 1978–2005). His 1984 apostolic letter *Redemptionis Anno* (Year of Redemption) anticipates the formal recognition of Israel to come later.[41] In the letter, the pope clearly states:

> For the Jewish people who live in the State of Israel and who preserve in that land such precious testimonies to their history and their faith, we must ask for the desired security and the due tranquility that is the prerogative of every nation and condition of life and of progress for every society.[42]

Although the pope desires the internationalization of Jerusalem, he eventually signs a "Fundamental Agreement" with Israel in 1993. In essence, the pact guarantees the Catholic Church certain rights in Israel and eradicates the possibility of theological arguments that might be made against the legitimacy of a Jewish state.[43] The pope also expresses sympathy numerous times for the "heavy sufferings for the Palestinian population" and meets with PLO leader Yasser Arafat at least twice. *Redemptionis Anno* balances the paragraph on Jewish rights with a paragraph on Palestinian rights:

> The Palestinian people, who find their historical roots in that land and who, for decades, have been dispersed, have the natural right in justice to find once more a homeland and to be able to live in peace and tranquility with the other peoples of the area.[44]

Jews may well despair over the mixed signals from liberal Protestants and Roman Catholics regarding the state of Israel: Yes to Israel; but Yes to Palestine as well. Moreover, Jews feel that the criticism of Israel goes beyond policy issues. "The use of double standards—harsher judgments and stricter demands made on Israel than on her Arab antagonists" is a fair description of the situation in 1979, according to a survey of American churches conducted by the American Jewish Committee, and remains true today.[45] A statement made by the Reformed Church in Holland illuminates the problem: "The Jewish people are called to exercise justice in an exemplary way. This ... is an essential aspect of their true identity." The Church's 1970 statement urges Israel not to be like other nations, but rather to shoulder the burden of Palestinian refugees. "It belongs to Israel's vocation that it should know itself to be responsible for them and that it should do all it can to put right the injustice done to them."[46] This captures the theological and political dilemma that liberals present to Jews.

Evangelicals and Christian Zionists also hold Israel to a different standard, believing in the "divinely ordained connection between the Jewish people and the land."[47] Rather than seeing the conflict between Israel and Palestine as the rivalry between two geopolitical entities with competing claims, Evangelicals regard it as "a contest over whether or not the word of God is true."[48] It is a supernatural, rather than secular, fight. The uncritical acceptance of policies regarding occupied territories and expansion indicates that Evangelicals do not hold Israel accountable as they might other nations. They, too, have a double standard, though it is more sympathetic to Israel than that of their liberal counterparts.

Cooperating for Peace and Equality

Christians have assisted the state of Israel in multiple ways: financially, politically, and morally. While American Jews may think this help is insufficient, Israelis have been grateful. Yet Jewish and Christian cooperation in support of either Israel or Palestine may not ensure safety and security as much as programs that bring Israelis and Palestinians together in face-to-face encounters. Many groups are attempting to resolve the tensions in such collaboration. Some focus on religious issues, such as Muslim–Jewish dialogue; some concentrate on nationalist issues, such as Palestinian and

Israeli peaceful engagement; and some emphasize single issues of joint concern, such as the environment or health. Cooperation is a key component of all of these endeavors.

The experiences of Rami Elhanan and Basaam Aramin exemplify cooperation at its deepest and most personal level. Both men lose their daughters to political violence—Elhanan's daughter to a Palestinian suicide bomber and Aramin's daughter to Israeli Defense Forces. Independently the two fathers join the Parents Circle-Families Forum. The PCFF is a joint program of more than 600 Palestinian and Israeli families who, having lost immediate family members, come together to promote dialogue, reconciliation, and peace.[49] The novel *Apeirogon*, by Colum McCann (2020), recounts the story of Elhanan and Aramin and the friendship that develops out of their shared losses. In a thousand short chapters, the book also hints at the infinite number of perspectives on the Israeli-Palestinian conflict. (An apeirogon is a polygon with an infinite number of sides—so many that it may look like a circle.) PCFF is just one of a number of organizations that bring Palestinians and Israelis together in common cause.

The most encouraging signs of peace are being negotiated on a daily basis by Israelis and Palestinians in direct contact with each other rather than by their friends and allies abroad, although mediation efforts by third-party intermediaries have been valuable. Like the historical case of Christians and Jews collaborating on the publication of shared religious texts, the present situation may be improved when Israelis and Palestinians team up on joint projects. The intense concern that Christians in North America and Europe express for their coreligionists and Jews in the Middle East is understandable but may not be helpful in the long run. This is true as well for Jews and Muslims living outside of Israel and Palestine. It is only through the ordinary, daily negotiation of difference, neighbor to neighbor, that deep equality can emerge.

Chapter 12

FINDING DEEP EQUALITY IN JEWISH AND CHRISTIAN RELATIONS

As Christians and Jews, following the example of the faith of Abraham, we are called to be a blessing to the world. This is the common task awaiting us. It is therefore necessary for us, Christians and Jews, to be first a blessing to one another.

—POPE JOHN PAUL II, ON THE FIFTIETH ANNIVERSARY OF THE WARSAW UPRISING, 1993[1]

The theoretical underpinnings of deep equality are clear: recognition of similarity and acceptance of difference, acknowledgment of complex identity, cooperation and neighborliness, repentance and forgiveness, and agonistic respect and generosity. These elements operate in dynamic tension with the reality of the human condition, which the expression complex identity captures. The notion of complexity serves as a check to both self-righteousness and self-abasement, as people holding different beliefs negotiate everyday relationships. "In some measure deep equality as it is practised in everyday life is everywhere once we are attuned to it," writes Lori Beaman. "The problem is to reorient one's framework to see it, and then to reflect more carefully on how it is achieved."[2]

Utilizing the vocabulary of deep equality, I have attempted to reorient the framework for considering Jewish and Christian relations. Instances of cooperation in biblical studies abound. Analyses of Jesus and Paul—who they were and what they taught—reveal not only significant differences between Jews and Christians but also many more similarities than most of the faithful would think. The Renaissance project of publishing religious literature in the original languages and in translation not only brings Jews and Christians together in common cause but has proven fruitful well into the twenty-first century. The distinctions that Christians and Jews take for granted develop over many centuries. The religious exclusivity we presume today is a modern development, not necessarily applicable in all times or all places.

This work toward deep equality progresses in the shadow of the Shoah. Was it only a catastrophe of this magnitude that could shake Christians out of their centuries-old contempt for Jews and Judaism? For whatever theological, metaphysical, or moral reasons, many churches and individual Christians are pierced with compunction over what happens to Jews in the Holocaust. Prompted by their own consciences, and with the help of Jews who have the courage to engage in dialogue, they examine the history of Christianity and its relationship with its nearest kin—those who also worship the God of Israel. As a consequence, they repent of sins of commission and omission in public statements and, more importantly, begin to institute actual reform of educational and liturgical materials. Listening without self-justification but not relinquishing faith commitments, and hearing without contradiction but accepting the importance of the other's faith commitments—these are the elements of agonistic respect that mark the dialogue process.

Deep equality does not mean sameness. "The quest for sameness," observes Beaman, can easily "produce injustices by erasing or ignoring differences that are important to individual, community, and group identities."[3] Recognizing similarity but accepting difference at the same time skirts the seductiveness of the quest for social cohesion and harmony, which are often achieved at the price of coercion or denial. It is important to note that deep equality does not imply that all religions or beliefs are equivalent, nor does it admit any suggestion of superiority or inferiority, of tolerance or sufferance. Rather, it illuminates the path to friendship between and among people holding radically different existential commitments. Rabbi Joseph Soloveitchik's admonition for Christians and Jews to engage at a mundane human level, rather than at a sophisticated theological level, seems helpful here. The usefulness of this approach for interreligious dialogue is self-evident, but it also appears that deep equality may be a way to work through other areas of difference—political, social, cultural, ethnic, gender, and racial.

Because historians focus on the conflict and competition that undeniably comprise the history of Jewish and Christian relations, they neglect the moments and eras marked by partnership and trust. This results in an inaccurate portrayal of both Christianity and Judaism. Although the study of Jewish and Christian relations is part of the larger examination of the history of the two faiths, it is also its own area of investigation.

What would the field of Jewish and Christian relations look like as an academic subject? The work of Sir Edward Kessler models this discipline. The British scholar writes prolifically on the topic, most notably the co-edited *Dictionary of Jewish-Christian Relations* and the textbook *Introduction to Jewish-Christian Relations*.[4] His scholarship is wide-ranging, however, and includes a biography of Claude Montefiore, an examination of Jewish and Christian interpretations of the Bible, an anthology of readings in English Liberal Judaism, and several co-edited volumes on themes and challenges to Jewish and Christian relations. While Kessler has recently turned his attention to Jewish, Christian, and Muslim dialogue, he continues to concentrate on the study of Jews and Christians.

Many institutions and organizations currently exist to promote the academic study of Jewish and Christian Relations, along with interreligious dialogue. Two of the oldest include the Institute of Judaeo-Christian Studies at Seton Hall University, founded in 1953, and the Dialogue Institute at Temple University, founded in 1978, which publishes *The Journal of Ecumenical Studies*. The Council of Centers on Jewish-Christian Relations is a network of groups throughout North America and abroad dedicated to advancing scholarship in the field. The discipline has developed far beyond what this brief list suggests.

Part of the difficulty in developing a counter-narrative to the master story of Jewish and Christian conflict is that research tends to utilize texts rather than other data. Thus, official church pronouncements and papal edicts, written reports by Jews undergoing persecution, and other documents largely comprise the accepted historical narrative. The stories of non-conflicts, in which Jews and Christians live side by side without being much interested in the other, are missing.[5] How can we describe something for which no apparent evidence exists? Church historian Wolfram Kinzig offers a few guideposts. Archaeological data, for example, such as inscriptions, buildings, artifacts, and other tangible items, are already telling a different story. In addition, social history, such as tax records, guild membership lists, construction permits, travelogues, and so on, also provide alternative data to religious and polemical texts from either side.

An example of the kind of microhistory Kinzig envisions might be historian Daniel Jütte's analysis of the memoir of a sixteenth-century merchant from Swabia in southern Germany. Hans Ulrich Krafft (1550–1621) demonstrates an instance of companionship between a Christian and Jews.[6] Krafft's diary, written five years before he dies, recounts the experiences the devout Lutheran has with several Jews over the course of his life. At one point, Krafft is imprisoned in Tripoli, where a Jew befriends him, securing him employment and even returning to prison to provide additional help. The Christian merchant then becomes friends with another Swabian—a "fellow countryman," in his words—who happens to be Jewish. Mayer Winterbach also aids Krafft on several occasions and, despite the Lutheran's expressed antipathy to Jews, the two develop a friendship that leads to several reunions over the course of Krafft's life.

Jütte argues that the history of tolerance and friendship is rarely studied from the bottom up, that is, from the actual experiences of real people. Usually the emphasis begins at the top, with a focus on social policy, legislation, and judicial decisions. And though Jütte is not expressly concerned with deep equality, he does observe that Christians tend to defend Jews when they have familiarity and close relationships with them. The historian also admits dissatisfaction with the premise that "when Jews and Christians met, they did so primarily as 'Jew' and as 'Christian' rather than as individuals embedded in a multifaceted reality."[7] Implicit in Jütte's admission is the notion of complex identity. Jütte, Kinzig, and many other scholars are opening doors—and minds—to alternative ways of seeing the shared history of Christians and Jews.

Rather than remaining stuck in the master narrative of unremitting Jewish sorrow and unrelenting Christian torment, I have shifted attention to people, events, activities, and eras characterized by elements of deep equality. While there has always been a counter-narrative, we have not always looked for it.[8] This is particularly understandable today, given the global upsurge in antisemitic activity. Yet we need to consider instances of everyday humanity, visible every day in news accounts of Jews helping Christians, Christians helping Jews, and members of the two religions teaming up to help others.

When we dig deeper, a compelling story unfolds. It is not completely at odds with the master narrative, but neither does it entirely confirm it. We find noteworthy examples throughout history of the ways in which Jews have shaped Christianity and in which Christians have influenced Rabbinic Judaism. Positive interactions are mutually beneficial—from the study of the Bible to uniting for social justice. This is nowhere more apparent than in the postwar era of Jewish and Christian dialogue in the twentieth century, which replaces hostility and misunderstanding with warmth and appreciation. That dialogue remains ongoing in the twenty-first century, as evidenced by continuing reflection and statements concerning Jewish and Christian relations and cooperation on interfaith projects.

But neither the master narrative nor the countervailing account is the end of the story. The dialogue has created surprising unanimity between Jewish and Christian scholars on one important issue: eschatology. Christian belief in the return of Christ and the Last Judgment, and Jewish faith in a coming Messiah or Messianic Age, make up the eschatological hope for each. However it is envisioned, eschatology always points to a future that God, rather than humans, determines. This future orientation allows for openness to others in the present, in the expectation that "all differences of faith between all humans will be overcome at last in a final divine act of redemption of Israel, of humankind, indeed of the entire created universe."⁹ This anticipation of the end avoids the problem of relativism. For believers, opposing claims to truth remain unresolved and mutually exclusive until God intervenes once and for all. Jews remain Jews, and Christians remain Christians, each appointed their own tasks under their own covenants. Therefore, each can agree that "it is God alone who will bring us to our unknown destination in a time pleasing to him."¹⁰

Indeterminacy in the face of God the absolute, as opposed to religious relativism, can be called a concluding element of deep equality. It connotes a state of living in the between-times, somewhere between creation and consummation for Jews and Christians. Indeterminacy is another way of admitting that the ultimate cannot be known absolutely in the present. As Paul the apostle says of the future, "For now we see in a mirror, dimly, but then we will see face to face" (1 Corinthians 13:12 NRSV). Writing two thousand years later, Abraham Joshua Heschel asserts, "The world in which we live is a mere supposition or hypothesis. The conclusion is still to come."¹¹

We don't know how the story ends. In fact, there are many stories, not only those recounted by Christians and Jews, but those of Hindus and Muslims and unbelievers and many others. Nevertheless, Jews and Christians are bound together by a common text, a shared past, and a mutual hope. For them, there is a story that awaits its ending.

NOTES

Introduction

1 Wolfram Kinzig, "Closeness and Distance: Towards a New Description of Jewish-Christian Relations," *Jewish Studies Quarterly* 10, no. 3 (2003): 290.

2 Bence Illyés, "A Jewish Cemetery in Hungary, Restored by a Christian," *Forward,* 16 October 2020, https://forward.com/author/bence-illyes/, retrieved 15 July 2021.

3 Loumay Alesali and Christina Zdanowicz, "A Jewish Synagogue Opened Its Doors to a Christian Congregation after Its Church Burned on Christmas," CNN, 14 March 2019, https://www.cnn.com/2019/03/14/us/synagogue-church-service-after-fire-trnd/index.html, retrieved 15 July 2021.

4 Greg Garrison, "Church Burned on Christmas Moves to Synagogue," *Alabama Life,* 12 March 2019, https://www.al.com/life/2019/03/church-burned-on-christmas-moves-to-synagogue.html, retrieved 15 July 2021.

5 Deborah E. Lipstadt, *Antisemitism Here and Now* (New York: Schocken, 2019).

6 I am following the current practice of spelling *antisemitism* without a hyphen. See, e.g., Lipstadt, 22–25.

7 Jules Isaac, *The Teaching of Contempt: Christian Roots of Anti-Semitism,* trans. Helen Weaver (New York: Holt, Rinehart and Winston, 1964).

8 Disputing that rosy assessment are David Engel, "Crisis and Lachrymosity: On Salo Baron, Neobaronianism, and the Study of Modern European Jewish History," *Jewish History* 20, no. 3/4 (2006): 243–264; and Adam Teller, "Revisiting Baron's 'Lachrymose Conception': The Meanings of Violence in Jewish History," *AJS Review* 38, no. 2 (November 2014): 431–439.

9   Jacques Berlinerblau, "On Philo-Semitism," *Occasional Papers—Jewish Civilization: The Importance of Discussing Philo-Semitism,* Georgetown University (Winter 2007): 8.

10 David S. Katz, "The Phenomenon of Philo-Semitism," in *Christianity and Judaism: Papers Read at the 1991 Summer Meeting and 1992 Winter Meeting of the Ecclesiastical History Society,* ed. D. Wood (Oxford, UK: Blackwell, 1992), 360.

11 Alan Edelstein, *An Unacknowledged Harmony: Philo-Semitism and the Survival of European Jewry* (Westport, CT: Greenwood Press, 1982), 13.

12 For example, Solomon Rappaport, *Jew and Gentile: The Philo-Semitic Aspect* (New York: Philosophical Library, 1980); William D. Rubinstein and Hilary L. Rubinstein, *Philosemitism: Admiration and Support in the English-Speaking World for Jews, 1840–1939* (New York: St. Martin's Press, 1999); and Edelstein, *An Unacknowledged Harmony.*

13 For example, Hans Joachim Schoeps, *Philosemitismus im Barock* (Tübingen: Mohr, 1952); David S. Katz, *Philo-Semitism and the Readmission of the Jews to England, 1603–1655* (Oxford, UK: Clarendon Press, 1982); Frank Stern, *The Whitewashing of the Yellow Badge: Antisemitism and Philosemitism in Postwar Germany,* trans. William Templer (New York: Pergamon, 1992); and Rebecca Shapiro, *"The Other Anti-Semitism: Philo-Semitism in Eighteenth- and Nineteenth-Century English Literature and Culture"* (Ph.D. dissertation, Purdue University, 1997).

14 Some books include: Irving Massey, *Philo-Semitism in Nineteenth-Century German Literature* (Tübingen: Niemeyer, 2000); Tony Kushner and Nadia Valman, eds., *Philosemitism, Antisemitism, and 'the Jews': Perspectives from the Middle Ages to the Twentieth Century* (New York: Routledge, 2004); Phyllis Lassner and Lara Trubowitz, eds., *Antisemitism and Philosemitism in the Twentieth and Twenty-First Centuries: Representing Jews, Jewishness, and Modern Culture* (Newark, DE: University of Delaware Press, 2008); Irene A. Diekmann and Elke-Vera Kotowski, eds., *Geliebter Feind, Gehasster Freund: Antisemitismus und Philosemitismus in Geschichte und Gegenwart* [Beloved Enemy, Hated Friend: Antisemitism and Philosemitism in Past and Present] (Berlin: Verlag Berlin Brandenburg, 2009); Jonathan Karp and Adam Sutcliffe, eds., *Philosemitism in History* (New York: Cambridge University Press, 2011); and David J. Wertheim,

ed. *The Jew as Legitimation: Jewish-Gentile Relations Beyond Antisemitism and Philosemitism* (New York: Palgrave Macmillan, 2017). See especially, Edward Kessler and Neil Wenborn, eds., *A Dictionary of Jewish-Christian Relations* (Cambridge, UK: Cambridge University Press, 2005) and Edward Kessler, *Introduction to Jewish-Christian Relations* (Cambridge, UK: Cambridge University Press, 2010).

15 Lori G. Beaman, *Deep Equality in an Era of Religious Diversity* (New York: Oxford University Press, 2017), 3.

16 Beaman, 129.

17 Beaman, 13.

18 Beaman, 11, 65; Jacques Derrida, "Avowing—The Impossible: 'Returns,' Repentance, and Reconciliation. A Lesson," in *Living Together: Jacques Derrida's Communities of Violence and Peace,* ed. Elisabeth Weber, trans. Gil Anidjar, 18–41 (New York: Fordham University Press, 2013). Thanks go to Lori Beaman for alerting readers to this essay.

19 Beaman, 78. Beaman develops the concept of contaminated diversity introduced by Anna Tsing in "Contaminated Diversity in 'Slow Disturbance': Potential Collaborators for a Liveable Earth," in *Why Do We Value Diversity? Biocultural Diversity in a Global Context,* ed. Gary Martin, Diana Mincyte, and Ursula Munsters, 95–97 (Munich: Rachel Carson Perspectives, 2012) and *The Mushroom at the End of the World: On the Possibility of Life in Capitalist Ruins* (Princeton, NJ: Princeton University Press, 2015).

20 Mark Krupnick, "The Rhetoric of Philosemitism," in *Rhetorical Invention and Religious Inquiry: New Perspectives,* ed. Walter Jost and Wendy Olmsted (New Haven, CT: Yale University Press, 2000), 357.

21 Bo Lidegaard, *Countrymen,* trans. Robert Maas (London: Atlantic Books, 2014), 20.

22 Lidegaard, 114.

23 Beaman, 93. For the concept of agonistic respect Beaman draws upon the work of William E. Connolly, *Neuropolitics: Thinking, Culture, Speed* (Minneapolis, MN: University of Minnesota Press, 2002).

24 Alan T. Levenson, "Writing the Philosemitic Novel: Daniel Deronda Revisited," *Prooftexts* 28, no. 2 (Spring 2008): 131.

25 Zygmunt Bauman, "Allosemitism: Premodern, Modern, Postmodern," in *Modernity, Culture and "the Jew,"* ed. Bryan Cheyette and Laura Marcus (Stanford, CA: Stanford University Press, 1998), 143.

Chapter 1. The Bible: Barrier and Bridge

1   Michael Wyschogrod, "Incarnation and God's Indwelling in Israel," in *Abraham's Promise: Judaism and Jewish-Christian Relations* (Grand Rapids, MI: Eerdmans, 2004), 167.

2   Amy-Jill Levine and Marc Zvi Brettler, *The Bible With and Without Jesus: How Jews and Christians Read the Same Stories Differently* (New York: HarperOne, 2020).

3   Claire Huchet Bishop, "Response to John Pawlikowski," in *Auschwitz: Beginning of a New Era? Reflections on the Holocaust,* ed. Eva Fleischner (New York: Ktav Publishing, Cathedral Church of St. John the Divine, and Anti-Defamation League of B'nai B'rith, 1977), 187.

4   André Lacoque, "The 'Old Testament' in the Protestant Tradition," in *Biblical Studies: Meeting Ground of Jews and Christians,* ed. Lawrence Boadt, C.S.P., Helga Croner, and Leon Klenicki, 120–143 (New York: Paulist Press, 1980).

5   Beryl Smalley, "Stephen Langton and the Four Senses of Scripture," *Speculum* 6, no. 1 (January 1931): 60.

6   Levine and Brettler, *The Bible With and Without Jesus,* 30, paraphrasing Michael Fishbane's commentary on the Song of Songs (Philadelphia: Jewish Publication Society, 2015).

7   Benedict de Spinoza [Baruch de Spinoza], *A Theologico-Political Treatise,* in *A Theologico-Political Treatise and A Political Treatise,* trans. R.H.M. Elwes (New York: Dover, 1951).

8   Jon D. Levenson, *The Hebrew Bible, the Old Testament, and Historical Criticism* (Louisville, KY: Westminster/John Knox, 1993).

9   Jorge Mejia, "A Christian View of Bible Interpretation," in Boadt, Croner, and Klenicki, *Biblical Studies,* 49.

10 Samuel Sandmel, *Anti-Semitism in the New Testament?* (Philadelphia: Fortress Press, 1978), 125–126.

11 Pontifical Biblical Commission, *The Interpretation of the Bible in the Church* (23 April 1993), http://catholic-resources.org/ChurchDocs/PBC_Interp-FullText.htm, retrieved 15 July 2021.

12 Jon D. Levenson, *The Hebrew Bible, the Old Testament, and Historical Criticism,* 69.

13 Pope Paul VI, *Dogmatic Constitution on Divine Revelation (Dei Verbum)*, 18 November 1965, in *Vatican Council II: The Conciliar and Post Conciliar Documents*, Vol. 1, rev. ed., ed. Austin Flannery, O.P. (Northport, NY: Costello Publishing, 1992), 755.

14 Pope Paul VI, *Dogmatic Constitution on Divine Revelation*, 756.

15 Bishop Kallistos Ware, *The Orthodox Way*, rev. ed. (Crestwood, NY: St. Vladimir's Seminary Press, 1995), 110, italics in original.

16 Sarah J. Tanzer, "The Problematic Portrayal of 'the Jews' and Judaism in the Gospel of John: Implications for Jewish-Christian Relations," in *Contesting Texts: Jews and Christians in Conversation about the Bible,* ed. Melody D. Knowles, Esther Menn, John Pawlikowski, O.S.M., and Timothy J. Sandoval, 103–118 (Minneapolis: Fortress Press, 2007).

17 Asher Finkel, "Scriptural Interpretation: A Historical Perspective," in *Evangelicals and Jews in Conversation on Scripture, Theology, and History*, ed. Marc H. Tanenbaum, Marvin R. Wilson, and A. James Rudin (Grand Rapids, MI: Baker Book House, 1978), 149–150.

18 Michael J. Cook, "The Bible and Catholic-Jewish Relations," in *Twenty Years of Jewish-Catholic Relations,* ed. Eugene J. Fisher, A. James Rudin, and Marc H. Tanenbaum (New York: Paulist Press, 1986), 112.

19 Willis Barnstone, *The Restored New Testament* (New York: W. W. Norton, 2009), 222.

20 Monika Hellwig, "From the Jesus Story to the Christ of Dogma," in *Antisemitism and the Foundations of Christianity,* ed. Alan T. Davies (New York: Paulist Press, 1979), 119.

21 David Tracy, "Religious Values After the Holocaust: A Catholic View," in *Jews and Christians After the Holocaust,* ed. Abraham J. Peck (Philadelphia: Fortress Press, 1982), 94.

22 A. Roy Eckardt, "End to the Christian-Jewish Dialogue: I. Contradictions in Catholic and Protestant Attitudes," *Christian Century* 83, no. 12 (23 March 1966), 362.

23 Wyschogrod, "Incarnation and God's Indwelling in Israel," 167.

24 Tikva Frymer-Kensky, David Novak, Peter Ochs, David Fox Sandmel, and Michael Signer, "*Dabru Emet*: A Jewish Statement on Christians and Christianity," in *Christianity in Jewish Terms*, ed.

Tikva Frymer-Kensky, David Novak, Peter Ochs, David Fox Sand-mel, and Michael Signer (Boulder, CO: Westview Press, 2000), xvi.

25 Levine and Brettler, *The Bible With and Without Jesus,* 421.

Chapter 2. Jesus the Jew

1 A. Roy Eckardt, *Elder and Younger Brothers: The Encounter of Jews and Christians* (New York: Charles Scribner's Sons, 1967), 142.

2 Amy-Jill Levine, *The Misunderstood Jew: The Church and the Scandal of the Jewish Jesus* (New York: HarperCollins, 2006), 6.

3 Albert Schweitzer, *The Quest of the Historical Jesus: A Critical Study of Its Progress from Reimarus to Wrede,* trans. William Montgomery (Tübingen: Mohr Siebeck, 1906; reprint Macmillan Publishing, 1968).

4 Susannah Heschel, *Abraham Geiger and the Jewish Jesus* (Chicago: University of Chicago Press, 1998), 1.

5 Susannah Heschel, 9.

6 Yaakov Ariel, "Christianity Through Reform Eyes: Kaufmann Kohler's Scholarship on Christianity," *American Jewish History* 89, no. 2 (June 2001): 189.

7 Annette Yoshiko Reed, "Messianism Between Judaism and Christianity," in *Rethinking the Messianic Idea in Judaism,* ed. Michael L. Morgan and Steven Weitzman, 23–62 (Bloomington: Indiana University Press, 2014), 42.

8 Susannah Heschel, 136.

9 Neta Stahl, "Jesus as the New Jew: Zionism and the Literary Repre-sentation of Jesus," *Journal of Modern Jewish Studies* 11, no. 1 (March 2012): 1–23.

10 Stahl, 5. Susannah Heschel has a different view of Klausner, 236.

11 Harry A. Wolfson, "Introductory," in Joseph Jacobs, *Jesus as Others Saw Him: A Retrospect A.D. 54,* (New York: Bernard G. Richards, 1925), n.p.

12 See, e.g., Joseph C. Weber, "Karl Barth and the Historical Jesus," *Journal of Bible and Religion* 32, no. 4 (October 1964): 350–354; and Paul E. Capetz, "The Old Testament as a Witness to Jesus Christ: Historical Criticism and Theological Exegesis of the Bible accord-

ing to Karl Barth," *Journal of Religion,* 90, no. 4 (October 2010): 475–506.

13 Rudolf Bultmann, *Jesus Christ and Mythology* (London: SCM Press, 1960; reprint SCM Press, 2012); and idem, *New Testament Mythology and Other Basic Writings,* trans. and ed. Schubert M. Ogden (Philadelphia: Fortress Press, 1984).

14 James Carleton Paget, "Quests for the Historical Jesus," in *The Cambridge Companion to Jesus,* ed. Markus Bockmuehl (New York: Cambridge University Press, 2001), 147.

15 E.P. Sanders, *Jesus and Judaism* (Philadelphia: Fortress Press, 1985), 267.

16 Sanders, *Jesus and Judaism,* 40.

17 See the articles in the "Special Section on Feminist Anti-Judaism" in *Journal of Feminist Studies in Religion* 7, no. 2 (Fall 1991).

18 Heschel, 148–150.

19 C.G. Montefiore, *Some Elements of the Religious Teaching of Jesus According to the Synoptic Gospels* (London: Macmillan, 1910; reprint Arno Press, 1973), 45.

20 Hyam Maccoby, *Jesus the Pharisee* (London: SCM Press, 2003), 192–193.

21 Harvey Falk, *Jesus the Pharisee: A New Look at the Jewishness of Jesus* (New York: Paulist Press, 1985), 8.

22 Samuel Sandmel, *A Jewish Understanding of the New Testament* (Cincinnati, OH: Alumni Association of the Hebrew Union College–Jewish Institute of Religion, 1956; 3rd ed. reprint Jewish Lights Publishing, 2005), xv.

23 Sandmel, *A Jewish Understanding of the New Testament,* 198.

24 Samuel Sandmel, *We Jews and Jesus: Exploring Theological Differences for Mutual Understanding* (New York: Oxford University Press, 1965; reprint Jewish Lights Publishing, 2006), xv.

25 Sandmel, *We Jews and Jesus,* 110.

26 Geza Vermes, *Jesus the Jew: A Historian's Reading of the Gospels* (Philadelphia: Fortress Press, 1973), 83.

27 Vermes, *Jesus the Jew,* 225, italics in original.

28 Amy-Jill Levine, *Short Stories by Jesus: The Enigmatic Parables of a Controversial Rabbi* (New York: HarperOne, 2014), 23.

29 Paula Fredriksen, *Jesus of Nazareth, King of the Jews: A Jewish Life and the Emergence of Christianity* (New York: Vintage Books, 1999), 124.

30 Daniel Boyarin, *The Jewish Gospels: The Story of the Jewish Christ* (New York: The New Press, 2012).

31 Boyarin, *The Jewish Gospels,* 57.

32 Daniel Boyarin, *Border Lines: The Partition of Judaeo-Christianity* (Philadelphia: University of Pennsylvania Press, 2004), 128–147.

33 Reed, 36.

34 David Van Biema, "#10: Re-Judaizing Jesus," *Time Magazine* (13 March 2008), at http://content.time.com/time/specials/2007/article/0,28804,1720049_1720050_1721663,00.html, retrieved 15 July 2021.

35 Peter Schäfer, *Two Gods in Heaven: Jewish Concepts of God in Antiquity* (Princeton, NJ: Princeton University Press, 2020); Daniel Boyarin, "The Gospel of the Memra: Jewish Binitarianism and the Prologue to John," *Harvard Theological Review* 94, no. 3 (July 2001): 243–284; and idem, *Border Lines,* 128–147.

36 Jonathan D. Brumberg-Kraus, "A Jewish Ideological Perspective on the Study of Christian Scripture," *Jewish Social Studies,* New Series, 4, no. 1 (Autumn 1997), 128.

37 Brumberg-Kraus, 133.

38 Amy-Jill Levine and Marc Zvi Brettler, eds., *The Jewish Annotated New Testament,* 2nd ed. rev. (New York: Oxford University Press, 2017).

39 Lori G. Beaman, *Deep Equality in an Era of Religious Diversity* (New York: Oxford University Press, 2017), 58, 62.

40 Levine, *The Misunderstood Jew,* 6.

Chapter 3. The Problem of Paul

1 Daniel Boyarin, *A Radical Jew: Paul and the Politics of Identity* (Berkeley: University of California, 1994), 2.

2 Jonathan D. Brumberg-Kraus, "A Jewish Ideological Perspective on the Study of Christian Scripture," *Jewish Social Studies,* New Series, 4, no. 1 (Autumn 1997): 121–152.

3 Daniel R. Langton, *The Apostle Paul in the Jewish Imagination: A Study in Modern Jewish-Christian Relations* (Cambridge, UK: Cambridge University Press, 2010), 43.

4   Daniel R. Langton, "The Myth of the 'Traditional View of Paul' and the Role of the Apostle in Modern Jewish-Christian Polemics," *Journal for the Study of the New Testament* 28, no. 1 (2005): 89.

5   Langton, "The Myth of the 'Traditional View of Paul' and the Role of the Apostle in Modern Jewish-Christian Polemics," 91.

6   C.G. Montefiore, "The Genesis of the Religion of St. Paul," in *Judaism and St. Paul: Two Essays* (London: Max Goschen, 1914; reprint Forgotten Books, 2015).

7   Modern scholars date the closing of the Babylonian Talmud to the eighth century CE.

8   Samuel Sandmel, *The Genius of Paul* (New York: Farrar, Straus and Cudahy, 1958; reprint Isha Books, 2013).

9   Hyam Maccoby, *The Mythmaker: Paul and the Invention of Christianity* (San Francisco: Harper and Row, 1986).

10 Rebecca Moore, "The Mythmaker: Hyam Maccoby and the Invention of Christianity," *Journal of Ecumenical Studies* 52, no. 3 (Summer 2017): 381–401.

11 Alan F. Segal, *Paul the Convert: The Apostolate and Apostasy of Saul the Pharisee* (New Haven, CT: Yale University Press, 1990), 194.

12 Segal, *Paul the Convert*, xi.

13 Boyarin, *A Radical Jew*, 52.

14 A formal analysis of the passage shows it is "a defense for the holiness and goodness of the Law" rather than a confession of sinfulness. Krister Stendahl, *Paul Among Jews and Gentiles and Other Essays* (Philadelphia: Fortress Press, 1976), 92.

15 William Wrede, *Paul*, trans. E. Lummis (London: Philip Green, 1907; reprint Wipf and Stock, 2001).

16 Albert Schweitzer, *The Mysticism of Paul the Apostle*, trans. William Montgomery (New York: Henry Holt, 1931), 377.

17 Stendahl, *Paul Among Jews and Gentiles and Other Essays*.

18 Stendahl, 16.

19 Donald A. Hagner, "Paul and Judaism. The Jewish Matrix of Early Christianity: Issues in the Current Debate," *Bulletin for Biblical Research* 3 (1993): 111.

20 James D.G. Dunn, "Introduction," in *The Cambridge Companion to St Paul*, ed. James D.G. Dunn (Cambridge, UK: Cambridge University Press, 2003), 10.

21 Kent L. Yinger, "The Continuing Quest for Jewish Legalism," *Bulletin for Biblical Research* 19, no. 3 (2009): 375.

22 Pamela Eisenbaum, *Paul Was Not a Christian: The Original Message of a Misunderstood Apostle* (New York: HarperCollins, 2009).

23 Eisenbaum, 202.

24 Eisenbaum, 241.

25 Mark D. Nanos, "A Jewish View," in *Four Views on The Apostle Paul,* ed. Michael F. Bird (Grand Rapids, MI: Zondervan, 2012), 166.

26 Lloyd Gaston, *Paul and the Torah* (Vancouver, B.C.: University of British Columbia Press, 1987; reprint Wipf and Stock, 2006), 114.

27 John G. Gager, *The Origins of Anti-Semitism: Attitudes Toward Judaism in Pagan and Christian Antiquity* (New York: Oxford University Press, 1983), 179.

28 Gager, 247.

29 Hagner, "Paul and Judaism," 123.

30 Yinger, 375–391.

31 Daniel R. Langton, "Modern Jewish Identity and the Apostle Paul: Pauline Studies as an Intra-Jewish Ideological Battleground," *Journal for the Study of the New Testament* 28, no. 2 (2005): 217–258.

32 Montefiore, "The Genesis of the Religion of St. Paul," 4–5.

33 Elaine Pagels describes their discovery in *The Gnostic Gospels* (New York: Random House, 1979).

34 All of the fragments are now available for free at The Leon Levy Dead Sea Scrolls Digital Library, Israel Antiquities Authority, https://www.deadseascrolls.org.il/?locale=en_US.

35 Geza Vermes, *Jesus and the World of Judaism* (Philadelphia: Fortress Press, 1983), 102, 69.

36 R.M. Price, "'Hellenization' and Logos Doctrine in Justin Martyr," *Vigiliae Christianae* 42, no. 1 (March 1988): 18–19.

37 Boyarin, *A Radical Jew,* 7.

38 Boyarin, *A Radical Jew,* 8.

39 Israel Jacob Yuval, "Christianity in Talmud and Midrash: Parallelomania or Parallelophobia?," in *Transforming Relations: Essays on Jews and Christians Throughout History in Honor of Michael Signer,* ed. Franklin T. Harkins (Notre Dame, IN: University of Notre Dame Press, 2010), 50.

40 Yuval, "Christianity in Talmud and Midrash," 50–57.

41 Yuval, "Christianity in Talmud and Midrash," 51.

42 Boyarin, *A Radical Jew,* 9.

43 Lori G. Beaman, *Deep Equality in an Era of Religious Diversity* (New York: Oxford University Press, 2017), 2.

44 Beaman, 29.

Chapter 4. Jewish Christians, Christian Jews, and the Quest for Purity

1 James Parkes, *The Conflict of the Church and the Synagogue: A Study in the Origins of Antisemitism* (London: Soncino Press, 1934; reprint World Publishing and Jewish Publication Society, 1961), 119–120.

2 Lori G. Beaman, *Deep Equality in an Era of Religious Diversity* (New York: Oxford University Press, 2017), 78.

3 The expression "parting of the ways" comes from Parkes, *The Conflict of the Church and the Synagogue.*

4 R.M. Price, "'Hellenization' and Logos Doctrine in Justin Martyr," *Vigiliae Christianae* 42, no. 1 (March 1988): 19.

5 Margaret H. Williams, ed., *The Jews Among the Greeks and Romans: A Diasporan Sourcebook* (Baltimore, MD: Johns Hopkins University Press, 1998), 163.

6 Louis H. Feldman, *Jew and Gentile in the Ancient World: Attitudes and Interactions from Alexander to Justinian* (Princeton, NJ: Princeton University Press, 1993), xi.

7 Williams, 139, quoting Codex Theodosianus (16.8.9).

8 Eliya Ribak, "Bright Beginnings: Jewish Christian Relations in the Holy Land, AD 400–700," *Studies in Christian-Jewish Relations* 6 (2011): 1–18.

9 Ribak, 19.

10 Wayne A. Meeks and Robert L. Wilken, *Jews and Christians in Antioch in the First Four Centuries of the Common Era* (Missoula, MT: Scholars Press, 1978), 6.

11 Meeks and Wilken, 6.

12 John G. Gager, *The Origins of Anti-Semitism: Attitudes Toward Judaism in Pagan and Christian Antiquity* (New York: Oxford University Press, 1983), 6–7.

13 Gager, 7.

14 Shaye J.D. Cohen, "The Significance of Yavneh: Pharisees, Rabbis, and the End of Jewish Sectarianism," *Hebrew Union College Annual* 55 (1984): 51.

15 Robert L. Wilken, *Judaism and the Early Christian Mind: A Study of Cyril of Alexandria's Exegesis and Theology* (New Haven, CT: Yale University Press, 1971), 27.

16 Robert L. Wilken, *John Chrysostom and the Jews: Rhetoric and Reality in the Late 4th Century* (Berkeley: University of California Press, 1983), 67.

17 Wilken, *John Chrysostom and the Jews,* 78–79.

18 Daniel Boyarin, *Dying for God: Martyrdom and the Making of Christianity and Judaism* (Stanford, CA: Stanford University Press, 1999), 8.

19 Marc Hirshman, *A Rivalry of Genius: Jewish and Christian Biblical Interpretation in Late Antiquity* (Albany: State University of New York Press, 1996), 75. The similar text appears in the *Mekhilta de-Rabbi Ishmael,* a third-century compilation of midrashim on selected chapters of Exodus concerning halakhah.

20 Hirshman, 87.

21 Ishay Rosen-Zvi, "Pauline Traditions and the Rabbis: Three Case Studies," *Harvard Theological Review* 110, no. 2 (2017): 169–194.

22 Naomi Janowitz, "Rabbis and their Opponents: The Construction of the 'Min' in Rabbinic Anecdotes," *Journal of Early Christian Studies* 6, no. 3 (Fall 1998): 454.

23 Adam H. Becker, "Beyond the Spatial and Temporal *Limes:* Questioning the 'Parting of the Ways' Outside the Roman Empire," in *The Ways That Never Parted: Jews and Christians in Late Antiquity and the Early Middle Ages,* ed. Adam H. Becker and Annette Yoshiko Reed (Minneapolis: Fortress Press, 2007), 392.

24 Ephraim Shoham-Steiner, "Jews and Healing at Medieval Saints' Shrines: Participation, Polemics, and Shared Cultures," *Harvard Theological Review* 103, no. 1 (January 2010): 111–129.

25 Dik van Arkel, *The Drawing of the Mark of Cain: A Socio-Historical Analysis of the Growth of Anti-Jewish Stereotypes* (Amsterdam: Amsterdam University Press, 2009), 65.

26 Hugh Nibley, "Christian Envy of the Temple," *Jewish Quarterly Review* 50, no. 3 (January 1960): 229–249.

27 Wilken, *John Chrysostom and the Jews,* 80.

28 Reimund Leicht, "The Legend of St. Eustachius (Eustasthius) as Found in the Cairo Genizah," in *Jewish Studies Between the Disciplines: Papers in Honor of Peter Schäfer on the Occasion of his 60th Birthday,* ed. Klaus Herrmann, Margarete Schlüter, and Giuseppe Veltri, 325–330 (Boston: Brill, 2003).

29 John Van Engen, "Introduction: Jews and Christians Together in the Twelfth Century," in *Jews and Christians in Twelfth-Century Europe,* ed. Michael A. Signer and John Van Engen (Notre Dame, IN: University of Notre Dame Press, 2001), 5.

30 Nicholas Vincent, "Two Papal Letters on the Wearing of the Yellow Badge, 1221 and 1229," *Jewish Historical Studies* 34 (1993–1996): 209–224.

31 For the role of the church in aggressively defining Christian culture, see R.I. Moore, *The Formation of a Persecuting Society: Power and Deviance in Western Europe, 950–1250* (New York: Oxford University Press, 1987); for the effect of shifting economics, van Arkel; for the impact of mendicant orders, see Jeremy Cohen, *The Friars and the Jews: The Evolution of Medieval Anti-Judaism* (Ithaca, NY: Cornell University Press, 1982). Cohen also assesses the twentieth-century Jewish scholars who find the First Crusade significant in "A 1096 Complex? Constructing the First Crusade," in *Jews and Christians in Twelfth-Century Europe,* 9–26.

32 Allison P. Coudert and Jeffrey S. Shoulson, "Introduction," in *Hebraica Veritas? Christian Hebraists and the Study of Judaism in Early Modern Europe,* ed. Allison P. Coudert and Jeffrey S. Shoulson (Philadelphia: University of Pennsylvania Press, 2004), 2.

33 Jonathan Elukin, *Living Together, Living Apart: Rethinking Jewish-Christian Relations in the Middle Ages* (Princeton, NJ: Princeton University Press, 2007), 8.

34 Elukin, 5.

Chapter 5. The Paradox of Christian Hebraism

1 Jerome Friedman, "Sixteenth-Century Christian Hebraica: Scripture and the Renaissance Myth of the Past," *Sixteenth Century Journal* 11, no. 4 (Winter 1980): 84, quoting Johannes Reuchlin.

2   David S. Katz, *Philo-Semitism and the Readmission of Jews to England, 1603–1655* (Oxford, UK: Clarendon Press, 1982), 44.

3   James Carroll, *Constantine's Sword: The Church and the Jews* (Boston: Houghton Mifflin, 2001), 218.

4   Paula Fredriksen, *Augustine and the Jews: A Christian Defense of Jews and Judaism* (New Haven, CT: Yale University Press, 2008), 275.

5   Lori G. Beaman, *Deep Equality in an Era of Religious Diversity* (New York: Oxford University Press, 2017), 82.

6   Rebecca Moore, *Jews and Christians in the Life and Thought of Hugh of St. Victor* (Atlanta, GA: Scholars Press, 1998).

7   Beryl Smalley, *The Study of the Bible in the Middle Ages* (Oxford, UK: Basil Blackwell and Mott, 1952; reprint University of Notre Dame Press, 1964), 156–172.

8   Smalley, *The Study of the Bible in the Middle Ages,* 149.

9   Rebecca Moore, *Jews and Christians in the Life and Thought of Hugh of St. Victor,* 86.

10 Smalley, *The Study of the Bible in the Middle Ages,* 156.

11 Jeremy Cohen, *The Friars and the Jews: The Evolution of Medieval Anti-Judaism* (Ithaca, NY: Cornell University Press, 1982), 62.

12 Deeana Copeland Klepper, *The Insight of Unbelievers: Nicholas of Lyra and Christian Reading of Jewish Text in the Later Middle Ages* (Philadelphia: University of Pennsylvania Press, 2007), 13–31.

13 Ram Ben-Shalom, *"Me'ir Nativ:* The First Concordance of the Hebrew Bible and Jewish Bible Study in the Fifteenth Century, in the Context of Jewish-Christian Polemics," *Aleph* 11, no. 2 (2011): 297.

14 Ben-Shalom, 297, quoting Isaac Nathan.

15 Ben-Shalom, 306.

16 Daniel O'Callaghan, ed. and trans. *The Preservation of Jewish Religious Books in Sixteenth-Century Germany: Johannes Reuchlin's "Augenspiegel"* (Leiden: Brill, 2013), 2–3.

17 Brian Copenhaver and Daniel Stein Kokin, "Egidio da Viterbo's *Book on Hebrew Letters:* Christian Kabbalah in Papal Rome," *Renaissance Quarterly* 67, no. 1 (Spring 2014): 1–42. The letters are tsade, yod, and he.

18 Copenhaver and Kokin, 3.

19 Deena Aranoff, "Elijah Levita, a Jewish Hebraist," *Jewish History* 23, no. 1 (2009): 31.

20 Aranoff, 25.

21 Jerome Friedman, 75.

22 Jerome Friedman, 82.

23 Sina Rauschenbach, "Mediating Jewish Knowledge: Menasseh ben Israel and the Christian *Respublica litteraria,*" *Jewish Quarterly Review* 102, no. 4 (Fall 2012): 569.

24 Jerome Friedman, 82.

25 Grant Underwood, "The *Hope of Israel* in Early Modern Ethnography and Eschatology," in *Hebrew and the Bible in America: The First Two Centuries,* ed. Shalom Goldman (Hanover, NH: University Press of New England, 1993), 91.

26 Rauschenbach, "Mediating Jewish Knowledge," 572.

27 Richard Popkin, "Jewish-Christian Relations in the Sixteenth and Seventeenth Centuries: The Conception of the Messiah," *Jewish History* 6, no. 1/2 (1992): 165.

28 Popkin, 166, quoting Menasseh ben Israel. Spelling as in original.

29 Jason P. Rosenblatt, "John Selden's *De Jure Naturali … Juxta Disciplinam Ebraeorum* and Religious Toleration," in *Hebraica Veritas?,* 103.

30 Rosenblatt, 119.

31 Arthur Hertzberg, "The New England Puritans and the Jews," in Goldman, *Hebrew and the Bible in America,* 105.

32 Shalom Goldman, "Introduction," in Goldman, *Hebrew and the Bible in America,* xvii.

33 Robert H. Pfeiffer, "The Teaching of Hebrew in Colonial America," *Jewish Quarterly Review* 45, no. 4 (April 1955): 363.

34 Pfeiffer, 366.

35 Goldman, "Introduction," xxii.

36 Popkin, 170.

37 Abraham Melamed, "The Revival of Christian Hebraism in Early Modern Europe," in *Philosemitism in History,* ed. Jonathan Karp and Adam Sutcliffe (New York: Cambridge University Press, 2011), 62.

38 Werner L. Gundersheimer, "Erasmus, Humanism, and the Christian Cabala," *Journal of the Warburg and Courtaud Institutes* 26, no. 1/2 (1963): 48, quoting Desiderius Erasmus.

39 Melamed, 53.

40 Adam Sutcliffe, "Hebrew Texts and Protestant Readers: Christian Hebraism and Denominational Definition," *Jewish Studies Quarterly* 7, no. 4 (2000): 326.

41 Sutcliffe, 326–327.

42 Sutcliffe, 324.

43 Sutcliffe, 327.

44 Melamed, 63.

Chapter 6. The Puzzle of Christian Zionism

1 Walter Roth, "Christian's [sic] 1891 Zionist Petition to U.S. President," *Society News* (Chicago Jewish Historical Society) XI, no. 1 (September 1987): 6.

2 Raphael Loewe, "Hebraists, Christian," *Encyclopedia Judaica,* ed. Michael Berenbaum and Fred Skonik, 2nd ed., Vol. 8 (Farmington Hills, MI: Gale, 2007 [1996]): 510–551.

3 Walter Jacob, *Christianity Through Jewish Eyes: The Quest for Common Ground* (Cincinnati, OH: Hebrew Union College Press, 1974), 15.

4 Daniel Jütte, "Interfaith Encounters Between Jews and Christians in the Early Modern Period and Beyond: Toward a Framework," *American Historical Review* 118, no. 2 (April 2013), 380–381.

5 Michael Berenbaum, "Pittsburgh Platform," *Encyclopedia Judaica,* ed. Michael Berenbaum and Fred Skonik, 2nd ed., Vol. 16 (Farmington Hills, MI: Gale, 2007), 190.

6 Michael Lipka, "Unlike U.S., Few Jews in Israel identify as Reform or Conservative," *FactTank,* Pew Research Center, https://www.pewresearch.org/fact-tank/2016/03/15/unlike-u-s-few-jews-in-israel-identify-as-reform-or-conservative/, retrieved 15 July 2021.

7 My discussion of dispensationalism is indebted to Yaakov Ariel, *On Behalf of Israel: American Fundamentalist Attitudes Toward Jews, Judaism, and Zionism, 1865–1945* (Brooklyn, NY: Carlson Publishing, 1991).

8 M[ordecai] M[anuel] Noah, *Discourse on the Restoration of the Jews: Delivered at the Tabernacle, Oct. 28 and Dec. 2, 1844* (New York: Harper and Brothers, 1845; reprint Arno Press, 1977), 50.

9 Noah, 33; italics in original.

10 Ariel, *On Behalf of Israel,* 17.

11 Ariel, *On Behalf of Israel*, 21.

12 Ariel, *On Behalf of Israel*, 48.

13 Ariel, *On Behalf of Israel*, 65.

14 Roth, 6.

15 Ariel, *On Behalf of Israel*, 88.

16 John S. Conway, "Protestant Missions to the Jews 1810–1980: Ecclesiastical Imperialism or Theological Aberration," *Holocaust and Genocide Studies* 1, no. 1 (1986): 131.

17 Conway, "Protestant Missions to the Jews 1810–1980," 129.

18 Agnieszka Jagodzińska, "Reformers, Missionaries, and Converts: Interactions Between the London Society and Jews in Warsaw in the First Half of the Nineteenth Century," in *Converts of Conviction: Faith and Scepticism in Nineteenth Century European Jewish Society*, ed. David B. Ruderman (Berlin: Walter de Gruyter, 2018), 14.

19 Conway, "Protestant Missions to the Jews 1810–1980," 129.

20 Carl Edwin Armerding, "The Meaning of Israel in Evangelical Thought," in *Evangelicals and Jews in Conversation on Scripture, Theology, and History*, ed. Marc H. Tanenbaum, Marvin R. Wilson, and A. James Rudin (Grand Rapids, MI: Baker Book House, 1978), 134.

21 Eitan Bar-Yosef, "Christian Zionism and Victorian Culture," *Israel Studies* 8, no. 2 (2003): 24.

22 Bar-Yosef, 29, quoting Lord Shaftesbury.

23 Todd M. Endelman, *Leaving the Jewish Fold: Conversion and Radical Assimilation in Modern Jewish History* (Princeton, NJ: Princeton University Press, 2015), 6.

24 Endelman, 11.

25 David B. Ruderman, ed., *Converts of Conviction: Faith and Scepticism in Nineteenth Century European Jewish Society* (Berlin: Walter de Gruyter, 2018).

26 David B. Ruderman, "Introduction," in *Converts of Conviction*, 3.

27 Elijah Zvi Soloveitchik, *The Bible, the Talmud, and the New Testament: Elijah Zvi Soloveitchik's Commentary to the Gospels*, ed. Shaul Magid, trans. Jordan Gayle Levy (Philadelphia: University of Pennsylvania Press, 2019).

28 Shaul Magid, "Introduction," in Soloveitchik, *The Bible, the Talmud, and the New Testament*, 15–16.

29 Magid, 16.

30 Michael Barkun, *A Culture of Conspiracy: Apocalyptic Visions in Contemporary America,* 2nd. ed. (Berkeley: University of California Press, 2013), 146.

31 David Biale, *Blood and Belief: The Circulation of a Symbol Between Jews and Christians* (Berkeley: University of California Press, 2007), 170.

32 Alan Levenson, "Missionary Protestants as Defenders and Detractors of Judaism: Franz Delitzsch and Hermann Strack," *Jewish Quarterly Review* 92, no's. 3–4 (January–April 2002): 391.

33 Susannah Heschel, *Abraham Geiger and the Jewish Jesus* (Chicago: University of Chicago Press, 1998), 197.

34 Susannah Heschel, 195.

35 "Strack, Hermann Leberecht," *Encyclopedia Judaica,* ed. Michael Berenbaum and Fred Skolnik, 2nd ed., Vol. 19 (Farmington Hills, MI: Gale, 2007): 240.

36 Alan Levenson, "Missionary Protestant Defenders and Detractors of Judaism," 412.

37 Bar-Yosef, 38.

38 Alexander Marx, "Review: Strack's Introduction to the Talmud and Midrash," *Jewish Quarterly Review,* New Series, 13, no. 3 (January 1923): 365.

Chapter 7. The Righteous and the Reprobate

1 Johannes M. Snoek, *The Grey Book: A Collection of Protests Against Anti-Semitism and the Persecution of Jews Issued by Non-Roman Catholic Churches and Church Leaders during Hitler's Rule* (Assen: Van Gorcum, 1969), 289.

2 Lori Beaman, personal email to author, 8 February 2021.

3 See, e.g., Robert P. Ericksen and Susannah Heschel, eds., *Betrayal: German Churches and the Holocaust* (Minneapolis: Fortress Press, 1999).

4 Doris L. Bergen, "Storm Troopers of Christ: The German Christian Movement and the Ecclesiastical Final Solution," in *Betrayal,* 40–67.

5 "What Are the Basic Criteria for Awarding the Title of Righteous?" *FAQs: The Righteous Among the Nations Program* (Jerusalem: Yad Vashem, n.d.), at https://www.yadvashem.org/righteous/faq.html, retrieved 15 July 2021.

6   Mordecai Paldiel, "Righteous Gentiles and Courageous Jews: Acknowledging and Honoring Rescuers of Jews," *French Politics, Culture, and Society,* 30, no. 2 (Summer 2012): 141.

7   Saul Friedländer, *Kurt Gerstein: The Ambiguity of Good* (New York: Alfred Knopf, 1969).

8   Snoek, 39.

9   Viewing the German Catholic Church critically is Guenter Lewy, *The Catholic Church and Nazi Germany* (New York: McGraw-Hill, 1964). Viewing it favorably, at least until 1933, is John Cornwell, *Hitler's Pope: The Secret History of Pius XII* (New York: Viking, 1999).

10   Cornwell, 108.

11   Cornwell, 109.

12   Cornwell, 133.

13   Bernard Lichtenberg, *The Righteous Among the Nations Database* (Jerusalem: Yad Vashem, 2004), https://righteous.yadvashem.org/?search=Bernhard%20Lichtenberg&searchType=righteous_only&language=en&itemId=4740137&ind=0, retrieved 15 July 2021.

14   Janet Sternfeld, *Homework for Jews: Preparing for Jewish-Christian Dialogue,* 2nd ed. (New York: National Conference of Christians and Jews, 1985), 24.

15   Benny Kraut, "Towards the Establishment of the National Conference of Christians and Jews: The Tenuous Road to Religious Goodwill in the 1920s," *American Jewish History* 77, no. 3 (March 1988): 399–412.

16   James W. Parkes, *The Jew and His Neighbor: A Study of the Causes of Anti-Semitism* (London: Student Christian Movement Press, 1930).

17   Anne Summers, "False Start or Brave Beginning? The Society of Jews and Christians, 1924–1944," *Journal of Ecclesiastical History* 65, no. 4 (October 2014): 840.

18   James Parkes, *The Conflict of the Church and the Synagogue: A Study in the Origins of Antisemitism* (London: Soncino Press, 1934; reprint World Publishing and Jewish Publication Society, 1961).

19   Snoek, 80–81.

20   Alice L. Eckardt, "Founding Father of Jewish-Christian Relations: The Rev. James Parkes (1896–1981)," *Studies in Christian-Jewish Relations* 3 (2008): CP9.

21   Snoek, 56.

22   Peter C. Kent, "A Tale of Two Popes: Pius XI, Pius XII, and the Rome-Berlin Axis," *Journal of Contemporary History* 23, no. 4 (October 1988): 601–602.

23   Snoek, 87.

24   "The Immigration of Refugee Children to the United States," *Holocaust Encyclopedia*, United States Holocaust Memorial Museum, https://encyclopedia.ushmm.org/content/en/article/the-immigration-of-refugee-children-to-the-united-states, retrieved 15 July 2021.

25   David I. Kertzer, "The Pope, the Jews, and the Secrets in the Archives," *Atlantic: Web Edition Articles*, 27 August 2020, https://www.theatlantic.com/ideas/archive/2020/08/the-popes-jews/615736/.

26   Michael Phayer, *The Catholic Church and the Holocaust, 1930–1965* (Bloomington and Indianapolis: Indiana University Press, 2000), xiii.

27   Kent, 603.

28   See John Cornwell for *Hitler's Pope*; defending Pius XII is Ralph McInerny, *The Defamation of Pius XII* (South Bend, IN: St. Augustine's Press, 2001), among others.

29   Michael R. Marrus, "Understanding the Vatican During the Nazi Period" (Jerusalem: Yad Vashem, 2000), https://www.yadvashem.org/articles/academic/understanding-the-vatican-during-the-nazi-period.html, retrieved 15 July 2021.

30   Hannah Arendt, "The Deputy: Guilt by Silence?" in *The Storm over the Deputy: Essays and Articles about Hochhuth's Explosive Drama*, ed. Eric Bentley (New York: Grove Press, 1964), 88.

31   Pinchas E. Lapide, *Three Popes and the Jews* (New York: Hawthorn Books, 1967), 218.

32   Marie Syrkin, *Blessed Is the Match: The Story of Jewish Resistance* (Philadelphia: Jewish Publication Society, 1974), xv.

33   Michael R. Marrus, *The Holocaust in History* (Hanover, NH: University Press of New England, 1987), 149.

34   Phayer, *The Catholic Church and the Holocaust,* xiii.

35   Phayer, *The Catholic Church and the Holocaust,* xvi.

36   Syrkin, 286–287.

37   Yuri Suhl, *They Fought Back: The Story of Jewish Resistance in Nazi Europe* (New York: Crown Publishers, 1967), 1.

38 For a different view of the Netherlands see Nechama Tec, *When Light Pierced the Darkness: Christian Rescue of Jews in Nazi-Occupied Poland* (New York: Oxford University Press, 1986), 9.

39 "The Netherlands," *Holocaust Encyclopedia,* United States Holocaust Memorial Museum, https://encyclopedia.ushmm.org/content/en/article/the-netherlands, retrieved 15 July 2021.

40 Syrkin, 283.

41 Michael Phayer, "Questions About Catholic Resistance," *Church History* 70, no. 2 (June 2001): 336.

42 Elizabeth Petuchowski, "Gertrud Luckner: Resistance and Assistance. A German Woman Who Defied Nazis and Aided Jews," in *Ministers of Compassion During the Nazi Period: Gertrud Luckner and Raoul Wallenberg* (South Orange, NJ: Institute of Judaeo-Christian Studies at Seton Hall University, 1999), 18.

43 John S. Conway, "Christian-Jewish Relations during the 1950s," *Kirchliche Zeitgeschichte* 3, no. 2 (Mai 1990): 26.

44 Tec, 70.

45 Tec, 153.

46 Rebecca Solnit, *A Paradise Built in Hell: The Extraordinary Communities that Arise in Disaster* (New York: Penguin Books, 2009).

47 Philip Friedman, *Their Brothers' Keepers* (New York: Crown Publishers, 1957), 10.

Chapter 8. Repentance and Forgiveness

1 F.E. Cartus, "Vatican II and the Jews," *Commentary* 39, no. 1 (January 1, 1965): 21, quoting Pope John XXIII. Attribution of this statement to Pope John XXIII is questioned in John Rothman, "An Incomparable Pope—John XXIII and the Jews (Extended)," *Inside the Vatican,* n.d., https://insidethevatican.com/magazine/vatican-watch/incomparable-pope-john-xxiii-jews-long/, retrieved 15 July 2021.

2 Robert P. Ericksen and Susannah Heschel, "Introduction," in *Betrayal: German Churches and the Holocaust,* ed. Robert P. Ericksen and Susannah Heschel (Minneapolis: Fortress Press, 1999), 9.

3 Raul Hilberg, *The Destruction of the European Jews,* 3rd ed., Vol. 1 (New Haven, CT: Yale University Press, 2003), xiii. Hilberg tracks

down the origin of the "six million" figure concerning the number of Jews killed. He himself comes up with the figure 5,100,000.

4 Zev Garber and Bruce Zuckerman, "Why Do We Call the Holocaust 'The Holocaust?' An Inquiry into the Psychology of Labels," *Modern Judaism* 9, no. 2 (May 1989): 210, endnote 14.

5 Eugene Fisher, "Anti-Semitism: A Contemporary Christian Perspective," *Judaism* 30, no. 3 (Summer 1981): 276.

6 Jacques Derrida, "Avowing—The Impossible: 'Returns,' Repentance, and Reconciliation. A Lesson," in *Living Together: Jacques Derrida's Communities of Violence and Peace,* ed. Elisabeth Weber, trans. Gil Anidjar, 18–41 (New York: Fordham University Press, 2013).

7 Hannah Arendt, *The Human Condition: A Study of the Central Dilemmas Facing Modern Man* (Garden City, NY: Doubleday, 1959), 240.

8 Simon Wiesenthal, *The Sunflower: On the Possibilities and Limits of Forgiveness* (New York: Schocken Books, 1976). An enlarged version is published in 1997.

9 Christian Rutishauser, "The 1947 Seelisberg Conference: The Foundation of the Jewish-Christian Dialogue," *Studies in Christian-Jewish Relations* 2, no. 2 (2007): 34–53.

10 Claire Huchet Bishop, "Jules Isaac: A Biographical Introduction," in Jules Isaac, *The Teaching of Contempt: Christian Roots of Anti-Semitism,* trans. Helen Weaver (New York: Holt, Rinehart and Winston, 1964), 9.

11 World Council of Churches, "Report of Committee IV—Concerns of the Churches: 3. The Christian Approach to the Jews," (Geneva: World Council of Churches, 1948), 160, at https://www.oikoumene.org/sites/default/files/Document/1948Christian_approach_Jews.pdf, retrieved 15 July 2021.

12 Micha Brumlik, "Post-Holocaust Theology: German Theological Responses since 1945," in Ericksen and Heschel, *Betrayal,* 175.

13 Complete text of the Berlin-Weissensee synod's declaration is in Brumlik, 175.

14 World Council of Churches, "Resolution on Anti-Semitism," Third Assembly, New Delhi (Geneva: World Council of Churches, 1961), https://archive.org/stream/newdelhireportth009987mbp/newdelhireportth009987mbp_djvu.txt, retrieved 15 July 2021.

15   George Faithful, *Mothering the Fatherland: A Protestant Sisterhood Repents for the Holocaust* (New York: Oxford University Press, 2014), 1.

16   Faithful, 5.

17   Faithful, 75.

18   Michael Phayer, *The Catholic Church and the Holocaust, 1930–1965* (Bloomington and Indianapolis: Indiana University Press, 2000), 144, quoting John J. McCloy.

19   Huchet Bishop, "Jules Isaac: A Biographical Introduction," 10–11.

20   Gavin d'Costa, *Vatican II: Catholic Doctrines on Jews and Muslims* (New York: Oxford University Press, 2014), 119.

21   Yigal Sklarin, "'Rushing in Where Angels Fear to Tread': Rabbi Joseph B. Soloveitchik, the Rabbinical Council of America, Modern Orthodox Jewry, and the Second Vatican Council," *Modern Judaism* 29, no. 3 (October 2009): 357.

22   Marc H. Tanenbaum, "Heschel and Vatican Council II—Jewish-Christian Relations," paper presented at a memorial symposium in honor of Abraham Joshua Heschel, at Jewish Theological Seminary, New York, NY, 21 February 1983, 6. From the Archives of the American Jewish Committee, at http://www.ajcarchives.org/ajcarchive/DigitalArchive.aspx, retrieved 15 July 2021.

23   Tanenbaum, "Heschel and Vatican Council II," 7.

24   Reuven Kimelman, "Rabbis Joseph B. Soloveitchik and Abraham Joshua Heschel on Jewish Christian Relations," *Modern Judaism* 24, no. 3 (October 2004): 253.

25   Abraham Joshua Heschel, "On Improving Catholic-Jewish Relations," New York, NY, 22 May 1962, Archives of the American Jewish Committee, http://www.ajcarchives.org/ajcarchive/DigitalArchive.aspx, retrieved 15 July 2021.

26   D'Costa, 119.

27   Leon Klenicki, "From Argument to Dialogue: *Nostra Aetate* Twenty-Five Years Later," in *In Our Time: The Flowering of Jewish-Catholic Dialogue,* ed. Eugene J. Fisher and Leon Klenicki (New York: Paulist Press, 1990), 78.

28   Sklarin, 356.

29   Tanenbaum, "Heschel and Vatican Council II," 16, quoting Abraham Joshua Heschel.

30 Tanenbaum, "Heschel and Vatican Council II," 17, quoting Abraham Joshua Heschel.

31 Arthur Gilbert, *The Vatican Council and the Jews* (Cleveland: World Publishing, 1968), viii.

32 Pope Paul VI, *Declaration on the Relation of the Church to Non-Christian Religions (Nostra Aetate)*, 28 October 1965, in *Vatican Council II: The Conciliar and Post Conciliar Documents*, Vol. 1, rev. ed., ed. Austin Flannery, O.P. (Northport, NY: Costello Publishing, 1992), 738–742.

33 This quote and all others from *Nostra Aetate* were translated by Father Killian, O.C.S.O., *in Vatican Council II: The Conciliar and Post Conciliar Documents,* rev. ed.

34 Eliezer Berkovits, *Faith after the Holocaust* (New York: Ktav Publishing, 1973), 26.

35 Samuel Sandmel, *We Jews and You Christians: An Inquiry Into Attitudes* (Philadelphia: J.B. Lippincott, 1967), 144–146.

36 Ben Zion Bokser, "Vatican II and the Jews," *Jewish Quarterly Review* 59, no. 2 (October 1968): 139.

37 Bokser, 147.

38 Gilbert, 214.

39 Gilbert, 216–217.

Chapter 9. Daring to Engage

1   Emil Fackenheim, *Quest for Past and Future: Essays in Jewish Theology* (Bloomington, IN: Indiana University Press, 1968), 22.

2   Yaakov Ariel, "Interfaith Dialogue and the Golden Age of Christian-Jewish Relations," *Studies in Christian-Jewish Relations* 6 (2011): 1–18.

3   Vatican Commission for Religious Relations with the Jews, "Guidelines and Suggestions for Implementing the Conciliar Declaration *Nostra Aetate* (no. 4)," January 1975 [1 December 1974], in *Stepping Stones to Further Jewish-Christian Relations,* ed. Helga Croner, 11–16 (New York: Stimulus Books, 1977). See also https://www.bc.edu/content/dam/files/research_sites/cjl/texts/cjrelations/resources/documents/catholic/Vatican_Guidelines.htm, retrieved 15 July 2021.

4   Vatican Commission for Religious Relations with the Jews, "Notes on the Correct Way to Present the Jews and Judaism in Preaching

and Catechesis in the Roman Catholic Church" (24 June 1985), at https://www.bc.edu/content/dam/files/research_sites/cjl/texts/cjrelations/resources/documents/catholic/Vatican_Notes.htm, retrieved 15 July 2021.

5   World Council of Churches, "Third Revised Text of British Working Group for World Council of Churches Consultation on the Church and the Jewish People: Guidelines/Recommendations on Jewish-Christian Relations, 1977," in *More Stepping Stones to Jewish-Christian Relations: An Unabridged Collection of Christian Documents 1975–1983,* ed. Helga Croner (New York: Paulist Press, 1985), 161.

6   World Council of Churches, "Third Revised Text of British Working Group," 162.

7   Marc H. Tanenbaum, "A Jewish Viewpoint on *Nostra Aetate,*" in *Twenty Years of Jewish-Catholic Relations,* ed. Eugene J. Fisher, A. James Rudin, and Marc H. Tanenbaum (New York: Paulist Press, 1986), 54.

8   Lori G. Beaman, *Deep Equality in an Era of Religious Diversity* (New York: Oxford University Press, 2017), 92.

9   Trude Weiss-Rosmarin, *Judaism and Christianity: The Differences* (New York: Jonathan David, 1943), 7.

10 Will Herberg, *Protestant–Catholic–Jew: An Essay in American Religious Sociology* (Chicago: University of Chicago Press, 1955; reprint University of Chicago Press, 1983), 256.

11 Emmanuel Nathan and Anya Topolski, "The Myth of a Judeo-Christian Tradition: Introducing a European Perspective," in *Is There a Judeo-Christian Tradition: A European Perspective,* ed. Emmanuel Nathan and Anya Topolski (Berlin: Walter de Gruyter, 2016), 1–2.

12 Arthur A. Cohen, *The Myth of the Judeo-Christian Tradition and Other Dissenting Essays* (New York: Schocken Books, 1957; reprint Schocken Books, 1971), xiii.

13 Arthur A. Cohen, 192.

14 Arthur A. Cohen, 82, 196; Herberg, 263.

15 According to Reuven Kimelman, the term "Integrationist Orthodoxy" better reflects Orthodox ideology. In "Rabbis Joseph B. Soloveitchik and Abraham Joshua Heschel on Jewish Christian Relations," *Modern Judaism* 24, no. 3 (October 2004), 251.

16 Yigal Sklarin, "'Rushing in Where Angels Fear to Tread': Rabbi Joseph B. Soloveitchik, the Rabbinical Council of America, Modern Orthodox Jewry, and the Second Vatican Council," *Modern Judaism* 29, no. 3 (October 2009): 362.

17 Joseph B. Soloveitchik, "Confrontation," *Tradition: A Journal of Orthodox Thought* 6, no. 2 (Spring 1964): 5–29.

18 Michael A. Chester, "Heschel and the Christians," *Journal of Ecumenical Studies* 38, no. 2/3 (Spring/Summer 2001): 255.

19 Joseph B. Soloveitchik, "Addendum to the Original Edition of 'Confrontation,'" in *A Treasury of Tradition,* ed. Norman Lamm and Walter S. Wurzburger (New York: Hebrew Publishing Company, 1967), 79.

20 Soloveitchik, "Addendum," 79.

21 Abraham Joshua Heschel, "No Religion Is an Island," *Union Seminary Quarterly Review* 21, no. 2 part 1 (January 1966): 117–134, and at https://utsnyc.edu/wp-content/uploads/Heschels-No-Religion-is-an-Island.pdf, retrieved 15 July 2021.

22 Abraham Joshua Heschel, "No Religion Is an Island," 122.

23 Abraham Joshua Heschel, "No Religion Is an Island," 127.

24 Martin Buber, *I and Thou,* trans. Walter Kaufmann (New York: Charles Scribner's Sons, 1970).

25 Buber, 59.

26 Ariel, "Interfaith Dialogue and the Golden Age of Christian-Jewish Relations," 10.

27 International Council of Christians and Jews, "Jews and Christians in Search of a Common Religious Basis for Contributing Towards a Better World," 1 March 1993, at https://www.bc.edu/content/dam/files/research_sites/cjl/texts/cjrelations/resources/documents/interreligious/ICCJ_1993.htm, retrieved 15 July 2021.

28 Tikva Frymer-Kensky, David Novak, Peter Ochs, and Michael Signer, "*Dabru Emet*: A Jewish Statement on Christians and Christianity," in *Christianity in Jewish Terms*, ed. Tikva Frymer-Kensky, David Novak, Peter Ochs, David Fox Sandmel, and Michael Signer, xv–xviii (Boulder, CO: Westview Press, 2000). *Dabru Emet* also available at https://www.bc.edu/content/dam/files/research_sites/cjl/texts/cjrelations/resources/documents/jewish/dabru_emet.htm, retrieved 15 July 2021.

29 Jon D. Levenson, "How Not to Conduct Jewish-Christian Dialogue," *Commentary* 112, no. 5 (December 2001): 36.

30 *To Do the Will of Our Father in Heaven: Toward a Partnership between Jews and Christians,* The Center for Jewish-Christian Understanding and Cooperation, 3 December 2015, https://www.cjcuc.org/2015/12/03/orthodox-rabbinic-statement-on-christianity/, retrieved 15 July 2021.

31 The Center for Jewish-Christian Understanding and Cooperation, "Groundbreaking Orthodox Rabbinic Statement on Christianity" (7 December 2015), at https://www.cjcuc.org/2015/12/07/groundbreaking-orthodox-rabbinic-statement-on-christianity/, retrieved 15 July 2021, quoting Rabbi Dr. Eugene Korn.

32 Israel Jacob Yuval, "'We Curse Christianity Three Times a Day': Can Jews and Christians Truly Reconcile?" *Haaretz,* 14 August 2020, at https://www.haaretz.com/life/books/.premium.MAGAZINE-we-curse-christianity-three-times-a-day-can-jews-and-christians-truly-reconcile-1.9072566, retrieved 15 July 2021.

33 Judith Hershcopf Banki, "Religious Education Before and After Vatican II," in *Twenty Years of Jewish-Catholic Relations,* 125.

34 Claire Huchet Bishop, "Response to John Pawlikowski," in *Auschwitz: Beginning of a New Era? Reflections on the Holocaust,* ed. Eva Fleischner (New York: Ktav Publishing, Cathedral Church of St. John the Divine, and Anti-Defamation League of B'nai B'rith, 1977), 180.

35 Philip A. Cunningham, *Education for Shalom: Religion Textbooks and the Enhancement of the Catholic and Jewish Relationship* (Philadelphia: The American Interfaith Institute, 1995), 78. The European studies are not underwritten by AJC.

36 Eugene J. Fisher, "A Content Analysis of the Treatment of Jews and Judaism in Current Roman Catholic Religion Textbooks and Manuals on the Primary and Secondary Levels," Ph.D. diss., New York University, 1976.

37 Ruth Seldin, *Image of the Jews: Teachers' Guide to Jews and Their Religion* (New York: Anti-Defamation League of B'nai B'rith, 1970), iii. The booklet includes lectures by Eugene Borowitz, Irving Greenberg, Jules Harlow, Max J. Routtenberg, Dore Schary, and Michael Wyschogrod.

38 J. Bruce Long, ed., *Judaism and the Christian Seminary Curriculum* (Chicago: Loyola University Press, 1966).

39 Bernard D. Weinryb and Daniel Garnick, *Jewish School Textbooks and Intergroup Relations: The Dropsie College Study of Jewish Textbooks* (New York: American Jewish Committee, 1965), 44–45.

40 Pinchas Lapide, *Israelis, Jews, and Jesus*, trans. Peter Heinegg (Garden City, NY: Doubleday, 1979).

41 Lapide, *Israelis, Jews, and Jesus*, 66–67.

42 Lapide, *Israelis, Jews, and Jesus*, 67.

43 Eugene J. Fisher, "The Roman Liturgy and Catholic-Jewish Relations since the Second Vatican Council," in *Twenty Years of Jewish-Catholic Relations*, 148.

44 American Jewish Committee, "Anti-Jewish Elements in Catholic Liturgy" (New York: American Jewish Committee, 1961), at http://www.ajcarchives.org/AJC_DATA/Files/6A2.PDF, retrieved 15 July 2021.

45 American Jewish Committee, "Anti-Jewish Elements in Catholic Liturgy," 10.

46 Elizabeth Palmer, "Reproach and Pleading," *Christian Century* 137, no. 8 (April 8, 2020): 10.

47 Evangelical Lutheran Church in America, *Evangelical Lutheran Worship* (Minneapolis, MN: Augsburg/Fortress, 2006).

48 Bishops' Committee for Ecumenical and Interreligious Affairs, *Criteria for the Evaluation of Dramatizations of the Passion* (Washington, DC: United States Conference of Catholic Bishops, 1988), at https://www.usccb.org/beliefs-and-teachings/ecumenical-and-interreligious/jewish/upload/Criteria-for-the-Evaluation-of-Dramatizations-of-the-Passion-1988.pdf, retrieved 15 July 2021.

49 Bishops' Committee for Ecumenical and Interreligious Affairs, 77.

50 Bishops' Committee for Ecumenical and Interreligious Affairs, 80.

51 Yom HaShoah occurs the 27th day of the month of Nissan each year, which is the fifth day following the eighth day of Passover.

52 Elizabeth Wright, "A Yom HaShoah Liturgy for Christians," Appendix B, in Franklin H. Littell, *The Crucifixion of the Jews* (New York: Harper and Row, 1975), 141–153.

53 Marcia Sachs Littell and Sharon Weissman Gutman, eds., *Liturgies on the Holocaust: An Interfaith Anthology*, new and rev. ed. (Valley Forge, PA: Trinity Press International, 1996).

54 Ariel, "Interfaith Dialogue and the Golden Age of Christian-Jewish Relations," 12.

Chapter 10. Rethinking Theology

1   David Novak, "From Supersessionism to Parallelism in Jewish-Christian Dialogue," in *Talking with Christians: Musings of a Jewish Theologian* (Grand Rapids, MI: Eerdmans, 2005), 11.

2   Mary C. Boys, S.N.J.M., "The Road Is Made by Walking," in *Faith Transformed: Christian Encounters with Jews and Judaism,* ed. John C. Merkle (Collegeville, MN: Liturgical Press, 2003), 173.

3   Irving Greenberg, "Cloud of Smoke, Pillar of Fire: Judaism, Christianity, and Modernity after the Holocaust," in *Auschwitz: Beginning of a New Era? Reflections on the Holocaust,* ed. Eva Fleischner (New York: Ktav Publishing, the Cathedral Church of St. John the Divine, and Anti-Defamation League of B'nai B'rith, 1977), 20–26.

4   Lori G. Beaman, *Deep Equality in an Era of Religious Diversity* (New York: Oxford University Press, 2017), 64–65.

5   Gregory Baum, "Introduction," in Rosemary Radford Ruether, *Faith and Fratricide: The Theological Roots of Anti-Semitism* (New York: Seabury Press, 1974), 11.

6   Baum, 5.

7   Rosemary Radford Ruether, *Faith and Fratricide: The Theological Roots of Anti-Semitism* (New York: Seabury Press, 1974), 228.

8   A. Roy Eckardt, *Elder and Younger Brothers: The Encounter of Jews and Christians* (New York: Charles Scribner's Sons, 1967).

9   Eckardt, *Elder and Younger Brothers, 71.*

10 Monika Hellwig, "From the Jesus Story to the Christ of Dogma," in *Antisemitism and the Foundations of Christianity*, ed. Alan T. Davies (New York: Paulist Press, 1979), 131.

11 Philip A. Cunningham, "The Sources Behind 'The Gifts and the Calling of God are Irrevocable' (Rom 11:29): A Reflection on Theological Questions Pertaining to Catholic-Jewish Relations on the Occasion of the 50th Anniversary of 'Nostra Aetate' (No. 4)," Commission of the Holy See for Religious Relations with the Jews, 10 December 2015, *Studies in Christian-Jewish Relations* 12, no. 1 (2017): 1–39, at https://ejournals.bc.edu/index.php/scjr/article/view/9792.

12 Michael Oppenheim, "Foreword," in *The Star of Redemption,* by Franz Rosenzweig, trans. Barbara E. Galli (Madison: University of Wisconsin Press, 2005), xi.

13 Rosenzweig, *The Star of Redemption,* 420.

14 Rosenzweig, 434–435.

15 Rosenzweig, 438.

16 Rosenzweig, 375.

17 James Parkes, "The Bible, The World and The Trinity," Chapter 12 in *Prelude to Dialogue: Jewish-Christian Relationships* (New York: Schocken, 1969), 202–221.

18 James Parkes, *God at Work in Science, Politics and Human Life* (New York: Philosophical Library, 1952).

19 E.P. Sanders, *Paul and Palestinian Judaism: A Comparison of Patterns of Religion* (Philadelphia: Fortress Press, 1977).

20 Sanders, *Paul and Palestinian Judaism,* 546.

21 Sanders, *Paul and Palestinian Judaism,* 549.

22 Sanders, *Paul and Palestinian Judaism,* 543.

23 E.P. Sanders, *Paul, the Law, and the Jewish People* (Philadelphia: Fortress Press, 1983), 46, 208.

24 Sanders, *Paul and Palestinian Judaism,* 550.

25 Jacob Neusner, "Judaism and Christianity, Their Relationship Then, Their Relationship to Come," in *Judaism in Monologue and Dialogue* (Lanham, MD: University Press of America, 2005), 83.

26 Neusner, "Judaism and Christianity, Their Relationship Then, Their Relationship to Come," 86.

27 Jacob Neusner, "The Absoluteness of Christianity and the Uniqueness of Judaism: Why Salvation Is Not of the Jews," in *Judaism in Monologue and Dialogue,* 94.

28 Pope Paul VI, *Declaration on the Relation of the Church to Non-Christian Religions (Nostra Aetate),* 28 October 1965, in *Vatican Council II: The Conciliar and Post Conciliar Documents,* Vol. 1, rev. ed., ed. Austin Flannery, O.P. (Northport, NY: Costello Publishing, 1992), 741.

29 A. Roy Eckardt, "Can There Be a Jewish-Christian Relationship?" *Journal of Bible and Religion* 33, no. 2 (April 1965): 130, 129.

30 Christian Scholars Group, *A Sacred Obligation: Rethinking Christian Faith in Relation to Judaism and the Jewish People,* in *Seeing Judaism*

Anew: Christianity's Sacred Obligation, ed. Mary C. Boys (Lanham, MD: Rowman and Littlefield, 2005), xiv.

31 Presbyterian Church (USA), *Christians and Jews: People of God,* Church Issues Series No. 7 (Louisville, KY: Office of Theology and Worship, n.d.), 9, 11, 13.

32 "United Methodist Guiding Principles for Christian-Jewish Relations," in *The Book of Resolutions of the United Methodist Church—2016* (Nashville, TN: United Methodist Publishing House, 2016), at https://www.umc.org/en/content/book-of-resolutions-united-methodist-guiding-principles-for-christian-jewish-relations, retrieved 15 July 2021.

33 Pontifical Biblical Commission, *The Jewish People and Their Sacred Scriptures in the Christian Bible* (Vatican City: Pontifical Biblical Commission, 2001), at https://www.vatican.va/roman_curia/congregations/cfaith/pcb_documents/rc_con_cfaith_doc_20020212_popolo-ebraico_en.html, retrieved 15 July 2021.

34 Tikva Frymer-Kensky, David Novak, Peter Ochs, and Michael Signer, "*Dabru Emet*: A Jewish Statement on Christians and Christianity," in *Christianity in Jewish Terms*, ed. Tikva Frymer-Kensky, David Novak, Peter Ochs, David Fox Sandmel, and Michael Signer (Boulder, CO: Westview Press, 2000), xvi.

35 Amy-Jill Levine and Mark Zvi Brettler, *The Bible With and Without Jesus: How Jews and Christians Read the Same Stories Differently* (New York: HarperOne, 2020), 424–425.

36 Rosemary Radford Ruether, "Theological Anti-Semitism in the New Testament," *Christian Century* 85, no. 7 (14 February 1968): 193.

37 Ruether, "Theological Anti-Semitism in the New Testament," 193.

38 Ruether, *Faith and Fratricide,* 249.

39 Ruether, *Faith and Fratricide,* 249–250.

40 David Tracy, "Religious Values after the Holocaust: A Catholic View," in *Jews and Christians after the Holocaust,* ed. Abraham J. Peck (Philadelphia: Fortress Press, 1982), 100.

41 Irving Greenberg, "The Case for a Positive Jewish Theology of Christianity," in *Post-Holocaust Jewish-Christian Dialogue: After the Flood, before the Rainbow,* ed. Alan L. Berger (Lanham, MD: Lexington Books, 2015), 27, italics in original.

42 Baum, 18.

43 John T. Pawlikowski, *Christ in the Light of the Christian-Jewish Dialogue* (New York: Paulist Press, 1982; reprint Wipf and Stock, 2001), 3.

44 Ellis Rivkin, *A Hidden Revolution: The Pharisees' Search for the Kingdom Within* (Nashville, TN: Abingdon Press, 1978).

45 Pawlikowski, *Christ in the Light of the Christian-Jewish Dialogue*, 114.

46 Pawlikowski, *Christ in the Light of the Christian-Jewish Dialogue*, 115.

47 Henry Siegman, "Jewish-Christian Relations: Still a Way to Go," *Judaism* 35, no. 1 (Winter 1986): 26.

48 Eliezer Berkovits, *Faith after the Holocaust* (New York: Ktav Publishing, 1973), 47.

49 Henry Bamberger, "Some Difficulties in Dialogue," *Judaism* 32, no. 2 (Spring 1983): 176–183.

50 Emil L. Fackenheim, "Jewish Faith and the Holocaust: A Fragment," in *The Jewish Return into History: Reflections in the Age of Auschwitz and a New Jerusalem* (New York: Schocken Books, 1978), 34.

51 David Novak, "A Jewish Response to a New Christian Theology," *Judaism* 31, no. 1 (Winter 1982): 115.

52 Michael Wyschogrod, "Paul, Jews, and Gentiles," in *Abraham's Promise: Judaism and Jewish-Christian Relations* (Grand Rapids, MI: Eerdmans, 2004), 191.

53 Wyschogrod, "Paul, Jews, and Gentiles," 200.

54 Wyschogrod, "Paul, Jews, and Gentiles," 200.

55 David Novak, *Jewish-Christian Dialogue: A Jewish Justification* (New York: Oxford University Press, 1989).

56 David Novak, "Introduction: What to Seek and What to Avoid in Jewish-Christian Dialogue," in *Christianity in Jewish Terms*, 5.

57 Novak, *Jewish-Christian Dialogue*, 135.

58 For his most developed articulation, see Irving Greenberg, *For the Sake of Heaven and Earth: The New Encounter Between Judaism and Christianity* (Philadelphia: Jewish Publication Society, 2004).

59 Greenberg, "The Case for a Positive Jewish Theology of Christianity," 12.

60 Greenberg, "The Case for a Positive Jewish Theology of Christianity," 23.

Chapter 11. Zionism and Evangelism

1   Hal Lindsey, with C.C. Carlson, *The Late Great Planet Earth* (Grand Rapids, MI: Zondervan, 1970), 45.

2   Joseph B. Soloveitchik, "The Community," *Tradition: A Journal of Orthodox Thought* 17, no. 2 (Spring 1978): 14.

3   Zwi Werblowsky, "The People and the Land," in *Speaking of God Today: Jews and Lutherans in Conversation*, ed. Paul D. Opsahl and Marc H. Tanenbaum (Philadelphia: Fortress Press, 1974), 76.

4   John Wesley, *The Journal of John Wesley*, vi.iii.v, 11 June 1739 (Grand Rapids, MI: Christian Classics Ethereal Library, n.d.), 65.

5   Arthur James Balfour, "Balfour Declaration 1917," *The Avalon Project*, Yale Law School, at https://avalon.law.yale.edu/20th_century/balfour.asp, retrieved 15 July 2021.

6   The 1916 Sykes-Picot Agreement predates the Balfour Declaration and lists the ways in which Great Britain and France will divide up the Middle East for commercial interests. It does say the two nations will "recognize and protect an independent Arab states [sic] or a confederation of Arab States." "The Sykes-Picot Agreement: 1916," *The Avalon Project*, Yale Law School, at https://avalon.law.yale.edu/20th_century/sykes.asp, retrieved 15 July 2021.

7   Gary Fields, *Enclosure: Palestinian Landscapes in a Historical Mirror* (Berkeley: University of California Press, 2017), 260.

8   Alan Dowty, "Much Ado about Little: Ahad Ha'am's 'Truth from Eretz Israel,' Zionism, and the Arabs," *Israel Studies* 5, no. 2 (Fall 2000): 157, quoting Ahad Ha'am.

9   Caitlin Carenen, "The American Christian Palestine Committee, the Holocaust, and Mainstream Protestant Zionism, 1938–1948," *Holocaust and Genocide Studies* 24, no. 2 (Fall 2010): 274.

10   Carenen, 277.

11   Carenen, 290.

12   Moshe Shemesh, "Did Shuqayri Call for 'Throwing Jews into the Sea'?" *Israel Studies*, 8, no. 2 (Summer 2003): 79, quoting announcer on Radio Damascus 23 May 1967.

13   Israel Ministry of Foreign Affairs, "This Week in Jewish History UNGA Rescinds 'Zionism is Racism' Resolution," World Jewish Congress, 16 December 2020, https://www.worldjewishcongress.

org/en/news/this-week-in-jewish-history--unga-rescinds-zionism-is-racism-resolution-12-3-2020, retrieved 17 July 2021.

14 Judith H. Banki, "The UN's Anti-Zionism Resolution: Christian Responses," Interreligious Affairs Department, American Jewish Committee 70th Anniversary Annual Meeting, Washington, D.C., 12–16 May 1976 (New York: American Jewish Committee, 1976), vii.

15 Marc H. Tanenbaum, "Preface," in "The UN's Anti-Zionism Resolution," iv.

16 A. Roy Eckardt and Alice L. Eckardt, "Again, Silence in the Churches: I, The Case for Israel," Appendix in A. Roy Eckardt, *Elder and Younger Brothers: The Encounter of Jews and Christians* (New York: Charles Scribner's Sons, 1967) 163.

17 Eckardt and Eckardt, "Again, Silence in the Churches: I," 165, 166.

18 A. Roy Eckardt and Alice L. Eckardt, "Again, Silence in the Churches: II, Christian and Arab Ideology," Appendix in Eckardt, *Elder and Younger Brothers,* 176.

19 Lucy S. Dawidowicz, "American Public Opinion," *The American Jewish Yearbook* 69 (1968): 218.

20 Dawidowicz, 219.

21 Study Group on Christian-Jewish Relations, "Statement to Our Fellow Christians" (1973), at https://www.bc.edu/content/dam/files/research_sites/cjl/sites/partners/csg/csg1973.htm, retrieved 15 July 2021.

22 Bumper sticker highlighting "USA" in the word *Jerusalem.*

23 Lindsey, 50–51.

24 Lindsey, 56.

25 Lindsey, 151.

26 Troy Anderson, "Where Your Israel Donation Really Goes," *Charisma News* (22 October 2013), at https://www.charismanews.com/opinion/standing-with-israel/47005-where-your-israel-donation-really-goes, retrieved 15 July 2021.

27 Tim LaHaye and Jerry Jenkins, *Left Behind* series (Wheaton, IL: Tyndale House, 1995–2007).

28 Yaakov Ariel, "From the Institutum Judaicum to the International Christian Embassy: Christian Zionism with a European Accent," in *Comprehending Christian Zionism: Perspectives in Comparison,* ed. Göran Gunner and Robert O. Smith (Minneapolis: Augsburg Fortress, 2014), 220.

29 Shalom L. Goldman, "Review Essay: Christians and Zionism," *American Jewish History* 93, no. 2 (June 2007): 253.

30 Jeffrey C. Pugh, *The Home Brewed Christianity Guide to the End Times: Theology After You've Been Left Behind* (Minneapolis: Augsburg Fortress, 2016), 150.

31 Dov Aharoni Fisch, *Jews for Nothing: On Cults, Intermarriage, and Assimilation* (Jerusalem and New York: Feldheim Publishers, 1984), 21.

32 Dan Cohn-Sherbok, *Messianic Judaism* (London: Continuum, 2000), 212.

33 Mark S. Kinzer, "Twenty-first Century Messianic Judaism: Evangelical and Post-Evangelical Trajectories," *Hebrew Studies* 57 (2016): 363, quoting the Hashivenu Forum.

34 Yaakov Ariel, "Theological and Liturgical Coming of Age: New Developments in the Relationship between Messianic Judaism and Evangelical Christianity," *Hebrew Studies* 57 (2016): 390.

35 Faydra Shapiro, "Jesus for Jews: The Unique Problem of Messianic Jews," *Marburg Journal of Religion* 16, no. 1 (2011): 12–16.

36 "Reflections on the Problem 'Church-Israel,' issued by the Central Board of the Union of Evangelical Churches in Switzerland, 1977," in *More Stepping Stones to Jewish-Christian Relations: An Unabridged Collection of Christian Documents 1975–1983,* ed. Helga Croner (New York: Paulist Press, 1985), 203.

37 Judith Hershcopf Banki, *Anti-Israel Influence in American Churches: A Background Report* (New York: American Jewish Committee, 1979).

38 World Council of Churches, "WCC Policy on Palestine and Israel 1948–2016 (summary)" (Geneva: World Council of Churches, 2017), at https://www.oikoumene.org/en/resources/documents/wcc-programmes/public-witness/peace-building-cf/wcc-policy-on-palestine-and-israel-1948-2016-summary, retrieved 15 July 2021.

39 World Council of Churches Central Committee, "Israeli-Palestinian Conflict—Minute [sic] on the situation in the Holy Land after the outbreak of the second Palestinian uprising," Potsdam, Germany, 29 January–6 February 2001, at https://www.oikoumene.org/en/resources/documents/commissions/international-affairs/regional-concerns/middle-east/israeli-palestinian-conflict-minute-on-the-situation-in-the-holy-land-after-the-outbreak-of-the-second-palestinian-uprising, retrieved 15 July 2021.

40 Olav Fykse Tveit, "On US Recognition of Jerusalem as Israel's Capital," 6 December 2017, at https://www.oikoumene.org/en/resources/documents/general-secretary/statements/on-us-recognition-of-jerusalem-as-israels-capital, retrieved 15 July 2021.

41 John T. Pawlikowski, "Land as an Issue in Jewish-Christian Dialogue," *Cross Currents* 59, no. 2 (June 2009): 202.

42 Pope John Paul II, *Redemptionis Anno,* 20 April 1984, in *The Saint for Shalom: How Pope John Paul II Transformed Catholic-Jewish Relations. The Complete Texts 1979–2005,* ed. Eugene J. Fisher and Leon Klenicki (New York: Crossroad, 2011), 82–83.

43 Pawlikowski, "Land as an Issue in Jewish-Christian Dialogue," 203.

44 Pope John Paul II, *Redemptionis Anno,* 83.

45 Marc H. Tanenbaum, "Preface," in *Anti-Israel Influence in American Churches,* n.p.

46 Synod of the Reformed Church, Holland, "Israel: People, Land and State: Suggestions for a Theological Evaluation [1970]," in *Stepping Stones to Further Jewish-Christian Relations,* ed. Helga Croner (New York: Stimulus Books, 1977), 105.

47 Faydra L. Shapiro, "'Thank you Israel, for Supporting America': The Transnational Flow of Christian Zionist Resources," *Identities: Global Studies in Culture and Power* 19, no. 5 (September 2012): 621.

48 Shapiro, "'Thank you Israel, for Supporting America,'" 621, quoting Senator James Inhofe.

49 Parents Circle-Families Forum, https://www.theparentscircle.org/en/about_eng/, retrieved 15 July 2021.

Chapter 12. Finding Deep Equality in Jewish and Christian Relations

1 Pope John Paul II, *Message of His Holiness John Paul II on the 50th Anniversary of the Warsaw Ghetto Uprising* (Vatican: Libreria Editrice Vaticana, 1993), at http://www.vatican.va/content/john-paul-ii/en/messages/pont_messages/1993/documents/hf_jp-ii_mes_19930406_ebrei-polacchi.html, retrieved 15 July 2021.

2 Lori G. Beaman, *Deep Equality in an Era of Religious Diversity* (New York: Oxford University Press, 2017), 15.

3 Beaman, 64.

4   Edward Kessler and Neil Wenborn, eds., *A Dictionary of Jewish-Christian Relations* (Cambridge, UK: Cambridge University Press, 2005); and Edward Kessler, *Introduction to Jewish-Christian Relations* (Cambridge, UK: Cambridge University Press, 2010).

5   Wolfram Kinzig, "Closeness and Distance: Towards a New Description of Jewish-Christian Relations," *Jewish Studies Quarterly* 10, no. 3 (2003): 288–289.

6   Daniel Jütte, "Interfaith Encounters Between Jews and Christians in the Early Modern Period and Beyond: Toward a Framework," *American Historical Review* 118, no. 2 (April 2013): 378–400.

7   Jütte, 382.

8   Kinzig, 290.

9   David Novak, "Avoiding Charges of Legalism and Antinomianism in Jewish-Christian Dialogue," in *Talking with Christians: Musings of a Jewish Theologian* (Grand Rapids, MI: Eerdmans, 2005), 30.

10 David Novak, *Jewish-Christian Dialogue: A Jewish Justification* (New York: Oxford University Press, 1989), 156.

11 Abraham Joshua Heschel, *A Passion for Truth* (New York: Farrar, Straus and Giroux, 1973; reprint Jewish Lights Publishing, 1995), 20.

WORKS CITED

Alesali, Loumay, and Christina Zdanowicz. "A Jewish Synagogue Opened Its Doors to a Christian Congregation after Its Church Burned on Christmas." CNN. 14 March 2019. At https://www.cnn.com/2019/03/14/us/synagogue-church-service-after-fire-trnd/index.html. Retrieved 15 July 2021.

American Jewish Committee. "Anti-Jewish Elements in Catholic Liturgy." New York: American Jewish Committee, 1961. At http://www.ajcarchives.org/AJC_DATA/Files/6A2.PDF. Retrieved 15 July 2021.

Anderson, Troy. "Where Your Israel Donation Really Goes." *Charisma News.* 22 October 2013. At https://www.charismanews.com/opinion/standing-with-israel/47005-where-your-israel-donation-really-goes. Retrieved 15 July 2021.

Aranoff, Deena. "Elijah Levita, a Jewish Hebraist." *Jewish History 23,* no. 1 (2009): 17–40.

Arendt, Hannah. "The Deputy: Guilt by Silence?" In *The Storm over the Deputy: Essays and Articles about Hochhuth's Explosive Drama.* Edited by Eric Bentley, 85–94. New York: Grove Press, 1964.

———. *The Human Condition: A Study of the Central Dilemmas Facing Modern Man.* Garden City, NY: Doubleday, 1959.

Ariel, Yaakov. "Christianity Through Reform Eyes: Kaufmann Kohler's Scholarship on Christianity." *American Jewish History* 89, no. 2 (June 2001): 181–191.

———. "From the Institutum Judaicum to the International Christian Embassy: Christian Zionism with a European Accent." In *Comprehending Christian Zionism: Perspectives in Comparison.* Edited by Göran Gunner and Robert O. Smith, 199–229. Minneapolis: Augsburg Fortress, 2014.

———. "Interfaith Dialogue and the Golden Age of Christian-Jewish Relations." *Studies in Christian-Jewish Relations* 6 (2011): 1–18.

————. *On Behalf of Israel: American Fundamentalist Attitudes Toward Jews, Judaism, and Zionism, 1865–1945.* Brooklyn, NY: Carlson Publishing, 1991.

————. "Theological and Liturgical Coming of Age: New Developments in the Relationship between Messianic Judaism and Evangelical Christianity." *Hebrew Studies* 57 (2016): 381–391.

Armerding, Carl Edwin. "The Meaning of Israel in Evangelical Thought." In *Evangelicals and Jews in Conversation on Scripture, Theology, and History.* Edited by Marc H. Tanenbaum, Marvin R. Wilson, and A. James Rudin, 119–140. Grand Rapids, MI: Baker Book House, 1978.

Balfour, Arthur James. "Balfour Declaration 1917." *The Avalon Project.* Yale Law School. At https://avalon.law.yale.edu/20th_century/balfour.asp. Retrieved 15 July 2021.

Bamberger, Henry. "Some Difficulties in Dialogue." *Judaism* 32, no. 2 (Spring 1983): 176–183.

Banki, Judith H. "The UN's Anti-Zionism Resolution: Christian Responses." Interreligious Affairs Department. American Jewish Committee 70th Anniversary Annual Meeting, Washington, D.C. 12–16 May 1976. New York: American Jewish Committee, 1976.

Banki, Judith Hershcopf. *Anti-Israel Influence in American Churches: A Background Report.* New York: American Jewish Committee, 1979.

————. "Religious Education Before and After Vatican II." In *Twenty Years of Jewish-Catholic Relations.* Edited by Eugene J. Fisher, A. James Rudin, and Marc H. Tanenbaum, 125–134. New York: Paulist Press, 1986.

Bar-Yosef, Eitan. "Christian Zionism and Victorian Culture." *Israel Studies* 8, no. 2 (2003): 18–44.

Barkun, Michael. *A Culture of Conspiracy: Apocalyptic Visions in Contemporary America*, 2nd ed. Berkeley: University of California Press, 2013.

Barnstone, Willis. *The Restored New Testament.* New York: W.W. Norton, 2009.

Baum, Gregory. "Introduction." In *Faith and Fratricide: The Theological Roots of Anti-Semitism.* By Rosemary Radford Ruether, 1–22. New York: Seabury Press, 1974.

Bauman, Zygmunt. "Allosemitism: Premodern, Modern, Postmodern." In *Modernity, Culture and "the Jew."* Edited by Bryan Cheyette and Laura Marcus, 143–156. Stanford, CA: Stanford University Press, 1998.

Beaman, Lori G. *Deep Equality in an Era of Religious Diversity*. New York: Oxford University Press, 2017.

Becker, Adam H. "Beyond the Spatial and Temporal *Limes*: Questioning the 'Parting of the Ways' Outside the Roman Empire." In *The Ways That Never Parted: Jews and Christians in Late Antiquity and the Early Middle Ages*. Edited by Adam H. Becker and Annette Yoshiko Reed, 373–392. Minneapolis: Fortress Press, 2007.

Ben-Shalom, Ram. "*Me'ir Nativ*: The First Concordance of the Hebrew Bible and Jewish Bible Study in the Fifteenth Century, in the Context of Jewish-Christian Polemics." *Aleph* 11, no. 2 (2011): 289–364.

Berenbaum, Michael. "Pittsburgh Platform." In *Encyclopedia Judaica*. Edited by Michael Berenbaum and Fred Skonik, 2nd ed., Vol. 16, 190–191. Farmington Hills, MI: Gale, 2007.

Bergen, Doris L. "Storm Troopers of Christ: The German Christian Movement and the Ecclesiastical Final Solution." In *Betrayal: German Churches and the Holocaust*. Edited by Robert P. Ericksen and Susannah Heschel, 40–67. Minneapolis: Fortress Press, 1999.

Berkovits, Eliezer. *Faith after the Holocaust*. New York: Ktav Publishing, 1973.

Berlinerblau, Jacques. "On Philo-Semitism." *Occasional Papers—Jewish Civilization: The Importance of Discussing Philo-Semitism*. Georgetown University (Winter 2007): 7–19.

Biale, David. *Blood and Belief: The Circulation of a Symbol Between Jews and Christians*. Berkeley: University of California Press, 2007.

Bishops' Committee for Ecumenical and Interreligious Affairs. *Criteria for the Evaluation of Dramatizations of the Passion*. Washington, DC: United States Conference of Catholic Bishops, 1988. At https://www.usccb.org/beliefs-and-teachings/ecumenical-and-interreligious/jewish/upload/Criteria-for-the-Evaluation-of-Dramatizations-of-the-Passion-1988.pdf. Retrieved 15 July 2021.

Bokser, Ben Zion. "Vatican II and the Jews." *Jewish Quarterly Review* 59, no. 2 (October 1968): 136–151.

Boyarin, Daniel. *Border Lines: The Partition of Judaeo-Christianity*. Philadelphia: University of Pennsylvania Press, 2004.

———. *Dying for God: Martyrdom and the Making of Christianity and Judaism*. Stanford, CA: Stanford University Press, 1999.

————. "The Gospel of the Memra: Jewish Binitarianism and the Prologue to John." *Harvard Theological Review* 94, no. 3 (July 2001): 243–284.

————. *The Jewish Gospels: The Story of the Jewish Christ*. New York: The New Press, 2012.

————. *A Radical Jew: Paul and the Politics of Identity*. Berkeley: University of California Press, 1994.

Boys, Mary C., S.N.J.M. "The Road Is Made by Walking." In *Faith Transformed: Christian Encounters with Jews and Judaism*. Edited by John C. Merkle, 162–181. Collegeville, MN: Liturgical Press, 2003.

Brumberg-Kraus, Jonathan D. "A Jewish Ideological Perspective on the Study of Christian Scripture." *Jewish Social Studies*, New Series, 4, no. 1 (Autumn 1997): 121–152.

Brumlik, Micha. "Post-Holocaust Theology: German Theological Responses since 1945." In *Betrayal: German Churches and the Holocaust*. Edited by Robert P. Ericksen and Susannah Heschel, 169–188. Minneapolis: Fortress Press, 1999.

Buber, Martin. *I and Thou*. Translated by Walter Kaufmann. New York: Charles Scribner's Sons, 1970.

Bultmann, Rudolf. *Jesus Christ and Mythology*. London: SCM Press, 1960; reprint SCM Press, 2012.

————. *New Testament Mythology and Other Basic Writings*. Edited and translated by Schubert M. Ogden. Philadelphia: Fortress Press, 1984.

Capetz, Paul E. "The Old Testament as a Witness to Jesus Christ: Historical Criticism and Theological Exegesis of the Bible according to Karl Barth." *Journal of Religion,* 90, no. 4 (October 2010): 475–506.

Carenen, Caitlin. "The American Christian Palestine Committee, the Holocaust, and Mainstream Protestant Zionism, 1938–1948." *Holocaust and Genocide Studies* 24, no. 2 (Fall 2010): 273–296.

Carroll, James. *Constantine's Sword: The Church and the Jews*. Boston: Houghton Mifflin, 2001.

Cartus, F.E. "Vatican II and the Jews." *Commentary* 39, no. 1 (January 1, 1965): 19–29.

The Center for Jewish-Christian Understanding and Cooperation. "Groundbreaking Orthodox Rabbinic Statement on Christianity." 7 December 2015. At https://www.cjcuc.org/2015/12/07/groundbreaking-orthodox-rabbinic-statement-on-christianity/. Retrieved 15 July 2021.

Chester, Michael A. "Heschel and the Christians." *Journal of Ecumenical Studies* 38, no. 2/3 (Spring/Summer 2001): 246–269.

Christian Scholars Group. *A Sacred Obligation: Rethinking Christian Faith in Relation to Judaism and the Jewish People.* In *Seeing Judaism Anew: Christianity's Sacred Obligation.* Edited by Mary C. Boys, xii–xix. Lanham, MD: Rowman and Littlefield, 2005.

Cohen, Arthur A. *The Myth of the Judeo-Christian Tradition and Other Dissenting Essays.* New York: Schocken Books, 1957; reprint Schocken Books, 1971.

Cohen, Jeremy. *The Friars and the Jews: The Evolution of Medieval Anti-Judaism.* Ithaca, NY: Cornell University Press, 1982.

———. "A 1096 Complex? Constructing the First Crusade." In *Jews and Christians in Twelfth-Century Europe.* Edited by Michael A. Signer and John Van Engen, 9–26. Notre Dame, IN: University of Notre Dame Press, 2001.

Cohen, Shaye J.D. "The Significance of Yavneh: Pharisees, Rabbis, and the End of Jewish Sectarianism." *Hebrew Union College Annual* 55 (1984): 27–53.

Cohn-Sherbok, Dan. *Messianic Judaism.* London: Continuum, 2000.

Conway, John S. "Christian-Jewish Relations during the 1950s." *Kirchliche Zeitgeschichte* 3, no. 2 (Mai 1990): 11–27.

———. "Protestant Missions to the Jews 1810–1980: Ecclesiastical Imperialism or Theological Aberration?" *Holocaust and Genocide Studies* 1, no. 1 (1986): 127–146.

Cook, Michael J. "The Bible and Catholic-Jewish Relations." In *Twenty Years of Jewish-Catholic Relations.* Edited by Eugene J. Fisher, A. James Rudin, and Marc H. Tanenbaum, 109–124. New York: Paulist Press, 1986.

Copenhaver, Brian, and Daniel Stein Kokin. "Egidio da Viterbo's *Book on Hebrew Letters:* Christian Kabbalah in Papal Rome." *Renaissance Quarterly* 67, no. 1 (Spring 2014): 1–42.

Cornwell, John. *Hitler's Pope: The Secret History of Pius XII.* New York: Viking, 1999.

Coudert, Allison P., and Jeffrey S. Shoulson. "Introduction." In *Hebraica Veritas? Christian Hebraists and the Study of Judaism in Early Modern Europe.* Edited by Allison P. Coudert and Jeffrey S. Shoulson, 1–17. Philadelphia: University of Pennsylvania Press, 2004.

Cunningham, Philip A. *Education for Shalom: Religion Textbooks and the Enhancement of the Catholic and Jewish Relationship.* Philadelphia: The American Interfaith Institute, 1995.

———. "The Sources Behind 'The Gifts and the Calling of God Are Irrevocable' (Rom 11:29): A Reflection on Theological Questions Pertaining to Catholic-Jewish Relations on the Occasion of the 50th Anniversary of 'Nostra Aetate' (No. 4)." Commission of the Holy See for Religious Relations with the Jews, 10 December 2015. *Studies in Christian-Jewish Relations* 12, no. 1 (2017): 1–39. At https://ejournals.bc.edu/index.php/scjr/article/view/9792. Retrieved 15 July 2021.

Dawidowicz, Lucy S. "American Public Opinion." *The American Jewish Yearbook* 69 (1968): 198–229.

D'Costa, Gavin. *Vatican II: Catholic Doctrines on Jews and Muslims.* New York: Oxford University Press, 2014.

Derrida, Jacques. "Avowing—The Impossible: 'Returns,' Repentance, and Reconciliation. A Lesson." In *Living Together: Jacques Derrida's Communities of Violence and Peace.* Edited by Elisabeth Weber, Translated by Gil Anidjar, 18–41. New York: Fordham University Press, 2013.

Diekmann, Irene A. and Elke-Vera Kotowski, eds. *Geliebter Feind, Gehasster Freund: Antisemitismus und Philosemitismus in Geschichte und Gegenwart.* Berlin: Verlag Berlin Brandenburg, 2009.

Dowty, Alan. "Much Ado about Little: Ahad Ha'am's 'Truth from Eretz Israel,' Zionism, and the Arabs." *Israel Studies* 5, no. 2 (Fall 2000): 154–181.

Dunn, James D.G. "Introduction." In *The Cambridge Companion to St Paul.* Edited by James D.G. Dunn, 1–15. Cambridge, UK: Cambridge University Press, 2003.

Eckardt, A. Roy. "Can There Be a Jewish-Christian Relationship?" *Journal of Bible and Religion* 33, no. 2 (April 1965): 122–130.

———. *Elder and Younger Brothers: The Encounter of Jews and Christians.* New York: Charles Scribner's Sons, 1967.

———. "End to the Christian-Jewish Dialogue: I. Contradictions in Catholic and Protestant Attitudes." *Christian Century* 83, no. 12 (March 23, 1966): 360–363.

Eckardt, A. Roy, and Alice L. Eckardt. Appendix, "Again, Silence in the Churches: I, The Case for Israel." In A. Roy Eckardt, *Elder and Younger Brothers: The Encounter of Jews and Christians*, 163–169. New York: Charles Scribner's Sons, 1967.

———. Appendix, "Again, Silence in the Churches: II, Christian and Arab Ideology." In A. Roy Eckardt, *Elder and Younger Brothers: The Encounter of Jews and Christians*, 169–177. New York: Charles Scribner's Sons, 1967.

Eckardt, Alice L. "Founding Father of Jewish-Christian Relations: The Rev. James Parkes (1896–1981)." *Studies in Christian-Jewish Relations* 3 (2008): CP1–9.

Edelstein, Alan. *An Unacknowledged Harmony: Philo-Semitism and the Survival of European Jewry*. Westport, CT: Greenwood Press, 1982.

Eisenbaum, Pamela. *Paul Was Not a Christian: The Original Message of a Misunderstood Apostle*. New York: HarperCollins, 2009.

Elukin, Jonathan. *Living Together, Living Apart: Rethinking Jewish-Christian Relations in the Middle Ages*. Princeton, NJ: Princeton University Press, 2007.

Endelman, Todd M. *Leaving the Jewish Fold: Conversion and Radical Assimilation in Modern Jewish History*. Princeton, NJ: Princeton University Press, 2015.

Engel, David. "Crisis and Lachrymosity: On Salo Baron, Neobaronianism, and the Study of Modern European Jewish History." *Jewish History* 20, no. 3/4 (2006): 243–264.

Ericksen, Robert P., and Susannah Heschel. "Introduction." In *Betrayal: German Churches and the Holocaust*. Edited by Robert P. Ericksen and Susannah Heschel, 1–21. Minneapolis: Fortress Press, 1999.

———, eds. *Betrayal: German Churches and the Holocaust*. Minneapolis: Fortress Press, 1999.

Evangelical Lutheran Church in America. *Evangelical Lutheran Worship*. Minneapolis, MN: Augsburg/Fortress, 2006.

Fackenheim, Emil. *Quest for Past and Future: Essays in Jewish Theology*. Bloomington, IN: Indiana University Press, 1968.

Fackenheim, Emil L. "Jewish Faith and the Holocaust: A Fragment." In *The Jewish Return into History: Reflections in the Age of Auschwitz and a New Jerusalem*, 30–36. New York: Schocken Books, 1978.

Faithful, George. *Mothering the Fatherland: A Protestant Sisterhood Repents for the Holocaust*. New York: Oxford University Press, 2014.

Falk, Harvey. *Jesus the Pharisee: A New Look at the Jewishness of Jesus.* New York: Paulist Press, 1985.

Feldman, Louis H. *Jew and Gentile in the Ancient World: Attitudes and Interactions from Alexander to Justinian.* Princeton, NJ: Princeton University Press, 1993.

Fields, Gary. *Enclosure: Palestinian Landscapes in a Historical Mirror.* Berkeley: University of California Press, 2017.

Finkel, Asher. "Scriptural Interpretation: A Historical Perspective." In *Evangelicals and Jews in Conversation on Scripture, Theology, and History.* Edited by Marc H. Tanenbaum, Marvin R. Wilson, and A. James Rudin, 142–153. Grand Rapids, MI: Baker Book House, 1978.

Fisch, Dov Aharoni. *Jews for Nothing: On Cults, Intermarriage, and Assimilation.* Jerusalem and New York: Feldheim Publishers, 1984.

Fisher, Eugene. "Anti-Semitism: A Contemporary Christian Perspective." *Judaism* 30, no. 3 (Summer 1981): 276–282.

Fisher, Eugene J. "A Content Analysis of the Treatment of Jews and Judaism in Current Roman Catholic Religion Textbooks and Manuals on the Primary and Secondary Levels." Ph.D. diss., New York University, 1976.

———. "The Roman Liturgy and Catholic-Jewish Relations since the Second Vatican Council." In *Twenty Years of Jewish-Catholic Relations.* Edited by Eugene J. Fisher, A. James Rudin, and Marc H. Tanenbaum, 135–155. New York: Paulist Press, 1986.

Fredriksen, Paula. *Augustine and the Jews: A Christian Defense of Jews and Judaism.* New Haven, CT: Yale University Press, 2008.

———. *Jesus of Nazareth, King of the Jews: A Jewish Life and the Emergence of Christianity.* New York: Vintage Books, 1999.

Friedländer, Saul. *Kurt Gerstein: The Ambiguity of Good.* New York: Alfred A. Knopf, 1969.

Friedman, Jerome. "Sixteenth-Century Christian Hebraica: Scripture and the Renaissance Myth of the Past." *Sixteenth Century Journal* 11, no. 4 (Winter 1980): 67–85.

Friedman, Philip. *Their Brothers' Keepers.* New York: Crown Publishers, 1957.

Frymer-Kensky, Tikva, David Novak, Peter Ochs, David Fox Sandmel, and Michael Signer. "*Dabru Emet*: A Jewish Statement on Christians and Christianity." In *Christianity in Jewish Terms.* Edited by Tikva

Frymer-Kensky, David Novak, Peter Ochs, David Fox Sandmel, and Michael Signer, xv–xviii. Boulder, CO: Westview Press, 2000.

Gager, John G. *The Origins of Anti-Semitism: Attitudes Toward Judaism in Pagan and Christian Antiquity*. New York: Oxford University Press, 1983.

Garber, Zev, and Bruce Zuckerman. "Why Do We Call the Holocaust 'The Holocaust'? An Inquiry into the Psychology of Labels." *Modern Judaism* 9, no. 2 (May 1989): 197–211.

Garrison, Greg. "Church Burned on Christmas Moves to Synagogue." *Alabama Life*. 12 March 2019. At https://www.al.com/life/2019/03/church-burned-on-christmas-moves-to-synagogue.html. Retrieved 15 July 2021.

Gaston, Lloyd. *Paul and the Torah*. Vancouver, B.C.: University of British Columbia Press, 1987; reprint Wipf and Stock, 2006.

Gilbert, Arthur. *The Vatican Council and the Jews*. Cleveland: World Publishing, 1968.

Goldman, Shalom. "Introduction." In *Hebrew and the Bible in America: The First Two Centuries*. Edited by Shalom Goldman, xi–xxx. Hanover, NH: Brandeis University Press, 1993.

Goldman, Shalom L. "Review Essay: Christians and Zionism." *American Jewish History* 93, no. 2 (June 2007): 245–260.

Greenberg, Irving. "The Case for a Positive Jewish Theology of Christianity." In *Post-Holocaust Jewish-Christian Dialogue: After the Flood, before the Rainbow*. Edited by Alan L. Berger, 5–28. Lanham, MD: Lexington Books, 2015.

———. "Cloud of Smoke, Pillar of Fire: Judaism, Christianity, and Modernity after the Holocaust." In *Auschwitz: Beginning of a New Era? Reflections on the Holocaust*. Edited by Eva Fleischner, 7–55. New York: Ktav Publishing, the Cathedral Church of St. John the Divine, and Anti-Defamation League of B'nai B'rith, 1977.

———. *For the Sake of Heaven and Earth: The New Encounter Between Judaism and Christianity*. Philadelphia: Jewish Publication Society, 2004.

Gundersheimer, Werner L. "Erasmus, Humanism, and the Christian Cabala." *Journal of the Warburg and Courtaud Institutes* 26, no. 1/2 (1963): 38–52.

Hagner, Donald A. "Paul and Judaism. The Jewish Matrix of Early Christianity: Issues in the Current Debate." *Bulletin for Biblical Research* 3 (1993): 111–130.

Hellwig, Monika. "From the Jesus Story to the Christ of Dogma." In *Antisemitism and the Foundations of Christianity*. Edited by Alan T. Davies, 118–136. New York: Paulist Press, 1979.

Herberg, Will. *Protestant–Catholic–Jew: An Essay in American Religious Sociology.* Chicago: University of Chicago Press, 1955; reprint University of Chicago Press, 1983.

Hertzberg, Arthur. "The New England Puritans and the Jews." In *Hebrew and the Bible in America: The First Two Centuries*. Edited by Shalom Goldman, 105–121. Hanover, NH: Brandeis University Press, 1993.

Heschel, Abraham Joshua. "No Religion Is an Island." *Union Seminary Quarterly Review* 21, no. 2 part 1 (January 1966): 117–134. At https://utsnyc.edu/wp-content/uploads/Heschels-No-Religion-is-an-Island.pdf. Retrieved 15 July 2021.

———. "On Improving Catholic-Jewish Relations." New York: Archives of the American Jewish Committee, 1962. At http://www.ajcarchives.org/ajcarchive/DigitalArchive.aspx. Retrieved 15 July 2021.

———. *A Passion for Truth.* New York: Farrar, Straus and Giroux, 1973; reprint Jewish Lights Publishing, 1995.

Heschel, Susannah. *Abraham Geiger and the Jewish Jesus.* Chicago: University of Chicago Press, 1998.

Hilberg, Raul. *The Destruction of the European Jews,* 3rd ed., Vol. 1. New Haven, CT: Yale University Press, 2003.

Hirshman, Marc. *A Rivalry of Genius: Jewish and Christian Biblical Interpretation in Late Antiquity.* Albany: State University of New York Press, 1996.

Huchet Bishop, Claire. "Jules Isaac: A Biographical Introduction." In Jules Isaac, *The Teaching of Contempt: Christian Roots of Anti-Semitism*. Translated by Helen Weaver. New York: Holt, Rinehart and Winston, 1964.

———. "Response to John Pawlikowski." In *Auschwitz: Beginning of a New Era? Reflections on the Holocaust.* Edited by Eva Fleischner, 179–190. New York: Ktav Publishing, Cathedral Church of St. John the Divine, and Anti-Defamation League of B'nai B'rith, 1977.

Illyés, Bence. "A Jewish Cemetery in Hungary, Restored by a Christian." *Forward,* 16 October 2020. At https://forward.com/author/bence-illyes/. Retrieved 15 July 2021.

"The Immigration of Refugee Children to the United States." *Holocaust Encyclopedia.* United States Holocaust Memorial Museum. At https://encyclopedia.ushmm.org/content/en/article/the-immigration-of-refugee-children-to-the-united-states. Retrieved 15 July 2021.

International Council of Christians and Jews. "Jews and Christians in Search of a Common Religious Basis for Contributing Towards a Better World." 1 March 1993. At https://www.bc.edu/content/dam/files/research_sites/cjl/texts/cjrelations/resources/documents/inter-religious/ICCJ_1993.htm. Retrieved 15 July 2021.

Isaac, Jules. *The Teaching of Contempt: Christian Roots of Anti-Semitism.* Translated by Helen Weaver. New York: Holt, Rinehart and Winston, 1964.

Israel Ministry of Foreign Affairs. "This Week in Jewish History UNGA Rescinds 'Zionism is Racism' Resolution." World Jewish Congress. 16 December 2020. At https://www.worldjewishcongress.org/en/news/this-week-in-jewish-history--unga-rescinds-zionism-is-racism-resolution-12-3-2020. Retrieved 17 July 2021.

Jacob, Walter. *Christianity Through Jewish Eyes: The Quest for Common Ground.* Cincinnati, OH: Hebrew Union College Press, 1974.

Jagodzińska, Agnieszka. "Reformers, Missionaries, and Converts: Interactions Between the London Society and Jews in Warsaw in the First Half of the Nineteenth Century." In *Converts of Conviction: Faith and Scepticism in Nineteenth Century European Jewish Society.* Edited by David B. Ruderman, 9–25. Berlin: Walter de Gruyter, 2018.

Janowitz, Naomi. "Rabbis and their Opponents: The Construction of the 'Min' in Rabbinic Anecdotes." *Journal of Early Christian Studies* 6, no. 3 (Fall 1998): 449–462.

Jütte, Daniel. "Interfaith Encounters Between Jews and Christians in the Early Modern Period and Beyond: Toward a Framework." *American Historical Review* 118, no. 2 (April 2013): 378–400.

Karp, Jonathan, and Adam Sutcliffe, eds. *Philosemitism in History.* New York: Cambridge University Press, 2011.

Katz, David S. "The Phenomenon of Philo-Semitism." In *Christianity and Judaism: Papers Read at the 1991 Summer Meeting and 1992*

Winter Meeting of the Ecclesiastical History Society. Edited by Diana Wood, 324–361. Oxford, UK: Blackwell, 1992.

———. *Philo-Semitism and the Readmission of the Jews to England, 1603–1655.* Oxford, UK: Clarendon Press, 1982.

Kent, Peter C. "A Tale of Two Popes: Pius XI, Pius XII, and the Rome-Berlin Axis." *Journal of Contemporary History* 23, no. 4 (October 1988): 589–608.

Kertzer, David I. "The Pope, the Jews, and the Secrets in the Archives." *Atlantic: Web Edition Articles.* 27 August 2020. At https://www.theatlantic.com/ideas/archive/2020/08/the-popes-jews/615736/. Retrieved 15 July 2021.

Kessler, Edward. *Introduction to Jewish-Christian Relations.* Cambridge, UK: Cambridge University Press, 2010.

Kessler, Edward, and Neil Wenborn, eds. *A Dictionary of Jewish-Christian Relations.* Cambridge, UK: Cambridge University Press, 2005.

Kimelman, Reuven. "Rabbis Joseph B. Soloveitchik and Abraham Joshua Heschel on Jewish Christian Relations." *Modern Judaism* 24, no. 3 (October 2004): 251–271.

Kinzer, Mark S. "Twenty-first Century Messianic Judaism: Evangelical and Post-Evangelical Trajectories." *Hebrew Studies* 57 (2016): 359–366.

Kinzig, Wolfram. "Closeness and Distance: Towards a New Description of Jewish-Christian Relations." *Jewish Studies Quarterly* 10, no. 3 (2003): 274–290.

Klenicki, Leon. "From Argument to Dialogue: *Nostra Aetate* Twenty-Five Years Later." In *In Our Time: The Flowering of Jewish-Catholic Dialogue.* Edited by Eugene J. Fisher and Leon Klenicki, 77–103. New York: Paulist Press, 1990.

Klepper, Deeana Copeland. *The Insight of Unbelievers: Nicholas of Lyra and Christian Reading of Jewish Text in the Later Middle Ages.* Philadelphia: University of Pennsylvania Press, 2007.

Kraut, Benny. "Towards the Establishment of the National Conference of Christians and Jews: The Tenuous Road to Religious Goodwill in the 1920s." *American Jewish History* 77, no. 3 (March 1988): 399–412.

Krupnick, Mark. "The Rhetoric of Philosemitism." In *Rhetorical Invention and Religious Inquiry: New Perspectives.* Edited by Walter Jost and Wendy Olmsted, 356–380. New Haven, CT: Yale University Press, 2000.

Kushner, Tony, and Nadia Valman, eds. *Philosemitism, Antisemitism, and "the Jews": Perspectives from the Middle Ages to the Twentieth Century.* New York: Routledge, 2004.

Lacoque, André. "The 'Old Testament' in the Protestant Tradition." In *Biblical Studies: Meeting Ground of Jews and Christians.* Edited by Lawrence Boadt, C.S.P., Helga Croner, and Leon Klenicki, 120–143. New York: Paulist Press, 1980.

LaHaye, Tim, and Jerry Jenkins. *Left Behind* series. Wheaton, IL: Tyndale House, 1995–2007.

Langton, Daniel R. *The Apostle Paul in the Jewish Imagination: A Study in Modern Jewish-Christian Relations.* Cambridge, UK: Cambridge University Press, 2010.

———. "Modern Jewish Identity and the Apostle Paul: Pauline Studies as an Intra-Jewish Ideological Battleground." *Journal for the Study of the New Testament* 28, no. 2 (2005): 217–258.

———. "The Myth of the 'Traditional View of Paul' and the Role of the Apostle in Modern Jewish-Christian Polemics." *Journal for the Study of the New Testament* 28, no. 1 (2005): 69–104

Lapide, Pinchas. *Israelis, Jews, and Jesus.* Translated by Peter Heinegg. Garden City, NY: Doubleday, 1979.

Lapide, Pinchas E. *Three Popes and the Jews.* New York: Hawthorn Books, 1967.

Lassner, Phyllis, and Lara Trubowitz, eds. *Antisemitism and Philosemitism in the Twentieth and Twenty-First Centuries: Representing Jews, Jewishness, and Modern Culture.* Newark, DE: University of Delaware Press, 2008.

Leicht, Reimund. "The Legend of St. Eustachius (Eustasthius) as Found in the Cairo Genizah." In *Jewish Studies Between the Disciplines: Papers in Honor of Peter Schäfer on the Occasion of his 60th Birthday.* Edited by Klaus Herrmann, Margarete Schlüter, and Giuseppe Veltri, 325–330. Boston: Brill, 2003.

The Leon Levy Dead Sea Scrolls Digital Library. Israel Antiquities Authority. At https://www.deadseascrolls.org.il/?locale=en_US.

Levenson, Alan. "Missionary Protestants as Defenders and Detractors of Judaism: Franz Delitzsch and Hermann Strack." *Jewish Quarterly Review* 92, nos. 3–4 (January–April 2002): 383–420.

Levenson, Alan T. "Writing the Philosemitic Novel: Daniel Deronda Revisited." *Prooftexts* 28, no. 2 (Spring 2008): 129–156.

Levenson, Jon D. *The Hebrew Bible, the Old Testament, and Historical Criticism*. Louisville, KY: Westminster/John Knox, 1993.

———. "How Not to Conduct Jewish-Christian Dialogue." *Commentary* 112, no. 5 (December 2001): 31–37.

Levine, Amy-Jill. *The Misunderstood Jew: The Church and the Scandal of the Jewish Jesus*. New York: HarperCollins, 2006.

———. *Short Stories by Jesus: The Enigmatic Parables of a Controversial Rabbi*. New York: HarperOne, 2014.

Levine, Amy-Jill, and Marc Zvi Brettler. *The Bible With and Without Jesus: How Jews and Christians Read the Same Stories Differently*. New York: HarperOne, 2020.

———, eds. *The Jewish Annotated New Testament*, 2nd ed. rev. New York: Oxford University Press, 2017.

Lewy, Guenter. *The Catholic Church and Nazi Germany*. New York: McGraw-Hill, 1964.

Lichtenberg, Bernard. *The Righteous Among the Nations Database*. Jerusalem: Yad Vashem, 2004. At https://righteous.yadvashem.org/?search=Bernhard%20Lichtenberg&searchType=righteous_only&language=en&itemId=4740137&ind=0. Retrieved 15 July 2021.

Lidegaard, Bo. *Countrymen*. Translated by Robert Maas. London: Atlantic Books, 2014.

Lindsey, Hal, with C.C. Carlson. *The Late Great Planet Earth*. Grand Rapids, MI: Zondervan, 1970.

Lipka, Michael. "Unlike U.S., Few Jews in Israel identify as Reform or Conservative." *FactTank*. Pew Research Center. At https://www.pewresearch.org/fact-tank/2016/03/15/unlike-u-s-few-jews-in-israel-identify-as-reform-or-conservative/. Retrieved 15 July 2021.

Lipstadt, Deborah E. *Antisemitism Here and Now*. New York: Schocken, 2019.

Littell, Marcia Sachs, and Sharon Weissman Gutman, eds. *Liturgies on the Holocaust: An Interfaith Anthology*, new and rev. ed. Valley Forge, PA: Trinity Press International, 1996.

Loewe, Raphael. "Hebraists, Christian." In *Encyclopedia Judaica*. Edited by Michael Berenbaum and Fred Skonik, 2nd ed., Vol. 8, 510–551. Farmington Hills, MI: Gale, 2007 [1996].

Long, J. Bruce, ed. *Judaism and the Christian Seminary Curriculum*. Chicago: Loyola University Press, 1966.

Maccoby, Hyam. *Jesus the Pharisee*. London: SCM Press, 2003.

———. *The Mythmaker: Paul and the Invention of Christianity*. San Francisco: Harper and Row, 1986.

Magid, Shaul. "Introduction." In *The Bible, the Talmud, and the New Testament: Elijah Zvi Soloveitchik's Commentary to the Gospels*. By Elijah Zvi Soloveitchik. Edited by Shaul Magid, 1–40. Translated by Jordan Gayle Levy. Philadelphia: University of Pennsylvania Press, 2019.

Marrus, Michael R. *The Holocaust in History*. Hanover, NH: University Press of New England, 1987.

———. "Understanding the Vatican During the Nazi Period." Jerusalem: Yad Vashem, 2000. At https://www.yadvashem.org/articles/academic/understanding-the-vatican-during-the-nazi-period.html. Retrieved 15 July 2021.

Marx, Alexander. "Review: Strack's Introduction to the Talmud and Midrash." *Jewish Quarterly Review*, New Series, 13, no. 3 (January 1923): 352–365.

Massey, Irving. *Philo-Semitism in Nineteenth-Century German Literature*. Tübingen: Niemeyer, 2000.

McInerny, Ralph. *The Defamation of Pius XII*. South Bend, IN: St. Augustine's Press, 2001.

Meeks, Wayne A., and Robert L. Wilken. *Jews and Christians in Antioch in the First Four Centuries of the Common Era*. Missoula, MT: Scholars Press, 1978.

Mejia, Jorge. "A Christian View of Bible Interpretation." In *Biblical Studies: Meeting Ground of Jews and Christians*. Edited by Lawrence Boadt, C.S.P., Helga Croner, and Leon Klenicki, 120–143. New York: Paulist Press, 1980.

Melamed, Abraham. "The Revival of Christian Hebraism in Early Modern Europe." In *Philosemitism in History*. Edited by Jonathan Karp and Adam Sutcliffe, 52–68. Cambridge, UK: Cambridge University Press, 2011.

Montefiore, C.G. "The Genesis of the Religion of St. Paul." In *Judaism and St. Paul: Two Essays*. London: Max Goschen, 1914; reprint Forgotten Books, 2015.

————. *Some Elements of the Religious Teaching of Jesus According to the Synoptic Gospels.* London: Macmillan, 1910; reprint Arno Press, 1973.

Moore, R.I. *The Formation of a Persecuting Society: Power and Deviance in Western Europe, 950–1250.* New York: Oxford University Press, 1987.

Moore, Rebecca. *Jews and Christians in the Life and Thought of Hugh of St. Victor.* Atlanta, GA: Scholars Press, 1998.

————. "The Mythmaker: Hyam Maccoby and the Invention of Christianity." *Journal of Ecumenical Studies* 52, no. 3 (Summer 2017): 381–401.

Nanos, Mark D. "A Jewish View." In *Four Views on The Apostle Paul.* Edited by Michael F. Bird, 159–193. Grand Rapids, MI: Zondervan, 2012.

Nathan, Emmanuel, and Anya Topolski. "The Myth of a Judeo-Christian Tradition: Introducing a European Perspective." In *Is There a Judeo-Christian Tradition? A European Perspective.* Edited by Emmanuel Nathan and Anya Topolski, 1–14. Berlin: Walter de Gruyter, 2016.

"The Netherlands." *Holocaust Encyclopedia,* United States Holocaust Memorial Museum. At https://encyclopedia.ushmm.org/content/en/article/the-netherlands. Retrieved 15 July 2021.

Neusner, Jacob. "The Absoluteness of Christianity and the Uniqueness of Judaism: Why Salvation Is Not of the Jews." In *Judaism in Monologue and Dialogue,* 91–103. Lanham, MD: University Press of America, 2005.

————. "Judaism and Christianity, Their Relationship Then, Their Relationship to Come." In *Judaism in Monologue and Dialogue,* 81–90. Lanham, MD: University Press of America, 2005.

Nibley, Hugh. "Christian Envy of the Temple." *Jewish Quarterly Review* 50, no. 3 (January 1960): 229–249.

Noah, M[ordecai] M[anuel]. *Discourse on the Restoration of the Jews: Delivered at the Tabernacle,* Oct. 28 and Dec. 2, 1844. New York: Harper and Brothers, 1845; reprint Arno Press, 1977.

Novak, David. "Avoiding Charges of Legalism and Antinomianism in Jewish-Christian Dialogue." In *Talking with Christians: Musings of a Jewish Theologian,* 26–45. Grand Rapids, MI: Eerdmans, 2005.

———. "From Supersessionism to Parallelism in Jewish-Christian Dialogue." In *Talking with Christians: Musings of a Jewish Theologian*, 8–25. Grand Rapids, MI: Eerdmans, 2005.

———. "Introduction: What to Seek and What to Avoid in Jewish-Christian Dialogue." In *Christianity in Jewish Terms*. Edited by Tikva Frymer-Kensky, David Novak, Peter Ochs, David Fox Sandmel, and Michael Signer, 1–6. Boulder, CO: Westview Press, 2000.

———. *Jewish-Christian Dialogue: A Jewish Justification*. New York: Oxford University Press, 1989.

———. "A Jewish Response to a New Christian Theology." *Judaism* 31, no. 1 (Winter 1982): 112–120.

O'Callaghan, Daniel, ed. and trans. *The Preservation of Jewish Religious Books in Sixteenth-Century Germany: Johannes Reuchlin's "Augenspiegel."* Leiden: Brill, 2013.

Oppenheim, Michael. "Foreword," xi–xv. In *The Star of Redemption*. By Franz Rosenzweig. Translated by Barbara E. Galli. Madison, WI: University of Wisconsin Press, 2005.

Pagels, Elaine. *The Gnostic Gospels*. New York: Random House, 1979.

Paget, James Carleton. "Quests for the Historical Jesus." In *The Cambridge Companion to Jesus*. Edited by Markus Bockmuehl, 138–155. New York: Cambridge University Press, 2001.

Paldiel, Mordecai. "Righteous Gentiles and Courageous Jews: Acknowledging and Honoring Rescuers of Jews." *French Politics, Culture, and Society*, 30, no. 2 (Summer 2012): 134–149.

Palmer, Elizabeth. "Reproach and Pleading." *Christian Century* 137, no. 8 (April 8, 2020): 10–11.

Parents Circle-Families Forum. At https://www.theparentscircle.org/en/about_eng/. Retrieved 15 July 2021.

Parkes, James. "The Bible, The World and The Trinity." Chapter 12. In *Prelude to Dialogue: Jewish-Christian Relationships*. New York: Schocken, 1969.

———. *The Conflict of the Church and the Synagogue: A Study in the Origins of Antisemitism*. London: Soncino Press, 1934; reprint World Publishing and Jewish Publication Society, 1961.

———. *God at Work in Science, Politics and Human Life*. New York: Philosophical Library, 1952.

————. *The Jew and His Neighbor: A Study of the Causes of Anti-Semitism*. London: Student Christian Movement Press, 1930.

Pawlikowski, John T. *Christ in the Light of the Christian-Jewish Dialogue*. New York: Paulist Press, 1982; reprint Wipf and Stock, 2001.

————. "Land as an Issue in Jewish-Christian Dialogue." *Cross Currents* 59, no. 2 (June 2009): 197–209.

Petuchowski, Elizabeth. "Gertrud Luckner: Resistance and Assistance. A German Woman Who Defied Nazis and Aided Jews." In *Ministers of Compassion During the Nazi Period: Gertrud Luckner and Raoul Wallenberg*, 5–21. South Orange, NJ: Institute of Judaeo-Christian Studies at Seton Hall University, 1999.

Pfeiffer, Robert H. "The Teaching of Hebrew in Colonial America." *Jewish Quarterly Review* 45, no. 4 (April 1955): 363–373.

Phayer, Michael. *The Catholic Church and the Holocaust, 1930–1965*. Bloomington and Indianapolis: Indiana University Press, 2000.

————. "Questions About Catholic Resistance." *Church History* 70, no. 2 (June 2001): 328–344.

Pontifical Biblical Commission. *The Interpretation of the Bible in the Church*. 23 April 1993. At http://catholic-resources.org/Church-Docs/PBC_Interp-FullText.htm. Retrieved 15 July 2021.

————. *The Jewish People and Their Sacred Scriptures in the Christian Bible*. Vatican City: Pontifical Biblical Commission, 2001. At https://www.vatican.va/roman_curia/congregations/cfaith/pcb_documents/rc_con_cfaith_doc_20020212_popolo-ebraico_en.html. Retrieved 15 July 2021.

Pope John Paul II. *Message of His Holiness John Paul II on the 50th Anniversary of the Warsaw Ghetto Uprising*. Vatican: Libreria Editrice Vaticana, 1993. At http://www.vatican.va/content/john-paul-ii/en/messages/pont_messages/1993/documents/hf_jp-ii_mes_19930406_ebrei-polacchi.html. Retrieved 15 July 2021.

————. *Redemptionis Anno*. 20 April 1984. In *The Saint for Shalom: How Pope John Paul II Transformed Catholic-Jewish Relations. The Complete Texts 1979–2005*. Edited by Eugene J. Fisher and Leon Klenicki, 79–84. New York: Crossroad, 2011.

Pope Paul VI. *Declaration on the Relation of the Church to Non-Christian Religions (Nostra Aetate)*. 28 October 1965. In *Vatican Council II: The Conciliar and Post Conciliar Documents*, Vol. 1, rev. ed. Edited by Austin Flannery, O.P., 738–742. Northport, NY: Costello Publishing, 1992.

———. *Dogmatic Constitution on Divine Revelation (Dei Verbum).* 18 November 1965. In *Vatican Council II: The Conciliar and Post Conciliar Documents*, Vol. 1, rev. ed. Edited by Austin Flannery, O.P., 750–765. Northport, NY: Costello Publishing, 1992.

Popkin, Richard. "Jewish-Christian Relations in the Sixteenth and Seventeenth Centuries: The Conception of the Messiah." *Jewish History* 6, no. 1/2 (1992): 163–177.

Presbyterian Church (USA). *Christians and Jews: People of God.* Church Issues Series No. 7. Louisville, KY: Office of Theology and Worship, n.d.

Price, R.M. "'Hellenization' and Logos Doctrine in Justin Martyr." *Vigiliae Christianae* 42, no. 1 (March 1988): 18–23.

Pugh, Jeffrey C. *The Home Brewed Christianity Guide to the End Times: Theology After You've Been Left Behind.* Minneapolis: Augsburg Fortress, 2016.

Rappaport, Solomon. *Jew and Gentile: The Philo-Semitic Aspect.* New York: Philosophical Library, 1980.

Rauschenbach, Sina. "Mediating Jewish Knowledge: Menasseh ben Israel and the Christian *Respublica litteraria.*" *Jewish Quarterly Review* 102, no. 4 (Fall 2012): 561–588.

Reed, Annette Yoshiko. "Messianism Between Judaism and Christianity." In *Rethinking the Messianic Idea in Judaism.* Edited by Michael L. Morgan and Steven Weitzman, 23–62. Bloomington: Indiana University Press, 2014.

"Reflections on the Problem 'Church-Israel,' issued by the Central Board of the Union of Evangelical Churches in Switzerland, 1977." In *More Stepping Stones to Jewish-Christian Relations: An Unabridged Collection of Christian Documents 1975–1983.* Edited by Helga Croner, 198–204. New York: Paulist Press, 1985.

Ribak, Eliya. "Bright Beginnings: Jewish Christian Relations in the Holy Land, AD 400–700." *Studies in Christian-Jewish Relations* 6 (2011): 1–18.

Rivkin, Ellis. *A Hidden Revolution: The Pharisees' Search for the Kingdom Within.* Nashville, TN: Abingdon Press, 1978.

Rosen-Zvi, Ishay. "Pauline Traditions and the Rabbis: Three Case Studies." *Harvard Theological Review* 110, no. 2 (2017): 169–194.

Rosenblatt, Jason P. "John Selden's *De Jure Naturali … Juxta Disciplinam Ebraeorum and Religious Toleration.*" In *Hebraica Veritas? Christian Hebraists and the Study of Judaism in Early Modern Europe.* Edited by Allison P. Coudert and Jeffrey S. Shoulson, 102–124. Philadelphia: University of Pennsylvania Press, 2004.

Rosenzweig, Franz. *The Star of Redemption.* Translated by Barbara E. Galli. Madison: University of Wisconsin Press, 2005.

Roth, Walter. "Christian's [sic] 1891 Zionist Petition to U.S. President." *Society News* (Chicago Jewish Historical Society), XI, no. 1 (September 1987): 6.

Rothman, John. "An Incomparable Pope—John XXIII and the Jews (Extended)." *Inside the Vatican,* n.d. At https://insidethevatican.com/magazine/vatican-watch/incomparable-pope-john-xxiii-jews-long/. Retrieved 15 July 2021.

Rubinstein, William D., and Hilary L. Rubinstein. *Philosemitism: Admiration and Support in the English-Speaking World for Jews, 1840–1939.* New York: St. Martin's Press, 1999.

Ruderman, David B. "Introduction." In *Converts of Conviction: Faith and Scepticism in Nineteenth Century European Jewish Society.* Edited by David B. Ruderman, 1–7. Berlin: Walter de Gruyter, 2018.

———, ed. *Converts of Conviction: Faith and Scepticism in Nineteenth Century European Jewish Society.* Berlin: Walter de Gruyter, 2018.

Ruether, Rosemary Radford. *Faith and Fratricide: The Theological Roots of Anti-Semitism.* New York: Seabury Press, 1974.

———. "Theological Anti-Semitism in the New Testament." *Christian Century* 85, no. 7 (14 February 1968): 191–196.

Rutishauser, Christian. "The 1947 Seelisberg Conference: The Foundation of the Jewish-Christian Dialogue." *Studies in Christian-Jewish Relations* 2, no. 2 (2007): 34–53.

Sanders, E.P. *Jesus and Judaism.* Philadelphia: Fortress Press, 1985.

———. *Paul and Palestinian Judaism: A Comparison of Patterns of Religion.* Philadelphia: Fortress Press, 1977.

———. *Paul, the Law, and the Jewish People.* Philadelphia: Fortress Press, 1983.

Sandmel, Samuel. *Anti-Semitism in the New Testament?* Philadelphia: Fortress Press, 1978.

———. *The Genius of Paul.* New York: Farrar, Straus and Cudahy, 1958; reprint Isha Books, 2013.

———. *A Jewish Understanding of the New Testament.* Cincinnati, OH: Alumni Association of the Hebrew Union College–Jewish Institute of Religion, 1956; 3rd ed. reprint Jewish Lights Publishing, 2005.

———. *We Jews and Jesus: Exploring Theological Differences for Mutual Understanding.* New York: Oxford University Press, 1965; reprint Jewish Lights Publishing, 2006.

———. *We Jews and You Christians: An Inquiry Into Attitudes.* Philadelphia: J.B. Lippincott, 1967.

Schäfer, Peter. *Two Gods in Heaven: Jewish Concepts of God in Antiquity.* Princeton, NJ: Princeton University Press, 2020.

Schoeps, Hans Joachim. *Philosemitismus im Barock.* Tübingen: Mohr, 1952.

Schweitzer, Albert. *The Mysticism of Paul the Apostle.* Translated by William Montgomery. New York: Henry Holt, 1931.

———. *The Quest of the Historical Jesus: A Critical Study of Its Progress from Reimarus to Wrede.* Translated by William Montgomery. Tübingen: Mohr Siebeck, 1906; reprint Macmillan Publishing, 1968.

Segal, Alan F. *Paul the Convert: The Apostolate and Apostasy of Saul the Pharisee.* New Haven, CT: Yale University Press, 1990.

Seldin, Ruth. *Image of the Jews: Teachers' Guide to Jews and their Religion.* New York: Anti-Defamation League of B'nai B'rith, 1970.

Shapiro, Faydra. "Jesus for Jews: The Unique Problem of Messianic Jews." *Marburg Journal of Religion* 16, no. 1 (2011): 1–16.

Shapiro, Faydra L. "'Thank you Israel, for Supporting America': The Transnational Flow of Christian Zionist Resources." *Identities: Global Studies in Culture and Power* 19, no. 5 (September 2012): 616–631.

Shapiro, Rebecca. "The Other Anti-Semitism: Philo-Semitism in Eighteenth- and Nineteenth-Century English Literature and Culture." Ph.D. diss., Purdue University, 1997.

Shemesh, Moshe. "Did Shuqayri Call for 'Throwing Jews Into the Sea'?" *Israel Studies*, 8, no. 2 (Summer 2003): 70–81.

Shoham-Steiner, Ephraim. "Jews and Healing at Medieval Saints' Shrines: Participation, Polemics, and Shared Cultures." *Harvard Theological Review* 103, no. 1 (January 2010): 111–129.

Siegman, Henry. "Jewish-Christian Relations: Still a Way to Go." *Judaism* 35, no. 1 (Winter 1986): 25–28.

Sklarin, Yigal. "'Rushing in Where Angels Fear to Tread': Rabbi Joseph B. Soloveitchik, the Rabbinical Council of America, Modern Orthodox Jewry, and the Second Vatican Council." *Modern Judaism* 29, no. 3 (October 2009): 351–385.

Smalley, Beryl. "Stephen Langton and the Four Senses of Scripture." *Speculum* 6, no. 1 (January 1931): 60–76.

———. *The Study of the Bible in the Middle Ages*. Oxford, UK: Basil Blackwell and Mott, 1952; reprint University of Notre Dame Press, 1964.

Snoek, Johannes M. *The Grey Book: A Collection of Protests Against Anti-Semitism and the Persecution of Jews Issued by Non-Roman Catholic Churches and Church Leaders during Hitler's Rule*. Assen: Van Gorcum, 1969.

Solnit, Rebecca. *A Paradise Built in Hell: The Extraordinary Communities that Arise in Disaster*. New York: Penguin Books, 2009.

Soloveitchik, Elijah Zvi. *The Bible, the Talmud, and the New Testament: Elijah Zvi Soloveitchik's Commentary to the Gospels*. Edited by Shaul Magid. Translated by Jordan Gayle Levy. Philadelphia: University of Pennsylvania Press, 2019.

Soloveitchik, Joseph B. "Addendum to the Original Edition of 'Confrontation.'" In *A Treasury of Tradition*. Edited by Norman Lamm and Walter S. Wurzburger, 78–80. New York: Hebrew Publishing Company, 1967.

———. "The Community." *Tradition: A Journal of Orthodox Thought* 17, no. 2 (Spring 1978): 7–24.

———. "Confrontation." *Tradition: A Journal of Orthodox Thought* 6, no. 2 (Spring 1964): 5–29.

"Special Section on Feminist Anti-Judaism." *Journal of Feminist Studies in Religion* 7, no. 2 (Fall 1991).

Spinoza, Benedict de. *A Theologico-Political Treatise*. In *A Theologico-Political Treatise and A Political Treatise*. Translated by R.H.M. Elwes. New York: Dover, 1951.

Stahl, Neta. "Jesus as the New Jew: Zionism and the Literary Representation of Jesus." *Journal of Modern Jewish Studies* 11, no. 1 (March 2012): 1–23.

Stendahl, Krister. *Paul Among Jews and Gentiles and Other Essays.* Philadelphia: Fortress Press, 1976.

Stern, Frank. *The Whitewashing of the Yellow Badge: Antisemitism and Philosemitism in Postwar Germany.* Translated by William Templer. New York: Pergamon, 1992.

Sternfeld, Janet. *Homework for Jews: Preparing for Jewish-Christian Dialogue,* 2nd ed. New York: National Conference of Christians and Jews, 1985.

"Strack, Hermann Leberecht." *Encyclopedia Judaica.* Edited by Michael Berenbaum and Fred Skolnik, 2nd ed., Vol. 19, 240 Farmington Hills, MI: Gale, 2007.

Study Group on Christian-Jewish Relations. "Statement to Our Fellow Christians." 1973. At https://www.bc.edu/content/dam/files/research_sites/cjl/sites/partners/csg/csg1973.htm. Retrieved 15 July 2021.

Suhl, Yuri. *They Fought Back: The Story of Jewish Resistance in Nazi Europe.* New York: Crown Publishers, 1967.

Summers, Anne. "False Start or Brave Beginning? The Society of Jews and Christians, 1924–1944." *Journal of Ecclesiastical History* 65, no. 4 (October 2014): 827–851.

Sutcliffe, Adam. "Hebrew Texts and Protestant Readers: Christian Hebraism and Denominational Definition." *Jewish Studies Quarterly* 7, no. 4 (2000): 319–337.

"The Sykes-Picot Agreement: 1916." *The Avalon Project.* Yale Law School. At https://avalon.law.yale.edu/20th_century/sykes.asp. Retrieved 15 July 2021.

Synod of the Reformed Church, Holland. "Israel: People, Land and State: Suggestions for a Theological Evaluation [1970]." In *Stepping Stones to Further Jewish-Christian Relations.* Edited by Helga Croner, 91–107. New York: Stimulus Books, 1977.

Syrkin, Marie. *Blessed Is the Match: The Story of Jewish Resistance.* Philadelphia: Jewish Publication Society, 1974.

Tanenbaum, Marc H. "Heschel and Vatican Council II—Jewish-Christian Relations." Paper Presented at a Memorial Symposium in honor of Abraham Joshua Heschel. New York: Jewish Theological Seminary, 1983. Archives of the American Jewish Committee. At http://www.ajcarchives.org/ajcarchive/DigitalArchive.aspx. Retrieved 15 July 2021.

————. "A Jewish Viewpoint on *Nostra Aetate.*" In *Twenty Years of Jewish-Catholic Relations.* Edited by Eugene J. Fisher, A. James Rudin, and Marc H. Tanenbaum, 39–60. New York: Paulist Press, 1986.

————. "Preface." In *Anti-Israel Influence in American Churches: A Background Report.* By Judith Hershcopf Banki, n.p. New York: American Jewish Committee, 1979.

————. "Preface." In "The UN's Anti-Zionism Resolution: Christian Responses." By Judith H. Banki, i–v. Interreligious Affairs Department, American Jewish Committee 70th Anniversary Annual Meeting, Washington, D.C. 12–16 May 1976. New York: American Jewish Committee, 1976.

Tanzer, Sarah J. "The Problematic Portrayal of 'the Jews' and Judaism in the Gospel of John: Implications for Jewish-Christian Relations." In *Contesting Texts: Jews and Christians in Conversation about the Bible.* Edited by Melody D. Knowles, Esther Menn, John Pawlikowski, O.S.M., and Timothy J. Sandoval, 103–118. Minneapolis: Fortress Press, 2007.

Tec, Nechama. *When Light Pierced the Darkness: Christian Rescue of Jews in Nazi-Occupied Poland.* New York: Oxford University Press, 1986.

Teller, Adam. "Revisiting Baron's 'Lachrymose Conception': The Meanings of Violence in Jewish History." *AJS Review* 38, no. 2 (November 2014): 431–439.

To Do the Will of Our Father in Heaven: Toward a Partnership between Jews and Christians. The Center for Jewish-Christian Understanding and Cooperation. 3 December 2015. At https://www.cjcuc.org/2015/12/03/orthodox-rabbinic-statement-on-christianity/. Retrieved 15 July 2021.

Tracy, David. "Religious Values after the Holocaust: A Catholic View." In *Jews and Christians after the Holocaust.* Edited by Abraham J. Peck, 87–107. Philadelphia: Fortress Press, 1982.

Tveit, Olav Fykse. "On US Recognition of Jerusalem as Israel's Capital." 6 December 2017. At https://www.oikoumene.org/en/resources/documents/general-secretary/statements/on-us-recognition-of-jerusalem-as-israels-capital. Retrieved 15 July 2021.

Underwood, Grant. "The *Hope of Israel* in Early Modern Ethnography and Eschatology." In *Hebrew and the Bible in America: The First Two Centuries.* Edited by Shalom Goldman, 91–101. Hanover, NH: University Press of New England, 1993.

"United Methodist Guiding Principles for Christian-Jewish Relations." In *The Book of Resolutions of the United Methodist Church—2016.* Nashville, TN: United Methodist Publishing House, 2016. At https://www.umc.org/en/content/book-of-resolutions-united-methodist-guiding-principles-for-christian-jewish-relations. Retrieved 15 July 2021.

Van Arkel, Dik. *The Drawing of the Mark of Cain: A Socio-Historical Analysis of the Growth of Anti-Jewish Stereotypes.* Amsterdam: Amsterdam University Press, 2009.

Van Biema, David. "#10: Re-Judaizing Jesus." *Time* Magazine. 13 March 2008. At http://content.time.com/time/specials/2007/article/0,28804,1720049_1720050_1721663,00.html. Retrieved 15 July 2021.

Van Engen, John. "Introduction: Jews and Christians Together in the Twelfth Century." In *Jews and Christians in Twelfth-Century Europe.* Edited by Michael A. Signer and John Van Engen, 1–8. Notre Dame, IN: University of Notre Dame Press, 2001.

Vatican Commission for Religious Relations with the Jews. "Guidelines and Suggestions for Implementing the Conciliar Declaration *Nostra Aetate* (no. 4)." January 1975 [1 December 1974]. In *Stepping Stones to Further Jewish-Christian Relations.* Edited by Helga Croner, 11–16. New York: Stimulus Books, 1977. See also https://www.bc.edu/content/dam/files/research_sites/cjl/texts/cjrelations/resources/documents/catholic/Vatican_Guidelines.htm. Retrieved 15 July 2021.

———. "Notes on the Correct Way to Present the Jews and Judaism in Preaching and Catechesis in the Roman Catholic Church." 24 June 1985. At https://www.bc.edu/content/dam/files/research_sites/cjl/texts/cjrelations/resources/documents/catholic/Vatican_Notes.htm. Retrieved 15 July 2021.

Vermes, Geza. *Jesus and the World of Judaism.* Philadelphia: Fortress Press, 1983.

———. *Jesus the Jew: A Historian's Reading of the Gospels.* Philadelphia: Fortress Press, 1973.

Vincent, Nicholas. "Two Papal Letters on the Wearing of the Yellow Badge, 1221 and 1229." *Jewish Historical Studies* 34 (1993–1996): 209–224.

Ware, Bishop Kallistos. *The Orthodox Way*, rev. ed. Crestwood, NY: St. Vladimir's Seminary Press, 1995.

Weber, Joseph C. "Karl Barth and the Historical Jesus." *Journal of Bible and Religion* 32, no. 4 (October 1964): 350–354.

Weinryb, Bernard D., and Daniel Garnick. *Jewish School Textbooks and Intergroup Relations: The Dropsie College Study of Jewish Textbooks*. New York: American Jewish Committee, 1965.

Weiss-Rosmarin, Trude. *Judaism and Christianity: The Differences*. New York: Jonathan David, 1943.

Werblowsky, Zwi. "The People and the Land." In *Speaking of God Today: Jews and Lutherans in Conversation*. Edited by Paul D. Opsahl and Marc H. Tanenbaum, 73–80. Philadelphia: Fortress Press, 1974.

Wertheim, David J., ed. *The Jew as Legitimation: Jewish-Gentile Relations Beyond Antisemitism and Philosemitism*. New York: Palgrave Macmillan, 2017.

Wesley, John. *The Journal of John Wesley*, vi.iii.v, 11 June 1739. Grand Rapids, MI: Christian Classics Ethereal Library, n.d.

"What Are the Basic Criteria for Awarding the Title of Righteous?" *FAQs: The Righteous Among the Nations Program*. Jerusalem: Yad Vashem, n.d. At https://www.yadvashem.org/righteous/faq.html. Retrieved 15 July 2021.

Wiesenthal, Simon. *The Sunflower: On the Possibilities and Limits of Forgiveness*. New York: Schocken Books, 1976.

Wilken, Robert L. *John Chrysostom and the Jews: Rhetoric and Reality in the Late 4th Century*. Berkeley: University of California Press, 1983.

———. *Judaism and the Early Christian Mind: A Study of Cyril of Alexandria's Exegesis and Theology*. New Haven, CT: Yale University Press, 1971.

Williams, Margaret H., ed. *The Jews Among the Greeks and Romans: A Diasporan Sourcebook*. Baltimore, MD: Johns Hopkins University Press, 1998.

Wolfson, Harry A. "Introductory." In *Jesus as Others Saw Him: A Retrospect A.D. 54*. By Joseph Jacobs, n.p. New York: Bernard G. Richards, 1925.

World Council of Churches. "Report of Committee IV—Concerns of the Churches: 3. The Christian Approach to the Jews." Geneva:

World Council of Churches, 1948. At https://www.oikoumene.org/
sites/default/files/Document/1948Christian_approach_Jews.pdf.
Retrieved 15 July 2021.

————. "Resolution on Anti-Semitism." Third Assembly, New
Delhi. Geneva: World Council of Churches, 1961. At https://
archive.org/stream/newdelhireportth009987mbp/newdelhireport-
th009987mbp_djvu.txt. Retrieved 15 July 2021.

————. "Third Revised Text of British Working Group for World Council
of Churches Consultation on the Church and the Jewish People:
Guidelines/Recommendations on Jewish-Christian Relations,
1977." In *More Stepping Stones to Jewish-Christian Relations: An
Unabridged Collection of Christian Documents 1975–1983*. Edited by
Helga Croner, 161–164. New York: Paulist Press, 1985.

————. "WCC Policy on Palestine and Israel 1948–2016 (summary)."
Geneva: World Council of Churches, 2017. At https://www.
oikoumene.org/en/resources/documents/wcc-programmes/
public-witness/peace-building-cf/wcc-policy-on-palestine-and-is-
rael-1948-2016-summary. Retrieved 15 July 2021.

World Council of Churches Central Committee. "Israeli-Palestinian Conflict—Minute [sic] on the situation in the Holy Land after the outbreak
of the second Palestinian uprising." Potsdam, Germany, 29 January–6 February 2001. At https://www.oikoumene.org/en/resources/
documents/commissions/international-affairs/regional-concerns/
middle-east/israeli-palestinian-conflict-minute-on-the-situation-in-
the-holy-land-after-the-outbreak-of-the-second-palestinian-uprising.
Retrieved 15 July 2021.

Wrede, William. *Paul*. Translated by E. Lummis. London: Philip Green,
1907; reprint Wipf and Stock, 2001.

Wright, Elizabeth. "A Yom HaShoah Liturgy for Christians." In *The
Crucifixion of the Jews*. By Franklin H. Littell. Appendix B, 141–153.
New York: Harper and Row, 1975.

Wyschogrod, Michael. "Incarnation and God's Indwelling in Israel." In
Abraham's Promise: Judaism and Jewish-Christian Relations, 165–
178. Grand Rapids, MI: Eerdmans, 2004.

————. "Paul, Jews, and Gentiles." In *Abraham's Promise: Judaism and
Jewish-Christian Relations*, 188–201. Grand Rapids, MI: Eerdmans,
2004.

Yinger, Kent L. "The Continuing Quest for Jewish Legalism." *Bulletin for Biblical Research* 19, no. 3 (2009): 375–391.

Yuval, Israel Jacob. "Christianity in Talmud and Midrash: Parallelomania or Parallelophobia?" In *Transforming Relations: Essays on Jews and Christians Throughout History in Honor of Michael Signer*. Edited by Franklin T. Harkins, 50–74. Notre Dame, IN: University of Notre Dame Press, 2010.

————. "'We Curse Christianity Three Times a Day': Can Jews and Christians Truly Reconcile?" *Haaretz*, 14 August 2020. At https://www.haaretz.com/life/books/.premium.MAGAZINE-we-curse-christianity-three-times-a-day-can-jews-and-christians-truly-reconcile-1.9072566. Retrieved 15 July 2021.

SOURCE INDEX

Rabbinic Literature

Early Christian Writings

SUBJECT INDEX